Women and Divorce/ Men and Divorce
Gender Differences in Separation, Divorce and Remarriage

Women and Divorce/ Men and Divorce
Gender Differences in Separation, Divorce and Remarriage

Sandra S. Volgy, PhD
Editor

The Haworth Press
New York • London

Women and Divorce/Men and Divorce: Gender Differences in Separation, Divorce and Remarriage has also been published as *Journal of Divorce & Remarriage*, Volume 14, Numbers 3/4 1991.

The Haworth Press, Inc., 10 Alice Street, Binghamton, NY 13904-1580
EUROSPAN/Haworth, 3 Henrietta Street, London WC2E 8LU England

Library of Congress Cataloging-in-Publication Data

Women and divorce/men and divorce : gender differences in separation, divorce, and remarriage / Sandra S. Volgy, editor.
    p. cm.
    Published also as v. 14, nos. 3/4 1991 of Journal of divorce & remarriage.
    ISBN 1-56024-114-4 (acid-free paper). (pbk.)
    1. Divorce — United States. 2. Divorced women — United States. 3. Divorced men — United States. 4. Remarriage — United States. 5. Sex role — United States. I. Volgy, Sandra Sue.
HQ834.W677   1991
306.89 — dc20
                          90-25066
                          CIP

Women and Divorce/
Men and Divorce
Gender Differences
in Separation, Divorce
and Remarriage

CONTENTS

ALL HAWORTH BOOKS & JOURNALS
ARE PRINTED ON CERTIFIED
ACID-FREE PAPER

ABOUT THE EDITOR

Sandra S. Volgy, PhD, is a clinical psychologist and family therapist who has specialized in the area of divorce and families for 15 years. She is currently in private practice in Tucson, Arizona, and is on the faculty of the Arizona Institute of Family Therapy. She was previously Child Advocate of the Conciliation Court of Pima County where she devised and established a comprehensive program for assisting families and children in the divorce process. She has co-authored a number of professional articles and has presented numerous national programs on the topic of children and divorce.

Introduction

This special volume on gender issues and differences in divorce represents a "coming of age" in the family studies and family therapy fields. In the past five years there has been a variety of major books published which finally begin to examine the theoretical and practical variables which attest to the reality of gender differences in the divorce process.

The compilation of recent research in this volume presents a mere suggestion of the potential breadth and depth of issues in the divorce field to be explored. Gender differences in parenting, in stepparenting, in areas of adjustment and accommodation to separation and divorce, in areas of sociological and economic adjustment to divorce are beginning to be studied with fascinating results. This group of studies also represents another reality in this field in that women and mothers are still being researched far more commonly than are men and fathers. However, there is a clearer trend now toward rebalancing this in the field.

Although the research presented in this volume may not break entirely new ground in the above arena, it nevertheless serves to lead us in new directions and points the way for greater recognition of these gender issues in future divorce studies.

Sandra S. Volgy
Editor

COMPARISON
OF GENDER DIFFERENCES

Self-Other Orientation
and Sex-Role Orientation
of Men and Women Who Remarry

Rebecca M. Smith
Mary Anne Goslen
Anne Justice Byrd
Linda Reece

SUMMARY. Remarried men and women were more oriented to a balance between self interests and the other's interest in the remarriage decision than in the first marriage decision. In-depth inter-

Rebecca M. Smith, PhD, is Professor and Mary Anne Goslen is Lecturer and a doctoral student in the Department of Child Development and Family Relations at the University of North Carolina, Greensboro, NC 27412. Anne Justice Byrd, PhD, is a 1986 doctoral graduate from the Department of Child Development and Family Relations and is Professor and Head of the Department of Sociology and Criminal Justice at Pfeiffer College, Misenheimer, NC 28109. Linda Reece is a doctoral student in the Department of Child Development and Family Relations and Associate Professor, Department of Nursing, Lenoir-Rhyne College, Hickory, NC 28601.

Funding for this project came from the UNCG Research Council and the School of Human Environmental Sciences Center for Research.

A version of this paper was presented at the Research and Theory Section of the annual conference of the National Council on Family Relations in Atlanta, GA, November, 1987.

3

views showed that these men and women used a similar balance when making the remarriage decision but that they arrived there by different avenues. The balance came from the women beginning to include self interests more and the men beginning to include the other's interest more. These remarried men and women also perceived themselves to be more nontraditional in sex-role orientation at the remarriage decision. Gilligan's Ethic of Care, a cogtnitive theory, was used to explain the change in self-other and sex-role orientation. Recommendations were made for using this theoretical framework in marital therapy.

Men and women enter a second marriage with previous experience, including divorce, which changes their expectations in remarriage. Their unwillingness to stay in a marriage that is inequitable was called "conditional commitment" by Furstenberg and Spanier (1984). They found that remarried persons commit themselves to a second marriage on the condition that the equity between self and others actually remains balanced. If the conditional commitment is based on the expectation of equity in all aspects of the marriage, then would this balance of self-other orientation really be a higher level of moral reasoning? In-depth interviews used in the present study showed that remarried men and women are alike in their expectation of an equitable self-other relationship, but they arrive at this similarity from different self-other stances in their first marriages.

The purpose of the present research was to explore the process of the decision to remarry from a moral cognitive theoretical perspective. A moral cognitive theory describes how people reason about issues concerning the rights of and responsibilities to self and others (Gilligan, 1977, 1982; Gilligan, Brown, & Rogers, 1990; Gilligan & Wiggins, 1987; Kohlberg, 1984; & Piaget, 1965).

REVIEW OF LITERATURE

In 1984 Pasley was concerned that theoretical advances were not very evident in reports of remarriage research at that time. She said that just knowing differences in static variables between first-married and remarried families was not enough. Since her challenge was presented, both theoretical applications to remarriage and studies about the process of the remarriage decision have been reported.

Remarriage Decisions

The process of the remarriage decision is increasingly being studied, although Roberts and Price (1985/86) reported few definitive conclusions in their review. Some researchers claim that remarried couples learn from their mistakes in the first marriage, but others claim there is little difference "in expectations and in the ability to make responsible decisions" (p. 9). However, Roberts and Price suggested that more research be done about the perception of self and others in the remarriage decision process, because people have different expectations of each other in a second marriage. They concluded that remarried persons want better communication, greater problem-solving outcome, and more understanding from their spouses. Most of the research they reviewed indicated that couples need to negotiate roles and boundaries prior to the decision to remarry.

Five research reports on remarriage since the Roberts and Price (1985/86) review showed that process variables as well as static variables were being studied. Instead of studying such broad variables as marital satisfaction, more narrowly defined variables were used to understand remarriage relationships. For example, Larson and Allgood (1987) compared 33 first-married and 33 remarried couples on marital intimacy and conflict resolution. They found that remarried couples have lower conflict resolution scores than first-married couples. This was explained by the probability that remarried couples use unproductive problem-solving strategies. When Byrd and Smith (1988) interviewed in-depth 23 remarried women about their decisions to marry and remarry, they found that these women considered personal, economic, and moral aspects. Using Gilligan's (1977, 1982) Ethic of Care to analyze the qualitative data, they found that almost all of the remarriage decisions were based on a realization that self-sacrifice in the first marriage was neither satisfying nor productive.

Although a secondary analysis of well-being and divorce-related stresses of remarried people showed statistically significant relationships with static variables, such findings could not explain the process of how remarried people come to their current, more satisfied state of well-being (Buehler, Hogan, Robinson, & Levy, 1987). Therefore, these researchers recommended a process of using " . . . a more realistic approach of conceptualizing and researching family transitions. . . . " (p. 418). They suggested that negotiation of new rules and roles necessary for remarriage should be studied.

Kalmuss and Seltzer (1986) did study negotiation and claim that remarried couples have the option of continuing behavior from the first marriage or renegotiating marital behavior. Their use of aggregated data from a large national survey did not permit the analysis of intrasubject change, but a study by Kvanli and Jennings (1987) did. They used videotaped interviews with 10 couples about their first and second marriages. When these couples described how they decided to remarry, they said they were aware of the new dimensions of themselves and what they wanted in a second partner. They made the decision to remarry, not from societal and family pressures but out of personal choice. Bowen's (1976) theory was used to explain that these couples were more differentiated from their families of origin and had a good balance of separateness and togetherness. These reviews suggest that couples may be using a higher level of moral reasoning when making a second marriage decision, however, none of the researchers explained the change in level of moral reasoning from a moral cognitive perspective.

The report from the 1987 Wingspread Conference on remarried families (Giles-Sims and Crosbie-Burnett, 1987) showed gaps in research on remarriage. One of the seven categories of research needs was the influence on the quality of remarried family relationships. In particular, one research question was about what remarried families expect of each other in time commitment, financial responsibilities, work roles, and parental roles.

The present research addresses these issues and gives further shape to a moral cognitive theory of remarriage which predicts that when remarriage decisions are made, they are often made on a more equitable level of moral reasoning. Such reasoning may explain why remarried people say they will not go into another marriage using a level of thinking that ties them to a self sacrificing role (Furstenberg & Spanier, 1984). A moral cognitive theory of remarriage may also provide a model for integrating research findings that remarried couples have the option of renegotiating roles, rules, and boundaries (Buehler et al., 1987; Kalmuss & Seltzer, 1986; Larson & Allgood, 1987; and Roberts & Price, 1985/86).

A Moral Cognitive Theory

The basic theoretical framework for this research was Gilligan's (1977, 1982; Gilligan, Brown, & Rogers, 1990) Ethic of Care. This theory claims that a moral dilemma can be viewed by each person from two perspectives, justice and care. Justice deals with issues of equality/inequality, and care deals with attachment/abandonment. Gilligan described the care perspective as one in which a person in a crisis situation may choose from three levels: concern for self by putting survival first; concern for others by putting nurturing first; and concern for self and others by realizing the truth that equality and connection are necessary for moral decisions. These three levels were described as successively more complex thinking. Care for others is the second level because at least it considers someone besides self; however, its denial of own self limits its moral value. Therefore, the highest level of moral concern is when both self and others are equally considered.

The transitions from one level to another occurs when the events in one's experiences do not seem to make sense with the old ways of thinking. Piaget (1965) called this inability to use old ways of thinking, to interpret what is now presented, a cognitive disequilibrium. That is, the old cognitive structures of the current moral level no longer can assimilate experiences in the same comfortable way. The transitions are the manifestation of this cognitive disequilibrium. The transition from care for self first (exclusion of others) to care for others first (exclusion of self) comes from a cognitive disequilibrium upon realizing that exclusion of others who need help may be selfish. The second transition from care for others to care for self and others comes from the cognitive disequilibrium that exclusion of self is not morally right, that is, sacrificing self cannot be equitable. A return to learning to care for self then precedes the transition to the highest level of care for self and others (inclusion of all concerned).

The two lower levels of moral reasoning, or levels of care, do not serve people well throughout long periods. Individuals who remain too long in the second level (exclusion of self) are at risk for abuse and depression. Likewise, people who remain at the first level too long (exclusion of others) are at risk for abandonment (Gilligan, Brown, & Rogers, 1990).

Making a marriage decision, especially when it is for the second time, involves beliefs about rights and relationships in conflicts between self and others, the essence of moral dilemmas. Perhaps for some men and some women, conventional sex roles in marriage, and the divorce provoke personal cognitive disequilibrium (Piaget, 1965) in self-other relationships. This disequilibrium then promotes higher cognitive development in self-other situations. If this is true, then remarriage decisions would be made from a more equitable level of dealing with self and others. When some of the respondents in Furstenberg and Spanier's (1984) study of remarriage implied that they were not going to be miserable again just for the sake of the marriage, they may have been showing a transition to a higher level of reasoning. The higher divorce rate among remarried persons may reflect the unwillingness to deal with marriage problems by serving the needs of the other to the detriment of self.

Although Gilligan described developmental levels of care in 1977 and 1982, she delayed the empirical study of development in order to validate her theory of different voices in moral development. The two voices identified are the care voice and the justice voice. The care voice is concerned with connection, and the justice voice is concerned with equality. Now that she has both empirical evidence and a methodology for studying moral voices (Brown, Argyris, Attanucci, Bardige, Gilligan, Johnston, Miller, Osborne, Ward, Wiggins, & Wilcox, 1988; Brown, Tappan, Gilligan, Miller, & Argyris, in press), Gilligan plans to reconsider development as a research issue. Her characterization of the levels has not changed, but she plans research to validate when and how development occurs. At the present time, she thinks that development along these three levels does not start in childhood with progressive changes by adulthood. Instead, these three levels are choices in each crisis situation that one meets throughout life.

Gilligan's theory has been used in a few studies that relate to marriage and family relations such as sex roles (Goldstein, 1987; Muus, 1988; & Rosenblum, 1986), religious attitudes (Yeaman, 1987), and sterilization (Abell, 1987). No studies in remarriage decisions using Gilligan's framework, except the one by Byrd and Smith (1988), were found even though it is a highly appropriate area.

Sex-Role Expectations in Remarriage

Sex-role expectations were used as a major variable in this research for understanding moral reasoning, since rights and responsibilities of self and others are essential to decisions regarding marriage expectations. That more men than women remarry and remarry more quickly (Glick & Lin, 1986) has been explained partially by differences in sex-role expectations of divorced men and women. Finlay, Starnes, and Alvarez (1985) found that divorced women would prefer a more nontraditional division of labor and power in remarriage, whereas divorced men would prefer more traditional sex roles in remarriage. They suggested that men may want to remarry in order to return to the traditional sex roles not so easy to maintain in the single lifestyle. Sex-role expectation appeared to be linked to the self-other aspect of moral cognition which men and women use in making the second marriage decision.

Understanding of intra-gender conflict may further illuminate what goes on in remarriage decisions. Rosenblum (1986) used Gilligan's (1977; 1982) self-other framework to show that inter-gender conflict pales beside the problem of intra-gender conflict. Each gender is taught to believe one way but reinforced by the culture to act in another. Men are taught to believe that equality and autonomy are the key concepts that guide higher levels of reasoning about conflicts between self and other; however, the culture reinforces behavior that is characterized by hierarchy, dominance, and personal achievement. Therefore, in marriage, men tend to act in a dominant and individually achieving manner. On the other hand, women are taught, in general, that nonviolence toward self and significant others in relationships is the guiding moral concept. Yet, they are reinforced to, and tend to, sacrifice self in service to others in marriage roles.

Some researchers who constructed instruments to measure attitudes about sex roles believed that (a) traditional sex-role orientation is associated with inequity and (b) nontraditional sex-role orientation is associated with equity (Osmond & Martin, 1975; Scanzoni, 1976; Tomeh, 1978). However, a pilot study with some people who claimed to be traditional did not seem to fit the description of having a lower level of moral reasoning. In addition, people who claimed to be nontraditional did not always seem to be using higher levels of moral reasoning. The conclusion from these interviews was that even when they choose a traditional sex-role expectation, their moral reasoning level could be the same as those who choose a nontraditional sex-role expectation. This was the basis for Smith & Bonar's suggestion in 1984 that a person could choose nontraditional sex roles with the belief that each person had rights but no responsibilities, classifying this thinking in a lower moral reasoning. It is certainly acknowledged that a person could choose traditional sex roles with the belief that each person had responsibilities but only certain people had rights which would classify their thinking in a lower level of moral reasoning. Traditional sex-role orientation could be classified as high moral if the couple chooses the traditional division of roles out of a sense of equity. Likewise, nontraditional sex-role orientation could be classified as high moral when there is a sense of equity in the decision.

RESEARCH QUESTIONS

Even though Byrd and Smith (1988) found that women used a higher level of self-other orientation in the second marriage decision, it was not known what level men would use. Therefore, the present study included both remarried men and women and compared them on the level of self-other orientation used in making the first marriage decision and the remarriage decision. Since sex-role expectations deal with self-other decisions, two other research questions were also asked. What sex-role orientation do men and women have at the first and second marriage decision? Is sex-role orientation related to self-other orientation? The answers to these questions will help to shape a moral cognitive theory of remarriage.

METHODOLOGY

This research was based on a retrospective multi-method design using two time periods in each person's life: the time of the first marriage decision and the time of the second marriage decision. The two dependent variables were self-other orientation (level of moral reasoning) and sex-role orientation (traditional and nontraditional). The major independent variables were time and sex. Other variables were (a) age and era of the first marriage decision; and (b) age, socioeconomic status variables (education, occupation, and income), and number of children under 18 living in the home at the time of the second marriage decision.

Sample

To be eligible for this remarriage research, the participants had to have been formerly divorced and remarried (once) within three years before the time of the interview. The names of the 64 men and women in the sample came through word of mouth from six counties and from the marriage records in one county in North Carolina. Potential respondents were contacted by telephone to ensure their eligibility and to set up an appointment for the interview. The age of the 32 men at the time of the interview ranged from 29 to 60 (mean = 42; sd = 8). The 32 women were somewhat younger (range = 23-52; mean = 36; sd = 7). Most of them had attended college and had middle- to upper-middle level jobs and family incomes. Although most of the remarried men and women had family incomes over $30,000, the personal income of more than two-thirds of the women was below $20,000 prior to remarriage. Only five of the men had personal incomes that low prior to remarriage. The remarried women were more likely to have children under 18 in the home although almost all men and women had children in their first marriages. Fifteen of the 32 women were interviewed as part of the Byrd and Smith (1988) sample in 1985. These respondents were not necessarily representative of the remarried population.

Data Collection Procedure

These data were collected in 1985, 1986, and 1987 in a one and one-half to two-hour tape recorded interview conducted in the interviewer's office, the respondent's home, or a place convenient for the respondent. After introductory remarks and signing the consent form, the tape recorder was turned on. The interview was set up in five sequential parts: (a) demographic data sheet either self-administered or read to the respondent;

(b) open-ended interview to measure Self-Other Orientation by asking respondents to tell their own story about what they considered when making the decision to marry the first time; (c) self-administered questionnaire which would reflect the Sex-Role Orientation at the time of the decision to marry the first time; (d) the same questionnaire repeated to reflect the Sex-Role Orientation at the time of the decision to marry the second time; and finally (e) open-ended interview to measure Self-Other Orientation by asking respondents to tell their own story about what they considered when making the decision to marry the second time.

By having the tape recorder operating the entire time, anything which respondents said, even if given out of sequence, was recorded. Also, having the recorder on during the time they were filling out the demographic data form and the Sex-Role Orientation forms was assumed to acclimate them for being recorded during the most important portions of the interview, the decision to marry and remarry. The same procedure was used with all but the 15 women from the Byrd and Smith (1988) study. The interview sequence for them was the same, but instead of a Sex-Role Orientation questionnaire, they responded to a relationship questionnaire. Therefore, they responded to the Sex-Role Orientation scale for their first marriage decision and for their second marriage decision by mail about one year after the interview.

Instruments and Scoring

Self-Other Orientation

The qualitative data for the major dependent variable, called "Self-Other Orientation" (a measure of levels of reasoning about equitable relationships) were collected in an open-ended interview essentially with variations from one prompt, "Tell me your story about how you decided to marry (remarry)." Other neutral prompts and probes were used to ensure that the following self-other areas were covered in their stories: (a) sex-role expectations; (b) why they had these expectations; (c) advantages and disadvantages in marrying (remarrying); and (d) how important decisions should be made. These data were transcribed verbatim.

A scoring guide was developed to gain a Self-Other Orientation score in the manner used by Abell (1987), Byrd and Smith (1988), Gilligan (1977 and 1982), Gilligan and Belenky (1980), and Skoe and Marcia (1987). Skoe and Marcia conducted a validation of Gilligan's care-based measure by comparing it with a Kohlbergian measure of morality (Gibbs & Widaman, 1982). They found a significant ($r = .37$) concurrent validity. When they compared Gilligan's measure with Marcia's (1966, 1980) ego identity status measure, they found a construct validity which indicated that people who have high level scores on the Gilligan measure also have high scores on identity.

The instrument used in this research was developed from the levels described by Gilligan in 1977 and 1982. Following the model of Colby and Kohlberg (1988), criterion judgments from previous interviews with remarried subjects were used in the Gilligan coding manual developed by Byrd and Smith (1988) and revised for the present study. Statements in context from the transcriptions were assessed as being in one of five levels of moral reasoning in self-other dilemmas in the following manner.

Level I: Care for self first with little real concern about the need of the other (exclusion of others). When there is a conflict of interests, the decision is for self. A typical response would be, "I wanted someone to take care of me." For women that meant financial and major decisions, but for men it meant cleaning, cooking, and sex.

Level I/II: The transition out of care for self first. The person shows cognitive disequilibrium when confronted with the need to be connected with others. Understanding the needs of others and beginning to see one's actions as selfish are characteristics of this first transition. Responses in this level were like this, "I felt obligated to marry her since she was so nice to me," or "He needed someone to look after him, too."

Level II: Care for others first with an overriding concern for the needs of others (exclusion of self). When there is a conflict of interest, the decision is for the other, thereby making the self the victim. This level is usually reinforced by society as the behavior of the "good" person, the hardworking provider, the self-sacrificing mother. These responses are conventional, "She's a good woman and I feel like I ought to provide for her," or "I expected and wanted to take care of him and his children," or "I wanted to keep house and him be head."

Level II/III: The transition out of caring for others first. Cognitive disequilibrium occurs from realizing that caring for others first is not the highest of ethical choices if self becomes the victim. The recognition of this transition comes with statements of self-sacrifice and resentment. Owning the cognitive change toward the highest of ethical self-other orientations is also important for moving out of Level II. These responses usually have the most emotion. Typically, they would be, "I was not going to keep up another man and do all the housework, too," or "I don't want to work and give it all to her; I need to think about myself, too."

Level III: Care for self and others equitably across time and situations (inclusion of self and others). This highest level not only considers self and others but also the need for the connection in the relationship. This level is also characterized by the ownership of the decision to care for both self and others. Such responses would sound like this, "I've learned you've got to consider her views or she won't help you," or "It's my responsibility to make myself happy, not his," or "I want an equal partner, no defined roles."

First and second marriage content in the responses can be different, but the essence of the levels is the same. The content for men and women may vary, but again, the level is discernible. Levels II/III and III were designated as meeting the requirements for higher moral self-other orientation.

The scoring manual gave a detailed description of the structure of each level as well as giving several criterion judgments for scoring the interview data. Each transcript was read first to get a feel for how the respondent used self-other orientation in making the first and second marriage decision. One of the researchers then marked small segments which dealt with the decisions. Each segment was numbered. Then each segment was scored for one of the five levels of Self-Other Orientation. Two other trained scorers read each transcript in full first and then scored the numbered segments. Scores were acceptable only when there was a 100% agreement between at least two trained scorers.

Final Self-Other Orientation scores were based on the mean score of the total number of nonrepeated segments. Each level was weighted by the following score: Level I = 100; Level I/II = 150; Level II = 200; Level II/III = 250; and Level III = 300. Each person received two Self-Other Orientation scores: one for the first marriage decision and one for the second marriage decision.

Sex-Role Orientation

The second dependent variable was Sex-Role Orientation. The Sex-Role Orientation questionnaire (Tomeh, 1978) has 24 items about responsibilities in the husband, wife, and parent roles. There was a four-point response to each item: very traditional (0); traditional (1); nontraditional (2); very nontraditional (3) with a range of total scores on the 24 items from 0 to 72. Each person in this research had two Sex-Role Orientation scores: one for the first marriage decision and one for the second marriage decision. Tomeh said that the instrument could be unidimensional although she constructed it from three dimensions, Wife-Mother Role, Husband-Father Role, and Husband-Wife Alteration Role. A factor analysis on the Sex-Role Orientation scores for the remarriage decision conducted in the present study did not support these three dimensions. A paper in preparation will give a detailed analysis of the Sex-Role Orientation instrument. For the present report, the total score of all 24 items was used in the analysis.

Independent Variables

The two major independent variables were (a) *time* of the decision to marry and to remarry and (b) *sex*. The era of the first marriage was also considered since era may have influenced the Sex-Role Orientation and the Self-Other Orientation. The eras were broken into the 1950s, 1960s, 1970s, and 1980s. Age at first marriage within era was also considered. Half of the women, but only four of the men, were under 21 when they married the first time. The era for the second marriage for all 64 respondents was the 1980s, however, their ages varied from 23 to 60.

DATA ANALYSIS AND RESULTS

Self-Other Orientation

The primary research question concerned Self-Other Orientation (moral reasoning level) (a) between the first and second marriage decisions and (b) between men and women. Both men and women showed a significant change in Self-Other Orientation scores from the first to the second marriage decision (see Table 1). Although the differences between men and women were not significantly different within each marriage decision, the pattern of the change was interesting (see Table 2).

Patterns of change from the first to the second marriage decision were similar for both men and women. All of the men and nearly all of the women scored at Level II or below (exclusion of self or exclusion of others) for the first marriage decision. Over half of the men and nearly two-thirds of the women were using Level II/III or III (inclusion of self *and* others) for the second marriage decision. At the second marriage decision, 22 of the 32 men had moved on to Levels II/III and III. Of the 30 women who had used Level II or below for the first marriage decision, 24 of them had begun to recognize exclusion of self (Level II/III) or had moved on to the highest level.

The large within-group variance as seen by the standard deviations for men as a group and women as a group (see Table 1) makes it necessary to look at how these men and women described their decisions. The highest Self-Other Orientation scores for both men and women or the greatest changes in scores at the second marriage decision, tended to come from some experiences prior to remarriage in which they had to perform the multiple roles of work, parenting, and housework causing them to under-

Table 1

Frequencies of Men and Women Using Self-Other Orientation Levels in First and Second Marriage Decisions

	Men (n = 32)		Women (n = 32)	
	First (Frequencies)	Second	First (Frequencies)	Second
Self-Other Orientation Level				
I Care for Self	11	0	17	0
I/II First Transition	14	1	9	1
II Care for Others	7	9	4	7
II/III Second Transition	0	19	0	19
III Care for Self and Others	0	3	2	5
Mean	162.25	258.91*	149.50	260.72**
SD	35.6	31.01	52.36	33.76
Range	100-228	183-300	100-300	185-300

15

TABLE 1 (continued)

Note: Cut-off scores for levels:
I = 100-149   I/II = 150-199
II = 200-249   II/III = 250-299   III = 300

Difference between first and second marriage for males:
*t = -12.87; p .000

Difference between first and second marriage for females:
**t = - 9.53; p .000

Difference between men and women for first marriage:
t = 1.14; p .26

Difference between men and women for second marriage:
t = -0.22; p .82

Table 2

Change in Level of Self-Other Orientation from First to Second
Marriage Decision for Men and Women

MEN (n = 32)

Second Marriage Decision Level

First Marriage Decision Level	I (n = 0)	I/II (n = 1)	II (n = 9)	II/III (n = 19)	III (n = 3)
I (n = 11)		1	1	9	
I/II (n = 14)			6	5	3
II (n = 7)			2	5	
II/III (n = 0)					
III (n = 0)					

TABLE 2 (continued)

WOMEN (n = 32)

First Marriage Decision Level	Second Marriage Decision Level				
	I (n = 0)	I/II (n = 1)	II (n = 7)	II/III (n = 19)	III (n = 5)
I (n = 17)		1	3	9	4
I/II (n = 9)			2	6	1
II (n = 4)				4	
II/III (n = 0)					
III (n = 2)			2		

stand the role conflict and role strain in work and family. Men's higher scores came from their realizing that they have to include others as well as self if they want more companionship. Women's higher scores at the second marriage decision were more likely to come from their learning to make it on their own and feeling good about it, wanting companionship but not needing it. The two women who made their first marriage decision from a Level III (see Table 2) reasoning but their second marriage decision from a lower level did so because they had wanted an equitable relationship in the first marriage. Instead they had husbands who would neither work for a living nor help with the housework. Their desire was for a little relief and being taken care of for a change.

Content Analysis

A content analysis (interrater reliability = .80) of the individual stories of the men and women about their marriage and remarriage decisions helps to understand how these changes came about. Men placed great emphasis on *companionship* in both the first and second marriage decision. Women, on the other hand, placed *companionship* high only in the second marriage decision. What women tended to want most in the first marriage was to have a traditional but romantic marriage. In the second marriage decision, the women wanted *sharing*, but they described it as equal input in the housework based on their being caught in the role strain of work, housework, and child care.

Interestingly enough, men also placed *sharing* high as a consideration in making the second marriage decision, but the concept had an entirely different etiology. These remarried men said they wanted *sharing* because they had learned from their first marriages that wives will not continue to be a companion without some sharing. Women arrived at *sharing* as important from the Self-Other Orientation Level II/III transition because they had felt self-sacrifice. For example, one woman said, "I was more willing to negotiate on things like family, work, financial support, and the real practical issues." Gilligan et al. (1990) called this learning to include self. Men arrived at *sharing* as important from the Self-Other Orientation Level I/II transition because they realized they had to consider the needs of others. One man said it this way, "I've learned a little about women. It's easy for a man to get lax . . . he gets other things on his mind. I plan to take time and give her more attention." Gilligan et al. (1990) called this learning to include others. When men felt self-sacrifice, Level II/III transition, it was usually from believing that they had done everything they could to make a good home while their wives had not.

Sex-Role Orientation

The Sex-Role Orientation scores for both men and women were in the "nontraditional" category at the first marriage decision, but were in the "very nontraditional" category with less within-group variance at the second marriage decision (see Table 3). As in Self-Other Orientation, the difference between men and women was not significantly different. The range and variance in the women's scores were somewhat greater than in the men's scores for the first marriage decision and for the second marriage decision as well.

Relationship Between Sex-Role Orientation and Self-Other Orientation

The difference in Sex-Role Orientation between the first and second marriage decisions could be attributed to the era of the first marriage decision and even the age of the person at that time. When the Sex-Role Orientation scores were plotted on age within era at first marriage, it was found that neither age nor era influenced the score. Even when young people married for the first time in the 1970s or the 1980s, their Sex-Role Orientation scores were as likely to be as low as were the people who had married in the 1950s or 1960s. Could a more traditional Sex-Role Orientation really be a first marriage decision phenomenon?

When sex-role instruments were developed, the notion was that a "very traditional" attitude was not equitable because such roles were accepted as a given with the male as the authority. On the other hand, a "very nontraditional" attitude was considered to be equitable because it encouraged individualism (Osmond & Martin, 1975; Scanzoni, 1976; Tomeh, 1978). In a paper presented at the NCFR Preconference Workshop (Smith & Bonar, 1984), this notion was challenged due to the fact that if people choose "traditional," then the very fact that they could choose, rather than be told to, would place them in a higher level of self-other concern (or equitable reasoning level). However, if people chose very nontraditional sex roles and at the same time pressed for too much individualism, their self-other concern could be on a lower level. From this thinking, it could be speculated that there would be no relationship between Sex-Role Orientation scores and Self-Other Orientation scores. That is, people who score very traditional might have any level, from self only or others only to self and others on the Self-Other Orientation measure. To test this notion, the Sex-Role Orientation scores and the Self-Other Orientation scores for the first marriage and then for the remarriage decision are presented for visual and statistical understanding (see Table 4).

Table 3

Sex-Role Orientation Scores for First and Second Marriage Decision by Sex

	Men (n = 32)		Women (n = 32)	
	First (Frequencies)	Second (Frequencies)	First (Frequencies)	Second (Frequencies)
Sex-Role Orientation				
Very Traditional	0	0	1	0
Traditional	5	1	5	0
Nontraditional	18	14	18	10
Very Nontraditional	9	17	8	22
Mean	47.09	55.28*	47.34	58.91**
SD	10.60	9.63	12.74	9.25
Range	24-68	29-71	15-72	38-72

21

TABLE 3 (continued)

Note: Cut-off scores:

Very Traditional = 0-18
Traditional = 19-36
Nontraditional = 37-54
Very Nontraditional = 55-72

Difference between first and second marriages for males:
*t = -4.01; p   .000

Difference between first and second marriage for females:
**t = -4.71; p   .000

Difference between men and women for first marriage:
t = -0.09; p   .932

Difference between men and women for second marriage:
t = -1.54; p   .13

Table 4

Frequencies of Men and Women for Self-Other Orientation
by Sex-Role Orientation by Marriage Decision

FIRST MARRIAGE

Self-Other Orientation

Sex-Role Orientation	I	I/II	II	II/III	III
Very Non-traditional	2 (+)a 5 (o)b	3 (+) 2 (o)	4 (+) 1 (o)		
Nontraditional	6 (+) 8 (o)	10 (+) 6 (o)	2 (+) 2 (o)	2 (o)	
Traditional	3 (+) 3 (o)		1 (+) 1 (o)		
Very Traditional	1 (o)	1 (+) 1 (o)			

23

TABLE 4 (continued)

SECOND MARRIAGE

Sex-Role Orientation	Self-Other Orientation				
	I	I/II	II	II/III	III
Very Non-traditional		1 {+} / 1 {o}	2 {+} / 4 {o}	12 {+} / 14 {o}	2 {+} / 3 {o}
Nontraditional			6 {+} / 3 {o}	6 {+} / 5 {o}	2 (o)
Traditional			1 (+)	1 (+)	1 (+)
Very Traditional					

a (+) = Men   b (o) = Women

When looking at the numbers of men and women on the various levels of Sex-Role Orientation by each level of Self-Other Orientation, there is no clear relationship. For example, there are several levels of Self-Other Orientation represented on any one level of Sex-Role Orientation. That is, just because a person scores on a "very traditional" level of Sex-Role Orientation, it does not follow that his or her scores will also be on a low level of Self-Other Orientation. Likewise, people who score "very non-traditional" do not automatically score on a very high level on the Self-Other Orientation instrument. Therefore, little support is given for the claims made by the designers of the Sex-Role Orientation instrument.

A correlation coefficient was computed between the Sex-Role and Self-Other Orientation scores for the first and second marriage decisions and for men and women. There was a very low nonsignificant correlation coefficient for all categories except for men in the first marriage decision (see Table 5). The coefficient was only .35 but was significant at the .025 level. Since all coefficients were low, the original proposal that sex-role orientation and self-other orientation are not necessarily related was supported when using the instruments described. Further support for no influence was shown when an analysis of variance of Self-Other Orientation scores for levels of Sex-Role Orientation by sex did not show any significant main effect or interaction effect.

Since there was little evidence for the relationship between Sex-Role Orientation and Self-Other Orientation, then it could be assumed that the expectation of no relationship could not be rejected. However, to gain more understanding of what goes into the Sex-Role Orientation scores, a step-wise multiple regression analysis was computed for the Sex-Role Orientation scores at the second marriage decision as the criterion variable and using (a) Self-Other Orientation at the second marriage decision and (b) education as the predictors. This procedure was done for women and then for men. The small sample size, 32 in each group, precluded using more than two predictors in the equation.

For women, the two predictors accounted for 41% of the variance in sex-role scores, education accounting for 21% of the variance in Sex-Role Orientation scores and Self-Other Orientation accounting for about the same amount of variance (20%). However, education was weighted more heavily (B = .45) than Self-Other Orientation (B = .10). The equation was significant (F = 4.78; p .02). On the other hand, for men, the two predictors accounted for less than a quarter of the variance in sex-role scores, education explaining 11% and Self-Other Orientation explaining an additional 12% of the total variance in Sex-Role Orientation (see Ta-

Table 5

Correlations Between Sex-Role Orientation and Self-Other
Orientation for Marriage by Sex

| | First Marriage | | Second Marriage | |
	Coefficient	Sig.	Coefficient	Sig.
Females (n = 32)	.046	.401 ns	.110	.275 ns
Males (n = 32)	.350	.025 *	.234	.098 ns
Total Sample (n = 64)	.152	.115 ns	.173	.086 ns

* Significant

ble 6). Again, education carried more weight than Self-Other Orientation. This equation was significant only at the .06 level (F = 3.06).

CONCLUSIONS

Two conclusions came from this research: (a) Traditional sex-role expectations are a first-marriage phenomenon and (b) men and women use different avenues of arriving at a higher level of moral reasoning for the remarriage decision. The assumption was that the respondents who married the first time before the 1970s would hold a more traditional sex-role orientation at their first marriage decision even though they were very young at that time. The surprising finding was that even if their first marriage occurred in the late 1970s and early 1980s, their sex-role orientation was more traditional than their remarriage decision. The conclusion, then, was that traditional sex-role orientation is a first-marriage phenomenon regardless of the age or the era. The 17 year-olds were as likely to be traditional as the 35 year-olds.

The second assumption was that men and women would make the second marriage decision from a higher level of moral reasoning from the care perspective (Gilligan, 1977, 1982; Gilligan et al., 1990), and they did. The surprising finding was that men and women come to this level of decision from different avenues. The highest level of care is to include both self and others. Lower levels are either (a) to exclude others or (b) to exclude self, both of which deny equity for all concerned. A content analysis of the interviews showed that men were more likely to have excluded others in their first marriages, whereas women were more likely to have excluded self. Of the two moral perspectives (rights and care), males are socialized to emphasize an individual rights perspective and to de-emphasize the care perspective in dealing with moral conflict. In so doing, they lean so much toward individual rights that the care perspective is not developed beyond the level of exclusion of others (care for self first). Females, on the other hand, are socialized to emphasize the care perspective and are reinforced to reach the level of inclusion of others to the exclusion of self (care for others first). In so doing, females de-emphasize the rights perspective in which individual rights are emphasized.

When men de-emphasize the care voice and use the rights perspective for dealing with moral conflict, they can think on a higher moral level from the rights perspective without making an effort to actually include others. In the rights perspective, individuals can be concerned about others' rights without ever being concerned about them as persons in a relationship. Women deal with moral conflict by excluding self, becoming the

Table 6

Regression of Sex-Role Orientation at Second Marriage
on Education and Self-Other Orientation for Women and Men

WOMEN

	b	B	R	Adjusted R-square	Cum. R-square	T	Sig.
Education	5.14	.45	.49	.21	.21	2.73	.01
Self-Other Orientation	.03	.10	.50	.20	.41	.61	.55

F = 4.78; p .02*

MEN

	b	B	R	Adjusted R-square	Cum. R-square	T	Sig.
Education	4.78	.41	.37	.11	.11	2.39	.02
Self-Other Orientation	.06	.21	.42	.12	.23	1.18	.25

F = 3.06; p .06

* Significant

28

selfless woman who puts others first. However, by excluding self, they are denying themselves and leaving out their individual right for care. Therefore, men and women go into their first marriages having been socialized to deal with moral conflict in different ways, one which excludes self and the other which excludes others. Yet both of them have been socialized to think they are doing what is morally right. This would guarantee unsatisfactory relationships.

The research findings in this study provide a different way to look at marital relationships, divorce, and the remarriage decision. Exclusion of others is a failure to respond, and it is difficult to live with someone who does not respond. It is equally difficult to live with someone who denies self in the continuing effort to care for others only. Usually a divorce results in one of two cases: (a) when couples cannot negotiate because they are still holding onto their former moral perspectives or (b) when couples cannot negotiate because one of them has learned to include both self and others, but the other has not.

By the time the men and women in this study had made the remarriage decision, they were alike in their realization that both self and others must be included; however, they came to this realization from different avenues. Since men were more likely to have excluded others in the first marriage, they arrived at inclusion of self and others by learning that women will not marry them if they do not include others. They were more willing to share responsibilities in the second marriage. Women were more likely to have excluded self in their first marriages; therefore they arrived at inclusion of self and others through a realization that exclusion of self was self-sacrifice. Women would not remarry unless there was an agreement about equal sharing of the responsibilities of the marriage.

Marital and family therapists can use these research findings to understand problems in a different way. When they can frame a marital problem as one of exclusion of self or others (or alternatively, lack of inclusion of self or others), they may be able to interpret a presenting problem more realistically. By doing so, an intervention could be designed which teaches clients to understand how their inclusion or exclusion of others has affected their relationship. This same framework might also explain cases of marital abuse. In abusive marriages, the victim might be the one who is denying self (excluding self as worthy) and the perpetrator may be the one who is excluding others. This same Ethic of Care (Gilligan, 1977 & 1982; Gilligan et al., 1990) can also explain how couples renegotiate and thus remain in long-term marriages. The realization of the use of the exclusion of self or the exclusion of others may occur within marriage with or without marital therapy. Goodwin and Smith (1988) found that couples in long-term marriages are more likely to have similar levels of moral reasoning. In some interviews prior to the final research interviews, they found that couples can describe how they moved to a higher level of moral reasoning within the marriage. Such movement was rarely simultaneous and the one reaching the higher level first made the effort to cause change in the other.

If men are socialized to emphasize an individual rights perspective over a care perspective, and if women are socialized to emphasize a care perspective over an individual rights perspective, there is little wonder that they cannot communicate in marriage. In this research, by using only the care perspective for analysis, the difference between men and women showed up when they described how they made the remarriage decision. The finding that in the remarriage decision men and women used a care perspective which included both self and others indicates that both of them continued to change. However, the finding that men come to remarriage from the level of exclusion of others and women come from the level of exclusion of self in their first marriage gives therapists a new way of examining communication problems in marriage. Further research should be done to test this notion that men and women move to the highest level of care by two different avenues.

REFERENCES

Abell, P. (1987). The decision to end childbearing by sterilization. *Family Relations*, *36*, 66-71.

Bowen, M. (1976). Theory in the practice of psychotherapy. In P. Guerin (Ed.), *Family therapy*. New York: Gardner Press.

Brown, L., Argyris, D., Attannuci, J., Bardige, B., Gilligan, C., Johnston, B., Miller, B., Osborne, R., Ward, J., Wiggins, G., & Wilcox, D. (1988). *A guide to reading narratives of moral conflict and choice for self and moral voice*. Cambridge: The Center for the Study of Gender, Education, and Human Development, Harvard University.

Brown, L., Tappan, M., Gilligan, C., Miller, B., & Argyris, D. (in press). Reading for self and moral voice: A method for interpreting narratives for real-life moral conflict and voice. In M. Packer & R. Addison (Eds.), *Interpretive investigations: Contributions to psychological research*. Albany: SUNY Press.

Byrd, A., & Smith, R. (in press). A qualitative analysis of the decision to remarry using Gilligan's Ethic of Care. *Journal of Divorce*, (Spring/Summer, 1988).

Buehler, C., Hogan, J., Robinson, B., & Levy, R. (1987). Remarriage following divorce: Stressors and well-being of custodial and noncustodial parents. *Journal of Family Issues*, *7*, 405-420.

Colby, A., & Kohlberg, L. (1988). *The measurement of moral judgment*. New York: Cambridge University Press.

Finlay, B., Starnes, C., & Alvarez, F. (1985). Recent changes in sex-role ideology among divorced men and women: Some possible causes and implications. *Sex Roles, 12,* 637-653.

Furstenberg, F., & Spanier, G. (1984). The risk of dissolution in remarriage: An examination of Cherlin's hypothesis of incomplete institutionalization. *Family Relations, 33,* 433-441.

Gibbs, J., & Widaman, K. (1982). *Social intelligence: Measuring the development of sociomoral reflection*. Englewood Cliffs, NJ: Prentice-Hall, Inc.

Giles-Sims, J., & Crosbie-Burnett, M. (1987). The remarried family: The status of research, clinical interventions and policy. Report on the Wingspread Conference, Racine, WI.

Gilligan, C. (1982). *In a different voice: Psychological theory and women's development*. Cambridge, MA: Harvard University.

Gilligan, C. (1977). In a different voice: Women's conceptions of self and morality. *Harvard Educational Review, 47,* 481-517.

Gilligan, C., & Belenky, M. (1980). A naturalistic study of abortion decisions. Pp. 69-103. In R. Selman & R. Yando (Eds.), *Clinical-developmental psychology*. San Francisco: Jossey-Bass.

Gilligan, C., Brown, L., & Rogers, A. (in press). Psyche embedded: A place for body, relationships, and culture in personality theory. In A. Rabil et al. (Eds.), *Studying persons and lives*. New York: Springer.

Gilligan, C., & Wiggins, S. (1987). The origins of morality in early childhood relationships. In J. Kagan and S. Lamb (Eds.), *The emergence of morality in young children*. Chicago, IL: University of Chicago Press.

Glick, P., & Lin, S. (1986). Recent changes in divorce and remarriage. *Journal of Marriage and the Family, 48,* 737-747.

Goldstein, H. (1987). The neglected moral link in social work practice. *Social Work, 32,* 181-186.

Goodwin, E., & Smith, R. (1988). Justice and responsibility reasoning in long-term marriages. (Paper to be presented at the National Council on Family Relations, Philadelphia.)

Kalmuss, D., & Seltzer, J. (1986). Continuity of marital behavior in remarriage: The case of spouse abuse. *Journal of Marriage and the Family, 48,* 113-120.

Kohlberg, L. (1984). *The psychology of moral development: Moral stages and the idea of justice*. New York: Harper & Row, Pub.

Kvanli, J., & Jennings, G. (1987). Recoupling: Development and establishment of the spousal subsystem in remarriage. *Journal of Divorce, 10,* 189-203.

Larson, J. & Allgood, S. (1987). A comparison of intimacy in first-married and remarried couples. *Journal of Family Issues, 8,* 319-331.

Marcia, J. (1966). Development and validation of ego identity status. *Journal of Personality and Social Psychology, 3,* 551-558.

Marcia, J. (1980). Identity in adolescence. Pp. 159-187. In J. Adelson (Ed.), *Handbook of adolescent psychology*. New York: Wiley & Sons, Inc.

Muus, R. (1988). Carol Gilligan's theory of sex differences in the development of moral reasoning during adolescence. *Adolescence, 23,* 229-243.

Osmond, M., & Martin, P. (1975). Sex and sexism: A comparison of male and female sex-role attitudes. *Journal of Marriage and Family, 37,* 146-154.

Pasley, K. (1984). Recognition of change: An introduction to the special issue on remarriage and stepparenting. *Family Relations, 33,* 351-353.

Piaget, J. (1965). *The moral judgment of the child.* New York: The Free Press.

Roberts, T., & Price, S. (1985/86). A systems analysis of the remarriage process: Implications for the clinician. *Journal of Divorce, 9,* 1-25.

Rosenblum, K. E. (1986). The conflict between and within genders: An appraisal of contemporary American femininity and masculinity. *Sociological Inquiry, 56,* 93-104.

Scanzoni, J. (1976). Sex role change and influences on birth intentions. *Journal of Marriage and Family, 38,* 43-58.

Skoe, E., & Marcia, J. (1987, September). The development and partial validation of a care-based measure of moral development. Paper presented at the Canadian Psychological Association Convention, Toronto. Department of Psychology, Simon Fraser University, Burnaby, British Columbia, Canada.

Smith, R., & Bonar, J. (1984, November). Sex-role attitudes: Moral reasoning or exchange theory. Paper presented at the Preconference on Theory Development and Research Methodology, National Council on Family Relations, San Francisco, California.

Tomeh, A. (1978). Sex-role orientation: An analysis of structural and attitudinal predictors. *Journal of Marriage and Family, 40,* 341-354.

Yeaman, P. (1987). Prophetic voices: Differences between men and women. *Review of Religious Research, 28,* 367-376.

Gender Differences in Divorce Adjustment

Patricia Diedrick

SUMMARY. Gender differences in divorce adjustment were investigated. It was concluded that there is sufficient evidence to demonstrate that males report less stress prior to the decision to divorce than do females, and that females fare better after separation and divorce than do males. It is argued that measures of divorce adjustment are either direct or indirect measures of self-esteem, and that gender differences in self-esteem exist prior to divorce and therefore account for gender differences in adjustment after divorce. It is further suggested that gender differences in the moderators of divorce adjustment (i.e., in attachment, initiation of divorce, and degree of social support) are related to gender roles and serve to reinforce gender differences in adjustment to divorce.

Divorce has been characterized as a highly disruptive life event creating effects that range from devastation to relief (Albrecht, 1980; Goode, 1956; Holmes & Rahe, 1967; Spanier & Thompson, 1983; Weiss, 1975). These differing effects have been characterized as indications of adjustment to divorce. Divorce adjustment has generally been measured in terms of self-esteem, or with measures which correlate highly with self-esteem. Gender differences in adjustment to divorce have been consistently noted, although Kitson and Raschke (1981) suggested that more research is required to determine whether such gender differences exist. The purpose of this literature review is to provide evidence that (a) gender differences in adjustment do exist, but (b) that the differences are the same ones that existed before the divorce, and relate to self-esteem. In addition, there are gender differences in behavior prior to, and after, divorce which

Patricia Diedrick, PhD, completed this study as a doctoral student in the Department of Child and Family Development at the University of Georgia. Correspondence should be addressed to the author at 64 Potawatomi Drive, Edgerton, WI 53534.

33

reinforce the gender differences in divorce adjustment and are related to sex roles.

ADJUSTMENT TO DIVORCE: GENERAL

The aftermath of divorce may be seen as a time requiring adjustment both to the loss of a spouse and to the gain of a new life-style (Spanier & Castro, 1979). Dasteel (1982) characterized the first type of adjustment as a process of individuation from a former partner involving grief and depression over the loss, and the second aspect of adjustment as reconstruction of self-concept and gain in self-efficacy. Dasteel suggested that stress after divorce results from the processes involved as individuals learn new skills, and those new skills can lead to greater feelings of self-esteem.

It has been pointed out that divorce adjustment begins during marriage at a time when one partner begins to withdraw his or her emotional involvement (Federico, 1979). Although historically adjustment was assumed to have occurred when an individual remarried (e.g., Goode, 1956), currently adjustment is being characterized as a process which may be more independent of marriage. Specifically, adjustment has been defined as the development of a separate identity and the ability to function adequately in new roles (Kitson & Raschke, 1981).

These two aspects of adjustment have been suggested as being separate processes, one characterizing the struggle with the loss (of a marriage, a spouse, a lover, a social status, and perhaps children) involved in divorce, and the other with the reorganization and changes of roles, and gain in new statuses, that occur because of the divorce (Spanier & Castro, 1979). Although these two processes of adjustment, to loss and to gain, overlap and affect each other, Spanier and Castro suggested that the creation of a new lifestyle appeared more important to overall adjustment.

The Impact of Divorce

Divorce, as a stressful event causing the loss of a partner and marriage, may lead to feelings of rejection and failure. As Knox (1985) suggested, divorce causes pain through the loss of intimacy; it shatters one's daily routine, and causes one to emphasize one's aloneness. Loss of a once intimate and loving partner, and possible loss of contact with children, can be devastating. The role of "wife" or "husband" becomes one of "former wife" or "former husband," and thus one's social status changes. Furthermore, one party, as the non-initiator of the divorce, likely feels rejected. Albrecht (1980) reported that the most common cause of stress after divorce was a feeling of personal failure.

It has been suggested that such feelings of failure injure self-esteem (Kessler, 1975). For both sexes, self-regard and self-acceptance have been found to be below normal after divorce (Gray, 1978). Complaints reflecting low self-esteem correlate with distress (Kitson & Sussman, 1982). As McCubbin and Dahl (1985, p. 306) suggested, "many experience divorce as a blow to their self-esteem." Although Thomas (1982) concluded that it has been well established that self-esteem is lowered by divorce, Erbes and Hedderson (1984) found that males who divorced had low self-esteem for several years prior to divorce. Thus, some question exists as to whether adjustment problems occur because of separation and divorce, or exist prior to divorce.

Along with the loss of a once intimate partner and possibly of self-esteem, divorce involves the creation of a new life-style, new roles, and thus changes in self-concept. Spanier and Castro (1979) suggested that adjustment to a new life is more difficult than to the loss of the marriage.

Thus, divorce adjustment has been described as a dual process involving adjustment to loss of love, status, and life-style, and adjustment to gain of a new life-style and the skills required to be mastered as a result of the change. The assumed effects of divorce, and stresses involved with making a new life, have led to a variety of measures of adjustment, all of which are related to self-esteem either directly or indirectly.

Measurement of Divorce Adjustment

Divorce adjustment has been measured primarily in terms of self-reported psychological, relational, and behavioral problems. Such measures emerge from the assumption that divorce leads to stressors which influence the individual in terms of psychological and behavioral changes. Measurement has, with few exceptions, been taken after actual separation or divorce, and thus conclusions concerning change because of divorce are difficult. Because divorce adjustment is assumed to begin prior to separation (Federico, 1979), data collected concerning that phase of divorce has been in terms of recollections of stress.

Psychological measures have involved areas of affect or personality assumed responsive to stress and related to well-being. Self-esteem (including self-acceptance, self-worth, and self-efficacy) has often been used as the primary ingredient in, or an aspect of, divorce adjustment measurement (e.g., Erbes & Hedderson, 1984; Granvold, Pedler, & Schellie, 1979; Gray, 1978; Pettit & Bloom, 1984; Salts & Zongker, 1983; Stewart, Schwebel, & Fine, 1986). Other psychological measures have involved questions dealing with general life satisfaction and happiness (Chiriboga & Thurnher, 1980; Keith, 1986; Mitchell, 1983), and measures of anxiety (Bloom & Clement, 1984; Granvold et al., 1979; Pettit & Bloom, 1984). These measures correlate highly with, and may be indications of, self-esteem (Burns, 1979). Instruments designed to measure interpersonal adjustment are also sometimes used to measure divorce adjustment, and these variables also correlate with self-esteem (Burns, 1979). Such measures have involved social adjustment and trust in others, and have been used by Nelson (1981), Erbes and Hedderson (1984) and others.

Behavioral indices have involved check lists of problems thought to reflect reactions to stress. These measures involve questions concerning behavioral problems such as difficulty in sleeping and alcohol usage (Stewart et al., 1986). Low self-esteem is believed to be a causal or contributing factor in the development of such problems (Burns, 1979).

Some measures of divorce adjustment have involved self-reports of stress that evolve from such areas as former spouse relationships, parenting, and financial concerns (e.g., Kurdek & Blisk, 1983). Reports of stress, however, do not necessarily relate to adjustment. For example, although Albrecht (1980) reported that females experienced more stress than males prior to the decision to divorce, and greater happiness after divorce, he concluded that females are more devastated by divorce due to their greater financial difficulties. But Keith (1985) found that females were actually more satisfied with their financial status than were males, despite females' lower economic status and stresses involved with financial problems. Thus, the mere existence of a problem is an inadequate measure of adjustment, for it is the individual's own perceptions of problems that influence adjustment.

GENDER DIFFERENCES IN ADJUSTMENT TO DIVORCE

Women face more stressors due to divorce than do men because of gender differences in income, social activity, and single parenthood. As previously discussed, this led Albrecht (1980) and others to conclude that women suffer more as a result of divorce. Yet there is overwhelming evidence that females actually fare better in terms of divorce adjustment than do males (Asher & Bloom, 1983; Bloom & Caldwell, 1981; Chiriboga, 1982; Wallerstein & Kelly, 1980; Zeiss, Zeiss, & Johnson, 1980). These differences are longlasting (Wallerstein, 1986).

Evidence exists that adjustment is more of a problem for women than for men prior to the decision to divorce, although such data is retrospective (Chiriboga & Cutler, 1977). Direct measurement of adjustment during the pre-decision period, although scant, has provided evidence that women may fare better at that time, at least in terms of self-esteem (e.g., Erbes & Hedderson, 1984; Klemer, 1971).

Preseparation Gender Differences in Adjustment

When women are asked to characterize the period prior to the divorce decision they report that period as being more stressful than do men (Bloom & Caldwell, 1981; Chiriboga & Cutler, 1977). Albrecht (1980) found that 8% of the women, compared with 22% of the men, rated the predivorce period as the best time (as compared with later times). Also, more females than males said prior to divorce was a more difficult time. Baruch, Barnett, and Rivers (1983) noted the predivorce period is difficult for women as they try desperately to hold together a marriage, but at the same time note the hopelessness of their efforts. The gender difference in retrospective reports of stress may reflect the degree to which men are unaware of marital problems. For example, it has been found that many men are unaware of even the possibility of divorce prior to the decision to divorce, and that the decision is more commmonly made by women (Kurdek & Blisk, 1983; Pettit & Bloom, 1984; Thomas, 1982; Zeiss et al., 1980). Furthermore, in giving reasons for the divorce, women are more likely to list specific problems, but men are more likely to report lack of knowledge concerning reasons for the divorce, or to report that their wives left simply to gain freedom (Thurnher, Fenn, Melichar, & Chiriboga, 1983). This also indicates that the predecision period is characterized by women's interest in the marital relationship and men's lack of attention concerning relationship problems.

It has been found that divorced and separated women report more disappointment and dissatisfaction with their past marriage than do men (Kitson & Sussman, 1982). Baruch et al. (1983, p. 167) noted that "freed from the tension of (a conflicted, unhappy) marriage, the divorced woman often finds she is beginning to feel better about herself than she has in years." These authors concluded that women had spent so much energy during the preseparation period trying to save an unhappy marriage that the actual separation represented a point of relief, and an opportunity for personal growth.

Postseparation Gender Differences
in Divorce Adjustment

During the postseparation period, females are generally found to be better adjusted in terms of health, happiness, and satisfaction with both self and others. Although some researchers have reported no gender differences in adjustment or mixed results (e.g., Gray, 1978; Rashke & Barringer, 1977; Weiss, 1975), most have found that gender differences in a wide variety of measures favor females as being better adjusted (Albrecht, 1980; Asher & Bloom, 1983; Bloom & Caldwell, 1981; Chiriboga, 1982; Gove, 1973; Wallerstein & Kelly, 1980; White & Bloom, 1981; Zeiss, Zeiss, & Johnson, 1980). Such differences have been found to exist for as long as ten years after divorce (Keith, 1985; Wallerstein, 1986).

Contrary results, although rare, have been reported. For example, Thomas (1982) reported that males scored better on a masculine-oriented measures of self-concept (i.e., dominance and aggressiveness). However, such results would be expected due to sex differences in gender role expectations. It has been suggested that females must fare more poorly because they generally have less money than do males after divorce (Albrecht, 1980). But as previously mentioned, females, despite their lower financial status, reported more satisfaction with their financial status, and with life in general, as compared with men (Keith, 1985). Thus, conclusions concerning adjustment, when based on assumptions of stress, may be inadequate.

After separation and divorce, males report more suicidal thoughts than do women (Gray, 1978; Zeiss et al., 1980). Anxiety and thoughts of suicide are further correlates of low self-esteem (Burns, 1979). And, it has been shown that men who divorce have low self-esteem in comparison with men who remain married, and that difference exists for years prior to, and years after, divorce (Erbes & Heddleson, 1984). Thus, it is possible that men struggle with adjustment problems long before divorce, and that their self-reported lack of stress prior to the separation period is an inadequate measure of their true adjustment pattern.

After separation, a change in roles, which may become a change in self-esteem sources and meaning, may evolve. For females, a sense of growth in self-esteem appears to result from divorce (Baruch et al., 1983; Haggman & Ashkenas, 1974; Wallerstein & Kelly, 1980). The effects of such changes appear long lasting (i.e., ten years later), with women having improved the quality of their lives more than did men (Wallerstein, 1986). This growth in self-esteem for women may be related to greater involvement in instrumental activities that can lead to a growing sense of self-esteem. Males, in gaining a feminine role (i.e., doing housework) after divorce, have not gained a role leading to self-esteem. As Gecas and Schwalbe (1986) pointed out, one cannot gain esteem from a role devalued in society. It is difficult to gain esteem from cleaning the toilet. But women on the other hand, add roles (such as "head of household," and "wage earner") from which esteem and greater confidence can be gained. Bardwick (1971) and others have contended that only as a woman gains an independent sense of self can she earn a true sense of self-esteem. Perhaps it is simply that women have much to gain whereas men have little to gain after divorce in terms of self-esteem that accounts for some of the gender difference noted in postseparation adjustment.

Gender Differences in the Moderators of Adjustment

A variety of psychological and relational variables have been determined as moderators of divorce adjustment difficulties. Such variables include social support, economic factors, personality factors such as self-esteem, relationship with former spouse, and circumstances surrounding the divorce (Kitson & Raschke, 1981; Pett, 1982). Gender differences exist in all of these moderator variables.

Personality variables have been found to be predictors of later divorce adjustment (Kurdek & Blisk, 1983). One important psychological variable associated with divorce adjustment appears to be self-esteem (Kitson & Rashke, 1981; Wallerstein & Kelly, 1980). As indicated, females reported a growth in feelings of self-esteem following divorce, whereas esteem remained low both prior to, and after, divorce for males (Baruch et al., 1983; Erbes & Hedderson, 1984). On the other hand, women with high self-esteem are more likely to divorce later in life (Klemer, 1971). Thus, gender differences in self-esteem may exist prior to divorce, and modify divorce adjustment. Furthermore, such gender differences in self-esteem continued to exist long after divorce (Wallerstein, 1986).

Initiation of divorce is associated with better divorce adjustment and this effect appears to continue to moderate improvement in the quality of life experienced long after divorce (Kurdek & Blisk, 1983; Pettit & Bloom, 1984; Wallerstein, 1986). Initiation of divorce may correspond with adjustment in that initiators may be those in pursuit of the greener pastures. Women are more likely to initiate divorce (Zeiss et al., 1980). In fact, Thomas (1982) found that half of the males reported having had no warning concerning divorce prior to the divorce. Women may fare better after divorce in part because they are more apt to initiate divorce.

Attachment, as a continued longing for, and love of, the former spouse, is negatively related to divorce adjustment (Kitson, 1982). Attachment has been described as an emotional dependence upon another individual, with a need for physical closeness (Spanier & Thompson, 1984). Weiss (1975) argued that the persistence of attachment made separation painful. Men report feeling a greater degree of attachment and desire to reconcile after divorce, as compared with women (Bloom & Kindle, 1985; Brown & Reimer, 1984; Zeiss et al., 1980).

Attachment tends to be less for those who initiated divorce (Berman, 1985), and women are more likely to initiate divorce (Thomas, 1982). Perhaps those who initiate divorce have begun the detachment process earlier. But, attachment, at least for men, appears so long lasting that this may not be an adequate explanation (e.g., Wallerstein, 1986).

Women apparently act in ways so as to decrease attachment. They prefer a greater distance in former spouse interactions and are less apt to profess love for, or act on longings to interact with, their former spouses, as compared with men (Goetting, 1979; Spanier & Thompson, 1984). Spanier and Thompson also reported that women, but not men, wanted decreased contact with their former spouses over time. Women's actions may be in part due to traditional gender roles that dictate male initiation of contact.

Degree of social activity correlates with adjustment (Spanier & Castro, 1979). Social support may aid in adjustment, providing therapeutic comfort. Women are more likely to find satisfaction in their friendships and to seek social support when they need help after divorce than are men (Chiriboga, Coho, Stein, & Roberts, 1979; Keith, 1986). In a longitudinal study, Keith found that divorced men were more socially isolated as compared with divorced women. And children, who typically remain with women rather than with men after divorce, may also be supportive. Many men, on the other hand, rarely have contact with their children after divorce, and some appear unable to recall the names of their children (Wallerstein, 1986). These gender differences in seeking social support are probably related to traditional gender roles. Men may behave in such ways as to deprive themselves of important sources of emotional support.

Gender differences exist in the variables that covary with adjustment, with each favoring females. Personality variables, such as self-esteem, and variations in gender roles, appear to moderate adjustment. Women's greater reliance on affiliation as a source of esteem, leading to a tendency to seek social support and receive custody of children, may aid in accounting for some of the gender differences after separation. Women's reliance on affiliation for esteem may also account for their greater stress during the preseparation phase, for they are more atuned to relational difficulties. Furthermore, as women gain independence and cope with new roles required as a result of divorce, they have an opportunity to gain self-esteem. For men, the addition of socially devalued tasks does not contribute to self-esteem. And traditional gender role activities, such as initiation of contact with individuals longed-for, may reinforce attachment for men. Non-reliance on social support may further inhibit men's adjustment.

DISCUSSION

Gender differences in adjustment to divorce exist both prior to the decision to divorce (with males reporting recollections of less stress at that time) and after the decision and separation (with females generally fairing better in terms of adjustment). But, gender differences in adjustment may exist prior to divorce, with low self-esteem males, and high self-esteem females, perhaps at risk to divorce.

These gender differences in adjustment after divorce parallel results of studies involving premarital relations and adjustment after death of a spouse. For example, Stroebe and Stroebe (1983) reviewed studies of adjustment after the death of a spouse and concluded that men suffer more in terms of depression and other psychological disorders, physical illnesses, death, and suicide rates, as compared with females. Also, in comparison with men, women are more likely to initiate an end to a dating relationship and adjust better to the ending of a relationship (Hochschild, 1975; Rubin, Peplau, & Hill, 1981). Therefore, gender differences, with females faring better than males after the end of a relationship, exist in premarital relations, in divorce, and after the death of a spouse.

Self-esteem and variables which correlate with esteem are common measures of divorce adjustment, based on the assumption that esteem is lowered by divorce, and that esteem is a general indicator of adjustment in life (Burns, 1979). It has been demonstrated in longitudinal studies that males who divorce, in comparison to males who remain married, had lower self-esteem and scored poorer in terms of other measures of adjustment for years both prior to and after divorce (Erbes & Hedderson, 1984). On the other hand, high self-esteem females appear more likely to divorce as compared with average or low self-esteem females (Klemer, 1971).

Perhaps high self-esteem females are more likely to initiate divorce and are better able to adjust to, and improve, their new lives.

Women, in contrast to men, have more to gain in terms of self-esteem as they add new roles and skills as a result of divorce. Women report feeling greater confidence and self-esteem after divorce (Baruch et al., 1983). Also, women more often than men act in ways that decrease attachment and bring in social support (Chiriboga et al., 1979; Keith, 1986; Spanier & Thompson, 1984), and the difference is probably related to gender role prescriptions.

Future research might best be directed to the determination of (a) what differentiates those who initiate divorce from those who do not, (b) what differentiates those who remain highly attached from those who are not, and (c) how self-esteem relates to these areas. Ideal research would involve measurement prior to separation and divorce. It is necessary to assess differences within groups. What differentiates those of each sex who adjust well from those who do not? It is ultimately more constructive to investigate why gender differences in divorce adjustment exist, and why there are differences in adjustment within gender groups, rather than to merely compare gender differences that now appear well-established.

REFERENCES

Albrecht, S. L. (1980). Reactions and adjustment to divorce: Differences in the experiences of males and females. *Family Relations, 29,* 59-68.

Asher, S. J. & Bloom, B. L. (1983). Geographic mobility as a factor in adjustment to divorce. *Journal of Divorce, 6,* 69-84.

Bardwick, J. (1971). *Psychology of women: A study of biocultural conflicts.* New York: Harper & Row.

Baruch, G., Barnett, R., & Rivers, C. (1983). *Lifeprints: New patterns of love and work for today's women.* New York: McGraw-Hill.

Berman, W. H. (1985). Continued attachment after legal divorce. *Journal of Family Issues, 6,* 375-392.

Bloom, B. L. & Caldwell, R. A. (1981). Sex differences in adjustment during the process of marital separation. *Journal of Marriage & the Family, 43,* 693-701.

Bloom, B. L. & Clement, C. (1984). Marital sex role orientation and adjustment to separation and divorce. *Journal of Divorce, 7,* 87-98.

Bloom, B. L. & Kindle, K. R. (1985). Demographic factors in the continuing relationship between former spouses. *Family Relations, 34,* 375-381.

Brown, S. D. & Reimer, D. A. (1984). Assessing attachment following divorce: Development and psychometric evaluation of the Divorce Reaction Inventory. *Journal of Counseling Psychology, 31,* 520-531.

Burns, R. B. (1976). *The self concept in theory, measurement, development and behaviour.* New York: Longman.

Chiriboga, D. A. (1982). Adaptation to marital separation in later and earlier life. *Journal of Gerontology, 37,* 103-114.

Chiriboga, D. A., Coho, A., Stein, J. A., & Roberts, J. (1979). Divorce, stress and social supports: A study in helpseeking behavior. *Journal of Divorce, 3,* 121-135.

Chiriboga, D. A. & Cutler, L. (1977). Stress responses among divorcing men and women. *Journal of Divorce, 1,* 95-106.

Chiriboga, D. A. & Thurnher, M. (1980). Marital lifestyles and adjustment to separation. *Journal of Divorce, 3,* 379-390.

Dasteel, J. C. (1982). Stress reactions to marital dissolution as experienced by adults attending courses on divorce. *Journal of Divorce, 5,* 37-47.

Erbes, J. T. & Hedderson, J. J. C. (1984). A longitudinal examination of the separation/divorce process. *Journal of Marriage & the Family, 46,* 937-940.

Federico, J. (1979). The marital termination period of the divorce adjustment process. *Journal of Divorce, 3,* 93-106.

Gecas, V. & Schwalbe, M. L. (1983). Beyond the looking-glass self: Social structure and efficacy-based self-esteem. *Social Psychology Quarterly, 46,* 77-88.

Goetting, A. (1979). The normative integration of the former spouse relationship. *Journal of Divorce, 2,* 395-414.

Goode, W. (1956). *After divorce.* Glencoe, IL: Free Press.

Gove, W. R. (1973). Sex, marital status, and mortality. *American Journal of Sociology, 79,* 45-67.

Granvold, D. K., Pedler, L. M., & Schellie, S. G. (1979). A study of sex-role expectance, and female post divorce adjustment. *Journal of Divorce, 2,* 383-393.

Gray, G. M. (1978). The nature of the psychological impact of divorce upon the individual. *Journal of Divorce, 1,* 289-301.

Haggman, K. & Ashkenas, R. (1974). *Single parent study: A preliminary investigation.* Paper presented at Massachusetts Children's Lobby Conference, Cambridge, March.

Hochschild, A. R. (1975). *Attending to, codifying, and managing feelings: Sex differences in love.* Paper presented at American Sociological Association, San Francisco.

Holmes, T. S. & Rashe, R. H. (1967). The social readjustment scale. *Psychosomatic Research, 11,* 213-218.

Keith, P. M. (1985). Financial well-being of older divorced/separated men and women: Findings from a panel study. *Journal of Divorce, 9,* 61-72.

Keith, P. M. (1986). Isolation of the unmarried in later life. *Family Relations, 35,* 389-395.

Kessler, S. (1975). *The American way of divorce: Prescriptions for change.* Chicago: Nelson-Hall.

Kitson, G. C. (1982). Attachment to spouse in divorce: A scale and its application. *Journal of Marriage & the Family, 44,* 379-393.

Kitson, G. C. & Raschke, H. J. (1981). Divorce research: What we know, what we need to know. *Journal of Divorce, 4*, 1-37.

Kitson, G. C. & Sussman, M. B. (1982). Marital complaints, demographic characteristics, and symptoms of mental distress in divorce. *Journal of Marriage & the Family, 44*, 87-101.

Klemer, R. H. (1971). Self-esteem and college dating experience as factors in mate selection and marital happiness: A longitudinal study. *Journal of Marriage and the Family, 33*, 183-187.

Knox, D. (1985). *Choices in relationships*. St. Paul, MN: West.

Kurdek, L. & Blisk, D. (1983). Dimensions and correlates of mothers' divorce experiences. *Journal of Divorce, 6*, 1-24.

McCubbin, H. & Dahl, B. B. (1985). *Marriage and family: Individuals and life cycles*. New York: Wiley.

Nelson, G. (1981). Moderators of women's and children's adjustment following parental divorce. *Journal of Divorce, 4*, 71-83.

Pett, M. G. (1982). Predictors of satisfactory social adjustment of divorced single parents. *Journal of Divorce, 5*, 1-17.

Pettit, E. J. & Bloom, B. L. (1984). Whose decision was it? The effects of initiator status on adjustment to marital disruption. *Journal of Marriage & the Family, 4*, 587-595.

Raschke, H. (1977). The role of social participation in postseparation and postdivorce adjustment. *Journal of Divorce, 1*, 129-140.

Rashke, H. J. & Barringer, K. D. (1977). Postdivorce adjustment among persons participating in Parents-Without-Partners organizations. *Family Perspective, 11*, 23-34.

Rubin, Z., Peplau, L. A., & Hill, C. I. (1981). Loving and leaving: Sex differences in romantic attachments. *Sex Roles, 7*, 821-835.

Salts, C. J. & Zongker, C. E. (1983). Effects of divorce counseling groups on adjustment and self concept. *Journal of Divorce, 6*, 55-67.

Spanier, G. B. & Castro, R. F. (1979). Adjustment to separation and divorce: An analysis of 50 case studies. *Journal of Divorce, 2*, 241-254.

Spanier, G. B. & Thompson, L. (1983). Relief and distress after marital separation. *Journal of Divorce, 7*, 32-49.

Spanier, G. B. & Thompson, L. (1984). *Parting: The aftermath of separation and divorce*. Beverly Hills: Sage.

Smart, L. S. (1979). An application of Erickson's theory to the recovery-from-divorce process. *Journal of Divorce, 1*, 67-79.

Stewart, J. R., Schwebel, A. I., & Fine, M. A. (1986). The impact of custodial arrangement on the adjustment of recently divorced fathers. *Journal of Divorce, 9*, 55-65.

Stroebe, M. S. & Stroebe, W. (1983). Who suffers more? Sex differences in health risks of the widowed. *Psychological Bulletin, 93*, 279-301.

Thomas, S. P. (1982). After divorce: Personality factors related to the process of adjustment. *Journal of Divorce, 5*, 19-36.

Thurnher, M., Fenn, C. B., Melchar, J., & Chiriboga, D. A. (1983). Sociodemographics: Perspectives on reasons for divorce. *Journal of Divorce, 6,* 25-35.

Wallerstein, J. S. (1986). Women after divorce: Preliminary report from a ten-year follow-up. *American Journal of Orthopsychiatry, 56,* 65-77.

Wallerstein, J. S. & Kelly, J. B. (1980). *Surviving the breakup: How children and parents cope with divorce.* New York: Basic Books.

Weiss, R. (1975). *Marital Separation.* New York: Basic Books.

White, S. W. & Bloom, B. L. (1981). Factors related to the adjustment of divorcing men. *Family Relations, 30,* 349-360.

Zeiss, A. M., Zeiss, R. H., & Johnson, S. M. (1980). Sex differences in initiation and adjustment to divorce. *Journal of Divorce, 4,* 21-33.

Gender Differences in College Students' Attitudes Toward Divorce and Their Willingness to Marry

Leora E. Black
Douglas H. Sprenkle

SUMMARY. This study compared the attitudes about divorce between young adults (college students) who had experienced parental divorce in their childhood and those from intact homes. While there were no overall group differences, a significant two-way interaction was found for parents' marital status and sex of their respondent. In the intact group, females had a slightly more positive attitude, but in the divorced group, males were considerably more positive in their attitudes towards divorce. The only relationship between the two groups that was near significance in terms of their readiness to marry was the divorced group's more favorable attitude towards pre-marital cohabitation. These young adults were also significantly more actively dating than the intact group. Intergenerational marital instability was also greater for college students who experienced parental divorce.

The purpose of the present study was to gain a better understanding of the effects of parental divorce experienced in childhood on young-adult adjustment. It involved the comparison of attitudes about divorce between young adults (college students) who have experienced parental divorce in their childhood and those from intact homes. Divorce adjustment is viewed as a constructive process which is influenced by many factors: individual coping skills, family coping skills, quality of family relationships, support networks available to parents and children, and societal and

Leora E. Black, PhD, is Adjunct Assistant Professor in Clinical Psychology, St. Michael's College, Colchester, VT 05439. Douglas H. Sprenkle, PhD, is Professor and Director of the Doctoral Program in Marriage and Family Therapy, MFT Building, Purdue University, 523 Russell Street, West Lafayette, IN 47907.

47

cultural norms regarding divorce. The study attempts to examine factors which could influence college students' attitudes toward divorce: marital status of parents, age at the time of divorce, sex, parents' socioeconomic status (occupation and level of income), and parents' level of education.

More research is needed in the area of long-term adjustment to parental divorce because (a) results from previous decades may no longer hold and (b) methodological problems in past investigations make results tenuous. Kulka and Weingarten (1979) cite three methodological problems which limit past studies' internal and external validity: (1) failure to distinguish between voluntary loss (parental death) and voluntary loss (parental divorce); (2) biased sampling through using clinical populations; and (3) lack of control for the effects of sociological variables (i.e., sex, age, social class, current marital status, marital history).

The current study diminishes these threats to internal and external validity by (1) distinguishing between involuntary and voluntary loss (students whose parents are divorced are compared with students whose parents are married to each other); (2) a nonclinical sample is used; (3) sociological variables are included in the analysis (i.e., parents' level of education, income, and occupation, current marital status (the samples were single, never married students). Investigation of the long-term adjustment of adults who have experienced parental divorce in childhood is limited and researchers agree that there needs to be further work (Kulka and Weingarten, 1979; Kurdek, Blisk, Siesky, 1981; Fine, Moreland, and Schwebel, 1983; and Montemayor, 1984).

LITERATURE REVIEW

Greenberg and Nay (1982) administered a Divorce Opinionnaire (Hardy, 1957) to 397 college students from homes where parents were separated/divorced, a parent was deceased, and parents were married to each other. The most significant finding was that students who experienced parental divorce had the most favorable attitude toward divorce. Rozendal (1983) found that college students who had experienced parental divorce gave more positive ratings to the term "divorce" than students from intact families and those who had experienced parental death.

Some studies have found that gender differences exist in how children react and adjust to their parents' divorce (Hetherington, Cox, and Cox 1981; Wallerstein, 1985). Wallerstein (1985) reports that 18 months after marital separation in the group of children who had experienced divorce prior to adolescence, boys appear to have significantly more problems in school and home than girls. At the five year mark no differences were found between males or females. However, at the ten year assessment of forty young adults ranging in age from 19 to 29, it was reported that

> . . . a significant number of men and women, and especially women, appear troubled and drifting. A minority consisting of one-third of the women appear especially wary of commitment and fearful of betrayal and seem caught up in a web of short-lived sexual relationships. The greater number, however, are strongly committed to the ideals of a lasting marriage and to values that include romantic love and fidelity. They are apprehensive about repeating their parents' unhappy marriage during their own adulthood and especially eager to avoid divorce for the sake of their still unborn children. (Wallerstein, 1985, p. 553)

During the ten year study, the process of adjustment varied in terms of the childrens' age at the time of divorce as well as gender. Initially, young children experiencing the separation reported more distress than older children. At the five year mark no differences in adjustment were found between the younger and older groups. At the ten year follow up, children who experienced the divorce at a younger age appear to be "less burdened" than those who were older at the time of the divorce (Wallerstein, 1984).

Although the major focus of the current study was on attitudes toward divorce, the authors thought it important to ascertain whether the intergenerational marital instability found in previous investigations (Pope and Mueller, 1976; Bumpass and Rindfuss, 1979; and Kulka and Weingarten, 1979), held true for this sample. Although not directly tested here, attitudes may be shaped not just by the marital experience of one's parents but by the marital status of one's grandparents.

Pope and Mueller (1976) concluded that children who have experienced marital instability (i.e., parental divorce or death) during childhood had higher rates of divorce or separation in their own first marriages. Bumpass and Rindfuss (1979) suggest that children who experience marital disruption are more likely to experience higher marital instability, lower level of education, and a lower socioeconomic status in adulthood. Kulka and Weingarten (1979) examined data from two cross-sectional surveys, performed in 1957 and 1976. They concluded that modest evidence existed for the intergenerational "transmission" of marital instability ". . . The difference is statistically reliable only for women in 1957, and, when controls for age and education are applied, only for men in 1976" (Kulka and Weingarten, 1979, p. 68).

Booth, Brinkerhoff, and White (1984) studied the impact of parental divorce on college students' courtship, another variable of interest in the current investigation. They examined "the impact of the amount of parental conflict before and after the divorce, change in the quality of parent-child relations, and parents' remarriage on the level and evaluation of courtship relations" (Booth, Brinkerhoff, and White, 1984, p. 85). The investigators suggest that the incidence of parental divorce correlates with the increase of courtship activity for the children. They conclude that the students' courtship activity increases "if the divorce is accompanied by acrimony during and after the divorce, parent-child relations deteriorate, and the custodial parent remains single" (Booth, Brinkerhoff, and White, 1984).

Stevenson and Black (1985) did a similar survey which supports the previous discussion. Also, they reported significant differences in college students' readiness for marriage, comparing students whose parents were divorced, widowed, or married to each other. The children from the divorce group were more skeptical about marriage, scoring significantly lower than the intact group or those who experienced parental death. Black (1984) surveyed college students to rank their priorities after school in terms of a job, time off, marriage, graduate school, and starting a family. A Spearman rank-order correlation indicated that students whose parents were divorced ranked marriage plans significantly lower than students whose families were intact.

After reviewing the literature, the following hypotheses were developed:

- *Hypothesis I*: Students from divorced homes will be more favorable in their attitudes towards divorce than students from intact homes.
- *Hypothesis II*: Males will be more positive in their attitudes toward divorce than females.
- *Hypothesis III*: Students who experienced their parents' divorce at a younger age, the pre-adolescent group, will be more positive in their attitudes toward divorce than those students who experienced their parents' divorce as adolescents.
- *Hypothesis IV*: Intergenerational marital instability will be greater in the group of students whose parents are divorced than those whose parents are still married to each other. Specifically, comparisons will be made between groups in terms of the marital status of the respondents' grandparents with the marital status of the respondents' parents.
- *Hypothesis V*: Students from divorced homes will report more dating behaviors/courtship activities than students from intact homes.

• *Hypothesis VI*: Students from intact homes will report a greater will-ingness to marry than students who experienced their parents' di-vorce.

In addition to the formal hypotheses, the authors also examined, using multivariate techniques, the potential contribution of a variety of variables to attitudes toward divorce: parents' occupation, level of education, stu-dents' location of upbringing, religious preference, religiosity, frequency of visitation by the noncustodial parent, and description of parents' present relationship.

METHOD

Subjects

The subjects were 348 undergraduate students enrolled in a marriage and family course at a large midwestern university. They were asked to participate in a study assessing college students' attitudes toward divorce and marriage. After administering the questionnaire, it was determined that 46 of the students had experienced their parents' divorce. Forty-three of the 46 were single and had never been married. In addition, 43 subjects were randomly selected from the intact group to match the divorce group in terms of their marital status.

Instrument

A questionnaire was initially developed after reviewing the literature on long-term adjustment to parental divorce and was piloted in 1983 and 1984. Additional refinements were made in 1986 using five marriage and family doctoral students who completed the questionnaire and critiqued the content. Content validity was also established by a panel of three na-tionally known experts on divorce. The questionnaire assessed the sub-jects' attitudes toward divorce and their willingness to marry. A five item scale assessed subjects' attitudes toward divorce. Four items were taken from Hardy's (1957) 12-item divorce attitude scale. Jorgensen and John-son (1980) computed item-total correlations and Cronbach's Alpha with these items. The correlations ranged from .64 to .77 and the Alpha coeffi-cient was .74. As noted below, Cronbach's Alpha was re-computed for the five item scale used in the current investigation.

The questionnaire included a number of demographic measures: par-ents' marital status, occupation, level of education, combined income, students' location of upbringing, religion, religiosity, sex, race, and age of the respondents. Students also were asked to describe their parents' present level of compatibility, perception of happiness during childhood and adolescence, past counseling experience(s), respondents' age at the time of the divorce, and amount of visitation by the non-custodial parent.

Data Analyses

This study attempted to find out if group differences existed between students from intact versus divorced homes and males vs. females in terms of students' attitudes toward divorce and their willingness to marry. A secondary emphasis involved the investigation of within-group differences for the students who experienced their parents' divorce. Comparisons were made between students who experienced the divorce prior to adolescence versus those who experienced it during adolescence.

Statistical analyses performed included: Chi-square statistics, Pearson's correlation, Spearman rank, and analyses of variance and regression. A Cronbach's alpha was calculated for the five item scale, "attitudes toward divorce." A composite score was computed and used throughout the analysis. Test-retest reliability was determined by computing Pearson's correlations (time 1 with time 2) for the "attitudes toward divorce" scale.

RESULTS

Reliability

A standardized alpha (SPSS update, 1981, p. 256) was used to calculate the internal reliability of the 5-item divorce scale (1 = negative attitude, through 5 = positive). Analysis is based on data collected at time 1 with a sample size of 86. The calculations indicated that the scale had an alpha equal to .73 and that a deletion of any of the items would not increase the alpha level.

The questionnaire was administered a second time one month later; 64% (55) of the students completed the questionnaire at time 2. A Pearson's correlation was computed for attitudes toward divorce time 1, (n = 55), with attitudes towards divorce time 2, (n = 55). A significant correlation was evident, r = .69, p = .001.

Demographics

The sample of 86 subjects was 52% female (45) and 46% male (40), with one incomplete response. The age range was 18 to 25, (M = 20.1). The sample was 88.4% Caucasian, 6% Black, 3.5% Hispanic, 1.2% Native American, and 1.2% Asian.

A comparison was made between students whose parents were divorced and those whose parents were still married to each other, in terms of parents' socioeconomic status (as indexed by: occupation, level of education, and combined incomes). The groups were similar except, not surprisingly, regarding mothers' occupation. In the married group, approximately 26% of the married mothers were homemakers, whereas only 7% of the divorced mothers were homemakers. Both groups were predominantly white collar versus blue collar with no significant differences between groups for either males or females.

In terms of parents' level of education, the parents who were married to each other were slightly (but not statistically significantly) more educated than the divorced parents. Fifty-two percent of the married fathers and 45% of the married mothers had at least a college education versus 42% of the divorced fathers and 33% of the divorced mothers. Also 48% of the fathers and 52% of the mothers married to each other had a high school education compared to 58% of the divorced fathers and 65% of the divorced mothers.

Analysis of the distribution of parents' combined income showed that both groups were predominantly middle to upper class. In the married group, 82% had combined income in the $30,000-$75,000+ range compared to 85% in the divorced group. Overall, the two groups were similar in terms of parents' socioeconomic status, with the exception of more mothers in the married group being homemakers.

Additional analysis showed there were no significant differences between groups in where they were raised, religious identification, or religiosity. Subjects came predominantly from small cities and small towns or rural areas. Approximately a third of each group was Catholic with the rest being mostly Protestant. Subjects identified themselves predominantly as "moderately religious."

The divorce subsample, N = 43, included 19 females (44%) and 23 males (53%), with one unknown. Age at time of the divorce was another variable of interest. Responses were dichotomized into two groups: pre-adolescent (birth through age 12) and adolescent (age 13 through 20). Approximately 58% (25) experienced the divorce in their pre-adolescent years, whereas, 41% (18) experienced it in their adolescent years.

Hypotheses

Hypothesis I. A t-test was computed for parents' marital status with the composite score of each student's attitude toward divorce. The composite scores range from five to 25, five indicating a negative attitude toward divorce and 25 a positive attitude. There were no significant differences between the intact group ($M = 14.37$) compared with the divorce group ($M = 14.52$). Overall, both groups appear to be neutral or indifferent in their attitudes toward divorce.

Hypothesis II. A t-test indicated that males ($M = 15.48$) were more positive in their attitudes toward divorce than females ($M = 13.49$). Further analysis showed that this difference occurred within the divorce group where males were more positive in their attitudes toward divorce ($M = 16.65$) than females ($M = 12.26$). Further analysis of the gender issue was done through multivariate statistics, repeated below.

Hypothesis III. The students who experienced their parents divorce at a younger age, the pre-adolescent group, would be more positive in their attitudes toward divorce than those students who experienced their parents divorce as adolescents. A t-test indicated no significant difference between students who experienced parental divorce as pre-adolescents ($M = 15.6$, $N = 25$) and those who experienced divorce as adolescents ($M = 13.05$, $N = 18$), $t = 1.64$, $p = .108$. Further analysis on this variable was done through multivariate statistics reported below.

Hypothesis IV. A Chi-square test of parents' marital status with grandparents' marital status (whether grandparents had ever been divorced) indicated that intergenerational marital instability was significantly greater for the divorced group ($\chi^2 = 3.7(1)$, $p = .05$).

Hypothesis V. A significant difference existed between groups in dating habits ($\chi^2 = 7.3 (2)$, $p = .03$) with 67.6% of the divorce group dating just one person, whereas, in the intact group 47.4% of the students were dating no one. A higher level of dating activity was found in the divorce group; only 18% reported that they were *not* dating vs. 47% in the intact group.

Hypothesis VI. Asked if "in (their) life time, do (they) want to get married?", 97.4% of the students whose parents are married responded "yes" versus 100% of the students who experienced their parents divorce. A t-test was run to determine if a significant difference existed between groups in term of their projected hypothetical age at marriage. The mean hypothetical age of the "married" group was 24.7 versus 25.1 for the "divorced" group. No significant differences emerged between the groups. A Spearman rank test indicated that there were no significant differences between groups in how students prioritized what they want to do after graduating college (career, marriage, graduate school, traveling/time off, and starting a family).

A chi-square test showed that parental status and whether students wanted to cohabitate with their partners before marriage was near significance ($\chi^2 = 3.5(1)$, p = .06). In the divorced group 54.1% (20) of the students wanted to live with their partner before getting married vs. 29.7% (11) in the intact group and 45.9% (17) students in the divorce group did not want to cohabitate vs. 70.3% (26) in the intact group.

A number of analyses of variance were computed to determine whether differences in students' attitudes toward divorce can be attributed to different levels of various independent variables: parents' marital status, parents' occupation, level of education, students' location of upbringing, religious preference, religiosity, sex of the respondent, description of parents' present relationship and age at time of the divorce. Analyses of variance were done by SPSS's ANOVA program, using the default strategy so cells were weighted by their sample sizes in order to deal with the unequal cell sizes (Tabachnick and Fidell, 1983, p. 219).

An analysis of variance was performed with three variables: parents' marital status, sex of the respondent and attitudes toward divorce (N = 85). The overall F was found to be significant, F $(2, 81)$ = 3.99, p = .011. A significant two-way interaction was found for parents' marital status and sex of the respondent in terms of their attitudes toward divorce (see Figure 1). In the intact group the more positive attitude was held by females (nonsignificant) but in the divorce group males were more positive (significant) in their attitudes toward divorce. The males and females in the intact group were more similar in their attitudes toward divorce than their counterparts in the divorce group. A significant main effect was found for the analysis of sex of the respondent with attitudes toward divorce (F $(1, 81)$ = 4.567, p = .04).

Another analysis of variance was done within the divorce subsample on attitudes toward divorce by sex of the respondent and age at the time of the divorce. A significant main effect for sex of the respondent was found (F $(1, 38)$ = 7.803, p = .01). Females were more negative in their attitudes toward divorce (M = 12.75) vs. males (M = 16.56). The multiple r squared indicates that 20% of the variance of students' reported attitudes toward divorce was explained by the students' gender and their age at the time of the divorce. A hierarchical regression analysis indicates that 18% of the variance is explained by the sex of the respondent and 2% is explained by the age at the time of the divorce. As can be seen by Figure 2,

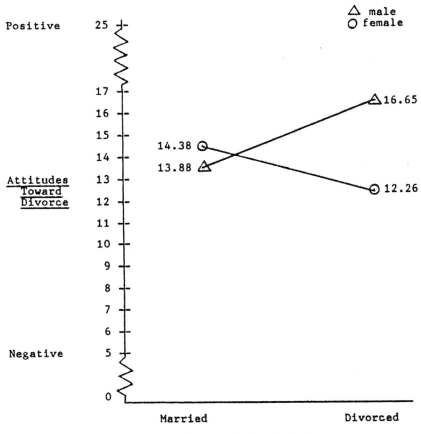

Figure 1

Two-way Interaction of Attitudes Toward Divorce With
Parents' Marital Status and Sex of The Respondent

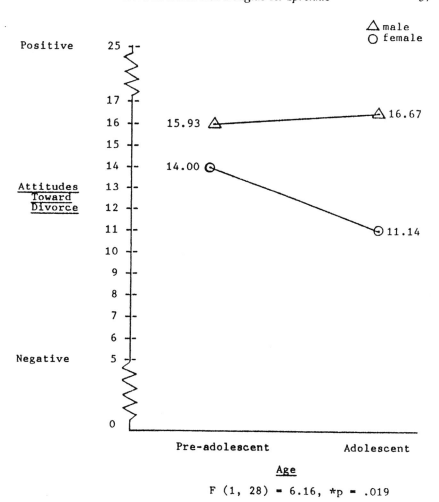

Figure 2

Two-way Interaction of Attitudes Toward Divorce With Sex of
The Respondent and Age at The Time of The Divorce

males were appreciably more positive in their attitudes toward divorce in families where the divorce occurred when the respondent was an adolescent as compared to females.

There were no significant relationships with parents' occupation, level of education, students' location of upbringing, religious preference, religiosity, and description of parents' present relationship.

DISCUSSION

The major finding of this study was that gender is the predominant variable that explains the unknown variance related to students' attitudes toward divorce. Although analysis of the entire sample indicated that males were more positive in their attitudes toward divorce than females, this was due entirely to male positivity in the divorced subsample.

The results of this study seem to be compatible with Wallerstein's ten year longitudinal study of 113 predominantly white middle class subjects in Northern California, (Harvard Medical School Mental Health Letter, 1985). The California study has found that boys have a difficult time dealing with the initial divorce but that "it was the girls who faced special difficulties as young adults. Many appeared to avoid commitment, fearing betrayal and rejection by men; they often became involved in short-lived sexual relationships . . ." (Harvard Medical School Mental Health Letter, 1985, p. 8). Perhaps gender differences can be explained by the process of socialization. Possibly females are socialized to maintain and value the family in a different way than males; therefore, females are less willing to endorse divorce as a positive outcome.

The only relationship between the two groups that was near significance in terms of their readiness to marry was whether or not they were favorable toward cohabitation prior to marriage. The divorced group was more favorable to cohabitating prior to marriage (54.1%), than the intact group (29.7%). These results can be interpreted in a number of ways. The results might be an indication that (1) young adults who experienced parental divorce are indeed more skeptical about getting married than children from intact homes or/and (2) young adults want to test out the relationship prior to making a more legal and personal commitment or/and (3) young adults want to build a stronger relationship prior to further commitment.

At the time which the questionnaire was administered, the divorced group reported to be significantly more actively dating (82%) than the intact group (53%). Not surprisingly there was a significant difference in how students described their parents' present level of compatibility. Fifty-two percent of the divorce group said that their parents were not compatible, whereas only 7.3% of the intact group described their parents as not compatible.

Limitations

The study has limited "generalizability" in that it is a cross-sectional survey of generally middle to upper middle class college students. It is retrospective in nature and also asks students to express their future expectations. The answers to such questions may or may not be accurate, although the method employed may be the best way of tapping current perceptions. Other disadvantages of using a survey include the loss of depth of information and potential problems related to social desirability (which was unfortunately not controlled).

In conclusion, the results of this study indicated that college students who experienced parental divorce and those whose parents are married to each other were not found to significantly differ in their readiness to marry and their attitudes toward divorce. College students who experienced parental divorce did report significantly more active dating behavior than the intact group. Also, those students who experienced parental divorce appeared to want to cohabitate with their spouse-to-be prior to marriage more so than the intact group. No group differences existed between the divorce or intact group, in terms of their attitudes toward divorce. Overall, college students reported neutral or indifferent attitudes toward divorce. However, differences did emerge between males and females in terms of their attitudes toward divorce. Males were more positive in their attitudes toward divorce than females within the divorce subsample. Intergenerational marital instability was greater for students from divorced homes than for students whose parents are married to each other.

REFERENCES

Black, L. College students' reactions and adjustment patterns to their parents' divorce. Unpublished undergraduate thesis, University of Vermont, 1984.

Booth, A.; Brinkerhoff, D.; and White, L. The impact of parental divorce on courtship. *Journal of Marriage and the Family*, 1984, 85-94.

Bumpass, L. and Rindfuss, R. Children's experience of marital disruption. *American Journal of Sociology*, 1979, *85*(1), 49-65.

Fine, M.; Moreland, J.; and Schwebel, A. Long-term effects of divorce on parent-child relationships. *Developmental Psychology*, 1983, *19*(5), 703-713.

Greenberg, E. and Nay, W. The intergenerational transmission of marital instability reconsidered. *Journal of Marriage and the Family*, 1982, 335-347.

Hardy, K. R. Determinants of conformity and attitude change. *Journal of Abnormal and Social Psychology*, 1957, *54*, 289-294.

Harvard Medical School, Mental Health Letter. (1985, September). Effect of divorce on children. Volume 2 (3), 8.

Hetherington, M.; Cox, M.; & Cox, R. Effects of divorce on parents and children. In M. Lamb (Ed.), *Non-traditional families*. New Jersey: Lawerence Erlbaum, 1982.

Jorgensen, S. and Johnson, A. (1980). Correlates of divorce liberality. *Journal of Marriage and the Family*, *42*(3), 671-626.

Kulka, R. and Weingarten, H. The long-term effects of parental divorce in childhood adjustment. *Journal of Social Issues*, 1979, *35*(4), 50-78.

Kurdek, L.; Blisk, D. and Siesky, A. Correlates of children's long-term adjustment to their parents' divorce. *Developmental Psychology*, 1981, *17*(5), 565-579.

Montemayor, R. Picking up the pieces: the effects of parental divorce on adolescents with some suggestions for school-based intervention programs. *Journal of Early Adolescence*, 1984, *4*(4), 289-314.

Pope, H. and Mueller, C. The intergenerational transmission of marital instability: comparisons by race and sex. *Journal of Social Issues*, 1976, *32*(1),49-66.

Rozendal, F. Halos vs. stigmas: long-term effects of parent's death or divorce on college students' concepts of the family. *Adolescence*, 1983, *18*(72), 947-955.

Stevenson, M. and Black, K. (1985) Parental death and divorce and offsprings' sexual attitudes and commitment. Unpublished paper, Purdue University.

Wallerstein, J. S. Children of divorce: preliminary report of a ten-year follow-up of older children and adolescents. *Journal of the American Academy of Child Psychiatry*, 1985, 24, 5, 545-553.

MEN
AND DIVORCE

Divorced Fathers Describe
Their Former Wives:
Devaluation and Contrast

David Schuldberg
Shan Guisinger

SUMMARY. This paper investigates the devaluation of women by their former husbands in a sample of sixty-one divorced fathers who had recently remarried. On the Adjective Check List (ACL) these husbands describe their former wives in highly negative and deviant terms as compared with the ACL norms and with their descriptions of themselves and the current partner. Devaluation of the former wife is not accompanied by idealization of either the present wife or the husbands' descriptions of themselves; a negative view of the

David Schuldberg, PhD, is Associate Professor, Department of Psychology, University of Montana, Missoula, MT 59812-1041. Shan Guisinger, PhD, is affiliated with the Department of Psychology, University of Montana.

An earlier version of this paper was presented at the annual meeting of the Rocky Mountain Psychological Association, Tucson, Arizona, April 24-27, 1985. The authors wish to thank Dr. Harrison G. Gough for many invaluable suggestions, and Dr. James A. Walsh for elucidating the componential nature of the correlation coefficient. They would also like to thank Drs. Judith S. Wallerstein and Philip A. Cowan.

former wife is slightly correlated with husbands' low self-esteem. There was a marked contrast between husbands' ACL descriptions of present and former wives on traits concerning interpersonal power, expressiveness, and control of aggression.

This paper investigates a pattern of devaluation of women by their former husbands. This pattern is remarkable because the devaluation is extreme and occurs in a non-clinical population of remarried fathers. It is of concern because there is strong evidence that interparental hostility is detrimental to children both in intact marriages and when the hostility continues into the post-divorce co-parenting relationship (Emery, 1982).

When a divorced father remarries, he must negotiate a number of relationships unique to remarriage and for which there are few social guidelines (Cherlin, 1978; Messinger, 1985; Sager et al., 1983; Wald, 1981). Perhaps most delicate, the new couple must work out a co-parenting relationship with the husband's wife. Yet, for many divorcing couples, hostility continues long after the official divorce (Wallerstein & Blakeslee, 1989). Weiss (1975) has noted: "Murderous phantasies in which the wife is the victim do not seem especially rare . . . shared parenting of the children provides a convenient vehicle for the expression of post-marital malice." Remarriage theories would benefit from our knowing the form of this "malice," yet little is known about parents' typical post-divorce relationship (Ahrons, 1981). Interviews with remarried fathers and their new wives suggested that a normal population of newly remarried individuals held a highly jaundiced view of the husband's former wife.

The question arises as to the extent that this hostile picture is a result of accurate perceptions of the spouse's behavior, or if it includes misperceptions and misattributions regarding the former partner. The fact that people are not objective perceivers of others or themselves is a central theme in the literature on person perception (Bender & Hastorf, 1950; Hastorf & Bender, 1952). Along with actual degree of similarity (Buss, 1985; Byrne & Nelson, 1965) and the presence of certain generally valued traits (Palmer & Byrne, 1970), accuracy in perception and in making predictions about the partner (Arias & O'Leary, 1985; Christensen & Wallace, 1976; Murstein & Beck, 1972), perceived similarity (Arias & O'Leary, 1985; Byrne & Blalock, 1963; Murstein & Beck, 1972) and types of attribution about a partner's behavior (e.g., Weiss, 1980; Jacobson et al., 1985) all contribute to marital satisfaction. Buss (1984) found generally positive correlations between spouses' traits across self-report, spouse ratings, and independent interviewers' ratings of the partners' personalities, as well as between preferences for mate characteristics (Buss & Barnes,

1986). Terman and Buttenwieser (1935) found that self-report responses of husbands and wives to a number of attitude and personality test items tend to be positively correlated, while these correlations are generally moderately negative for unhappy and divorced couples.

Despite research on person perception and marriage, no recent study has examined the perceptions of the formerly married of each other. Clinical observations suggest that comparison and contrast in two different relationships might contribute to a husband's negative view of the former wife. First, the husband might contrast himself and his former wife, with the former wife generally being seen as all bad: "I really tried to make the marriage work; she was just too self-centered for the give and take of marriage." A contrast between two others occurs when the former wife is perceived as very different from the present wife: "They are as unlike as night and day; my first wife was a real witch; my second wife is an angel." Both of these contrasts between spouses could result from the defense mechanism of *splitting*, a psychological process generally attributed to disturbed individuals and observed less frequently in normal adult populations. Splitting represents a failure to achieve integration of both good and bad aspects of a person (Fairbairn, 1961; Kernberg, 1980; Kohut, 1984) and generally involves contrasting two individuals (or the self and an other), with one being devalued while the other is simultaneously overvalued or idealized. This paper presents data indicating that some, but not all, of these processes operate in husbands' relationships with their former wives.

This research uses the Adjective Check List (ACL; Gough & Heilbrun, 1980) to examine the pattern of remarried husbands' perceptions of their former wives, their present wives, and themselves. We examine four hypotheses:

First, we expect that because of the need for amicable co-parenting of their children, divorced fathers' descriptions of their former wives will be only moderately negative, and will become less negative over the course of the remarriage.

Secondly, when it occurs, devaluation of the former wife will occur as part of the defense mechanism of splitting, and will thus be accompanied by an idealization of either the present wife or the husband himself.

Third, extreme devaluation of the former wife will be symptomatic of the husband's intrapersonal difficulties involving self-worth, and will be correlated with his low self-esteem.

Finally, the husbands' perceptions of the former wife will be *dissimilar from* and *contrast with* their descriptions of themselves and their present wives. *Dissimilarity* refers to how far apart two different personality profiles are. *Contrast* occurs when one person is rated as low on a particular trait while another person is described as high. In this case the two descriptions are polarized; for example, the husbands may use the present wife or themselves as a reference point for describing the former wife, and rate one as high on a particular trait and the other as low, and vice versa.

METHODS

Subjects

The participants in this study are sixty-one divorced fathers who had recently remarried. Thirty-eight remarried couples were seen in their first year of marriage, and twenty-three couples were seen in their third, fourth, or fifth years of marriage. Seventeen couples were seen at two points in the remarriage, once at one year and once at three to five years.[1]

Couples were recruited primarily from the marriage license records recorded in 1979, 1980 and 1983 in four counties in the San Francisco Bay area of California. Participants were also recruited through referrals from subjects, informal contacts, newspaper advertisements, and contacting stepparent organizations.

The men had been married an average of 1.9 years (SD = 1.5), after having been divorced an average of 4.7 years (SD = 3.0). Their mean age was 36.0 years (SD = 5.0). Most were college graduates, white, and middle to upper middle class, with an average of 16 years of education (SD = 3.0) and a mean annual income of \$40,246 (SD = \$1,880) in 1981-83. They had an average of 1.6 children (SD = .6). As a group these fathers reported a great deal of involvement with their children as compared with national statistics (Furstenberg & Nord, 1985), spending an average of 12.5 days per month (SD = 9.8) with them. Eleven and one-half percent of the fathers had sole custody of their children, and 46% were involved in joint custody arrangements. Thirty-eight percent of the new wives also had children from a previous marriage. At the time the data were collected, eight of the fathers (13%) had had a child with the new wife. This sample, of course, is not a representative one due to the selection procedures employed, the families' high income, and the fathers' high degree of involvement with their children. Nevertheless, a highly-functioning sample can provide useful information if the subjects exhibit behavior that is more deviant than expected.

In most cases, data were gathered in the course of a home visit that included an interview and the completion of a number of other questionnaires. Usually both members of the couple were present, and they were instructed not to look at the partner's responses or discuss the instrument.[2]

The Adjective Check List

The measure of self and other evaluation used in this study is the Adjective Check List (Gough & Heilbrun, 1980), consisting of 300 adjectives and adjectival phrases commonly used to describe a person's attributes. Each Adjective Check List can be scored for thirty-seven empirically derived personality scales.[3] Each partner in this study filled out a total of four ACL's in a fixed order, the first describing themselves, then their spouse, the husband's former spouse, and their Ideal self. Adjective Check Lists with fewer than twenty responses were eliminated from the analyses. The Adjective Check List descriptions are analyzed to examine the components of comparison and contrast in these remarried husbands' perceptions of their former wives.

Overall description of the former wife. A composite adjectival description of the former wife provides a qualitative picture of the husbands' perceptions of and relationships with the former wives. Then, three ACL *modus operandi* scales are examined for the husbands' ACL descriptions of the former wife. These scales, *Favorable* adjectives, *Unfavorable* adjectives, and *Communality* (a measure of the usualness of the adjectives checked), allow a comparison of the overall favorability and degree of deviance in the husbands' descriptions of the former wives. *T*-tests are used to examine the degree to which husbands' evaluations of the former wife differ on these scales for men remarried for different lengths of time.

Idealization of the self or present wife. To test the hypothesis that a negative evaluation of the former wife is accompanied by an idealization of either the self or the present wife, the husbands' self-descriptions and descriptions of the present wife are compared to the ACL norms for the three *modus operandi* scales to determine whether these ACL descriptions reflect idealized or devalued descriptions.

Husbands' devaluation of the former wife and low self-esteem. A measure of self-esteem based on self-ideal congruence was calculated as the reflected sum of absolute differences between the husbands' ACL self-descriptions and descriptions of the Ideal self on eight ACL scales (Gough, Fioravanti, & Lazzari, 1983). Self-esteem is correlated with the husbands' descriptions of the former wife on *Favorable* adjectives, *Unfavorable* adjectives, and *Communality* to assess the degree to which a negative evaluation of the former wife is associated with the husband's own intrapersonal difficulties measured by low self-esteem.

Dissimilarity and contrast in descriptions of the former wife, present wife, and self. Differences between descriptions of the former wife, the present wife, and self are examined in two ways. To test the hypothesis that the husbands' perceptions of the former wife are *dissimilar* from their perceptions of present wife and self, the differences in profile elevation between descriptions of the former wives, the present wives, and the husbands' self-descriptions are examined. Multivariate Analysis of Variance (MANOVA) is used to determine whether pairs of profiles differ overall on the thirty-seven ACL scales, with *t*-tests used to examine individual scale differences between descriptions. Cronbach and Gleser's (1953) *D* statistic is also computed for pairs of descriptions for each subject and used as an index of the mean distance or dissimilarity between pairs of descriptions.[4] The ACL Likability index (Gough & Heilbrun, 1980, p. 43), a ratio of *Favorable* adjectives to *Favorable* plus *Unfavorable* adjectives, is also compared for the present and former wives.

Secondly, the scale by scale correlations between pairs of ACL descriptions are used to provide indices of attributional *contrast*.[5] If devaluing of the former wives occurs as the result of polarization, comparison, and contrast in the husbands' attributions, then the adjectival descriptions of the contrasted individuals should be negatively correlated on particular salient traits. In addition, the husbands' ACL descriptions of the Ideal self are examined for contrast between the negatively evaluated ex-wife and the husbands' Ideal self.

RESULTS

Overall Description of the Former Wife

At the level of the individual adjectives, the composite person who emerges from the husbands' descriptions of the former wives is characterized by a conflicting mixture of traits, with both positive and negative adjectives checked. At one year of remarriage, the husbands ($n = 38$), in order of frequency checked, saw their former wives as defensive (82% of the subjects used this descriptor), dissatisfied (66%), attractive (63%), emotional (63%), resentful (63%), confused (61%), demanding (58%), friendly (58%), capable (55%), complaining (55%), fault-finding (55%), opinionated (55%), argumentative (53%), bitter (53%), good-looking (53%), healthy (53%), and intelligent (53%).

At three years of remarriage, the men ($n = 37$)[6] most frequently chose these adjectives to describe their former wives: attractive (70%), capable (68%), defensive (68%), emotional (57%), healthy (57%), intelligent (57%), demanding (54%), dissatisfied (54%), good-looking (54%), stubborn (54%), hard-headed (51%), self-centered (51%), friendly (49%), headstrong (49%), resentful (49%), argumentative (46%), and assertive (46%).[7]

While these composite descriptions do include some positive adjectives, overall scores on the ACL scales are extremely negative. The mean descriptions of the former wife on the *modus operandi* Scales *Favorable*, *Unfavorable*, and *Communality* are from 1.9 to 2.5 standard deviations from the standardization sample mean in the negative direction, and the mean profile for the former wives is strikingly deviant on a large number of scales. These negative evaluations are extremely unusual in research using the ACL.[8]

Figure 1 shows the mean ACL scale elevations for husbands' descriptions of the the current and former wife, and the husbands' self-descriptions. Appendix 1 contains the mean scale scores for each of these three descriptions, along with the results of univariate tests of scale differences. Since the subjects in this study are drawn from a non-clinical population and since these negative evaluations are extreme in relation to the ACL literature, it is likely that these perceptions of the former wife are indeed unrealistic, although no direct data were gathered on the personalities or behavior of the former wives themselves.

Contrary to the first hypothesis, descriptions of the former wife do not become significantly less negative on the *modus operandi* scales in the third year of remarriage, although there is a non-significant trend toward a more positive view, also found in the present wives' descriptions of the ex-wife, and much more apparent in interviews with the couple (Guisinger, Cowan, & Schuldberg, 1989).[9]

Are the Men Splitting?

Is devaluation of the former wife accompanied by an idealization or over-valuation of either self or present wife? While the husbands' descriptions of the former wives are remarkably negative, their self-descriptions and descriptions of the present wife are within normal limits. Mean scores for husbands' descriptions of the partner on these three *modus operandi* scales fall within 0.7 standard deviations of the standardization sample mean, and husbands' mean self-descriptions are within 0.4 standard deviations of the mean.

The husbands' descriptions of the present wife are positive but not extreme, and as a group the present wives were rated slightly *below* the standardization sample mean on *Communality*. The current wife does not appear to be idealized, nor do the husbands tend to describe themselves in

FIGURE 1. Husbands' descriptions of themselves and their present and former wives: Mean Adjective Check List profiles. Reproduced by special permission of the publisher, Consulting Psychologists Press, Inc., from the Manual for the Adjective Check List, by Harrison Gough, PhD, and Alfred Heilbrun, PhD, copyright 1980.

THE ADJECTIVE CHECK LIST PROFILE

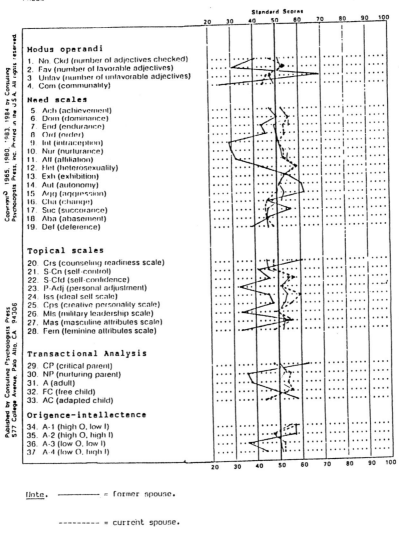

Note. ——— = former spouse.

- - - - - - - = current spouse.

——— ·· = Self Description

an inflated manner. This means that technically, in the group as a whole, splitting is not responsible for the devaluation of the former wife.

Is a Negative Evaluation of the Former Wife Related to Husbands' Low Self-Esteem?

This study finds a non-significant trend for devaluation of the former wife to be correlated with husband's low self-esteem. For *Favorable* adjectives, the correlation with the self-ideal congruence measure is .18 ($p < 0.10$, one-tailed test). For *Unfavorable* adjectives, $r = -.19$, $p < 0.10$.[10]

Do Husbands' Perceptions of Former Wives Differ from or Contrast with Their Perceptions of Self and the Present Wife?

Dissimilarity in scale elevations. All of the pairs ACL profiles examined in this study differed significantly in elevation when repeated-measures MANOVA's were conducted, although the magnitudes of these differences vary greatly. The relative sizes of the profile differences are evident in the magnitude of Cronbach and Gleser's D statistic (and of the F statistic from each MANOVA). The value of the D statistic for the the mean difference in profiles from the husbands' descriptions of the present and former wives is 114.8 ($SD = 38.4$).[11] The distance between profiles of the former wife and the husbands' self-descriptions yields a mean value of D of 108.5 ($SD = 35.8$).[12] This compares with a value of D of 65.7 ($SD = 26.3$) for the profiles of self and present wife.

Contrast in the husbands' perceptions of pairs of individuals in the self, present wife, and former wife triad. On the whole, scale score correlations across pairs of descriptions of self, partner, former wife, and Ideal self tend to be positive in this study. This may reflect a general tendency for people to use the same adjectives in different descriptions and is expected in a repeated measures situation.[13] When negative correlations occur, they are in contrast to this trend. Over the 37 ACL scales, husbands' descriptions of themselves tend to be positively correlated with their descriptions of their present wives. Husbands' self-descriptions and descriptions of the former wife are also correlated for a number of scales. Only the scale for *Dominance* is negatively correlated across descriptions of self and former wife.[14]

Evidence for contrast and polarization appears for husbands' descriptions of their present and former wives. The scales of *Dominance, Exhibitionism, Autonomy, Aggression, Abasement, Deference, Self Control,* and

Masculine attributes are negatively correlated at the the .05 level or better for descriptions of the present and former wife.[15] Appendix 2 contains the correlations between husbands' ACL descriptions of themselves and their present wives, themselves and their former wives, and their present and former wives.

DISCUSSION

These data show extreme devaluation of former wives in a normal and highly-functioning population of recently remarried men. These husbands' descriptions of their former wives are strikingly and surprisingly negative. While there is persuasive evidence for the devaluation of former wives by their former husbands, this does not appear to be a result of the operation of *splitting* in these men's relationships. There is no evidence for unrealistic overvaluation or idealization in their perceptions of either themselves or their present wives. Thus, as a group, these husbands are *not* splitting in the psychoanalytic sense of seeing the self or present wife as all good and the former wife as all bad; rather, they simply devalue the former wife.

The evidence is weak for a relationship between devaluation of the former wife and low self-esteem in the men; there is a non-significant trend for men with higher self-esteem to devalue the former wife less, and scores on the ACL Likability index indicate that men who "like themselves more" (in terms of the positive vs. negative adjectives in their self descriptions) also tend to like the former wife more ($r = .24, p = .03$, one-tailed test). The small magnitude of these correlations tends to normalize and minimize the compensatory or defensive aspects of the negative evaluations made by these remarried husbands.

However, the descriptions of the former wife are strikingly *dissimilar* and quantitatively very different from the husbands' views of themselves, the present wife, or their Ideal self. The degree to which the former wife is viewed as deviant is unusual in the literature on ACL descriptions. It is not clear from these data whether this is a reflection of the former wives' actual traits or behavior, or rather represents a consistent misperception on the part of the husbands. The study does find evidence for a process of *contrast* in the husbands' perceptions of their past and present marital relationships, but no such contrast involving self-perceptions. Husbands tend to describe the former wife as low on certain traits when they describe the present partner as high on the trait, and vice versa. This attributional contrast is virtually unique to the husbands' perceptions of the present and former spouse and is distinct from the findings of Terman and

Buttenwieser (1935) and Buss (1984). The eight ACL scales where this contrast occurs shed light on the personality traits that are salient in the process of comparison and polarization of perceptions of the present and former wife. The lack of a correlation on the Likability index for the present and former wife ($r = .09, p > 0.10$) indicates that the contrast is not simply global devaluation, but rather involves specific traits. The negatively correlated scales suggest that the husbands contrast the two women in the salient areas of power (as evidenced by negative correlations for *Dominance, Abasement, Deference, Autonomy,* and *Masculine attributes*), expressiveness and responsibility (*Exhibitionism*), and the control of hostile and angry impulses (*Aggression* and *Self-control*).

Explanations for Negative Evaluations of the Former Wife

We considered alternative explanations for these negative evaluations of the former wife. While outside observers (or the former wives themselves) would have been unlikely to have evaluated these 61 women as negatively as their ex-husbands and their new partners did, our interviews suggested that these men's deviant descriptions are partially influenced by their real experiences with the former wives' behavior, either during the marriage or during the period of marital separation and divorce. It is highly likely that the former wives sometimes *were* "emotional," "defensive," and "demanding" in *situations* where they dealt with the former husband and his new partner. The stress of marital separation and divorce often elicits atypical behavior, and divorce researchers have well chronicled the uncharacteristic behavior, sexual activity, child neglect, drug and alcohol abuse, and even violence of separating marital partners (Wallerstein & Kelly, 1979; Wallerstein & Blakeslee, 1989; Weiss, 1975). Husbands may excuse their own atypical behavior while making trait attributions about the former wife, a pattern observed in the literature on attribution and marriage (e.g., Jacobson et al., 1985). The husbands may also have now forgotten their own post-divorce behavior while still vividly remembering the spouse's. It is also possible that the devaluation of the former wife serves a defensive function and helps to protect the integrity of the remarried family. One would not guess from the negative descriptions of the former wives in interviews as well as on the ACL scales that these husbands and their former wives were once in love, although the husbands include the adjectives "attractive," "good-looking," and "intelligent" in their descriptions. Men and women going through divorce often continue to have feelings of attachment toward their former wives (Ahrons, 1981; Kitson, 1982; Spanier & Casto, 1979;

Weiss, 1975); a way to fight this attraction may be to devalue the former spouse, and this negative evaluation may function to solidify the new family's boundaries.

Conversely, a strong negative evaluation of the former wife could indicate that the current marriage is in trouble and that scapegoating of the former wife is occurring. We have found that those couples who were relatively more negative in their evaluation of the former wife tended to be *less* satisfied with their new marriages, data suggestive of this second hypothesis (Guisinger, Cowan, & Schuldberg, 1989).[16] Additional explanations for this hostility toward the former wife can be made in terms of displaced anger toward the husband's children or in terms of cognitive dissonance (Festinger, 1957).

The findings of very negative perceptions of the former wife which do not moderate significantly in the first three to five years of remarriage are troubling because these former spouses are also parents and, for their children's sake, need to negotiate an effective co-parenting relationship. Interparental hostility has negative implications for child adjustment in general (Emery, 1982) and contributes to lessened contact with the non-custodial parent in divorcing families (Wallerstein & Kelly, 1980; Wallerstein & Blakeslee, 1989). The present data indicate that interventions with divorcing families and their children need to address attributions and perceptions, as well as the interpersonal, behavioral, and social aspects of the relationship between former spouses.

NOTES

1. Except when explicit comparisons are made across time, only the first set of data from these subjects is used.

2. Two couples were seen in a university Psychology Clinic, and four returned their questionnaires by mail. This research did not contact the former wife, and so no data are available regarding her perspective regarding her self, the ex-husband, or his new wife.

3. Nineteen of these scales are based on Murray's (1938) needs; nine topical scales were derived for special purposes; five are based on Transactional analysis theory (Williams & Williams, 1980), and four relate to Welsh's (1975) two factor theory of creativity and intelligence. Scores are computed as sums of endorsed indicative adjectives, minus the number of endorsed contraindicative adjectives, and are transformed into T-scores (Gough & Heilbrun, 1980).

4. The overall D statistic is used for these analyses, combining the contributions of profile elevation, scatter, and shape to the dissimilarity of profiles.

5. Studies of similarities and differences between personality descriptions

commonly ignore differences in the elevation of trait measures and examine only these correlations.

6. Data from the seventeen subjects who were seen a second time at three to five years of remarriage are included here.

7. At three to five years, 46% of the men also described their former wife as responsible and temperamental.

8. The ACL manual (Gough & Heilbrun, 1980) suggests that profiles with T-scores of less than 20 on Communality, and for which 2 * Communality + Military Leadership—Unfavorable is less than 50 T are suspect as possibly resulting from random responding. While these decision rules may not apply to these ACL descriptions of others, when they are applied to the ACL descriptions of the former wives, 68% are flagged as suspicious, as compared to 7% of the husbands' Self-descriptions and 8% of the descriptions of the present wife. 74% of the new wives' descriptions of the former wife also appear suspect by these rules.

9. The seventeen subjects who were seen at two points in their remarriage were included in these analyses. For *Favorable* adjectives, $t[73] = 0.97$; for *Unfavorable* adjectives, $t[73] = 0.81$; for *Communality*, $t[73] = 0.68$. $p > .10$ in all cases.

10. *Communality* scores for the husbands' descriptions of the former wife are not significantly correlated with self-esteem ($r = -.01, p > .10$).

11. The repeated-measures Multivariate Analysis of Variance for the 37 ACL scales indicates that descriptions of the present and former wives differ significantly ($F[37, 58] = 9.8, p < 0.0001$). Univariate t-tests for differences in mean elevations of each scale show that all but five of the ACL scales differ significantly in elevation at the 0.05 level. The present wives also received a mean Likability index score of 0.91, while the former wives received a mean score of 0.51 ($t[60] = 10.1, p < 0.001$). Since all pairs of descriptions differ significantly in elevation in this study, it is useful to examine the extent of agreement between self-report and spouse ACL descriptions of the two current partners themselves. These self- and other-descriptions of the same individual provide a benchmark for evaluating the differences in profile elevations found in this study. Husbands' self-descriptions and their wives' descriptions of them also differ significantly ($F[37,60] = 4.4, p < .0001$). D is 54.2 ($SD = 15.7$) for this set of profiles. The husbands' descriptions of their wives are also significantly different overall from the wives' self-descriptions ($F[37, 60] = 2.5, p = 0.01$), with $D = 58.7$ ($SD = 16.7$). These values of D (and the multivariate F's) highlight the much larger magnitude of the differences between the husbands' descriptions of the present and former wives and themselves and the former wife.

12. The mean ACL profile for the former wives also differs significantly from the husbands' mean self description ($F[37,58] = 19.7, p < 0.0001$). Univariate tests of individual scale differences indicate that the profiles differ significantly on all but seven of the 37 ACL scales. Surprisingly, when the husbands' overall descriptions of themselves and the present wife are compared, these two perceptions are significantly different as well. ($F[37, 59] = 3.4. p = .002$); eight of the 37 scales differ significantly at the 0.05 level. The mean magnitude of the D

statistic for this pair of profiles is smaller. The present wives also describe themselves as significantly different from their husbands ($F[37, 61] = 5.1$, $p <$ .0001). For this pair of profiles, $D = 68.6$, $SD = 22.4$.

13. At the level of the 300 ACL *items*, the four ACL descriptions tend to be positively intercorrelated.

14. The trait of *Dominance* has been an interesting exception in other studies as well. See Palmer & Byrne (1970) and Buss (1984).

15. The husbands' ACL scores for Self and their Ideal self tend to be positively correlated over many scales. The partner and Ideal self ACL's are also positively correlated, on a smaller number of scales. The husbands' ACL's for former wife and Ideal self tend to be unrelated, non-significantly correlated for all but two scales, *Number checked* ($r = .40$, $p < .05$) and *Self-control*, ($r = -0.32$; $p < 0.05$). In terms of profile elevation, the former wife is seen as very different from the husbands' Ideal self ($F[37,57] = 21.2$, $p < 0.0005$), and the distance between the former wife and the husbands' Ideal self profiles is large ($D = 130.2$, $SD = 42.3$). The husbands' descriptions of their Ideal selves were curiously unrelated (either in terms of positive or negative correlations) to their descriptions of the former wife.

16. For example, the correlation between husbands' marital satisfaction and *Communality* for the description of the former wife is .27 ($p = .02$, one-tailed test).

REFERENCES

Ahrons, C. (1981). The continuing coparental relationship between divorced spouses. *American Journal of Orthopsychiatry, 5*, 415-428.

Arias, H. & O'Leary, K.D. (1985). Semantic and perceptual discrepancies in discordant and nondiscordant marriages. *Cognitive Therapy and Research, 9*, 51-61.

Bender, I.E. & Hastorf, A.H. (1950). The perception of persons: Forecasting another person's responses on three personality scales. *Journal of Abnormal and Social Psychology, 45*, 557-561.

Buss, D. M. (1984). Marital assortment for personality dispositions: Assessment with three different data sources. *Behavior Genetics, 14*, 111-123.

Buss, D. (1985). Human mate selection. *American Scientist, 73*, 47-51.

Buss, D.M. & Barnes, M. (1986). Preferences in human mate selection. *Journal of Personality and Social Psychology, 50*, 559-570.

Byrne, D. (1963). *The attraction paradigm*. N.Y.: Academic.

Byrne, D. & Blalock, B. (1963). Similarity and assumed similarity of attitudes between husbands and wives. *Journal of Abnormal and Social Psychology, 67*, 636-640.

Byrne, D. & Nelson, D. (1965). Attraction as a linear function of positive reinforcements. *Journal of Personality and Social Psychology, 1*, 659-663.

Cherlin, A. (1978). Remarriage as an incomplete institution. *American Journal of Sociology, 84*, 634-650.

Christensen, L. & Wallace, L. (1976). Perceptual accuracy as a variable in marital adjustment. *Journal of Sex and Marital Therapy, 2,* 130-136.

Cronbach, L.J. & Gleser, G.C. (1953). Assessing similarity between profiles. *Psychological Bulletin, 50,* 456-473.

Emery, R. (1982). Interparental conflict and the children of discord and divorce. *Psychological Bulletin, 92,* 310-330.

Fairbairn, W.R.D. (1952). *An Object Relations Theory of Personality.* N.Y.: Basic.

Festinger, L. (1957). *A theory of cognitive dissonance.* Evanston, Ill.: Row-Peterson.

Furstenberg, F.F. & Nord, C. W. (1985). Parenting apart: Patterns of childrearing after marital disruption. *Journal of Marriage and the Family, 47,* 893-904.

Gage, N. L., & Cronbach, L. J. (1955). Conceptual and methodological problems in interpersonal perception. *Psychological Review, 62,* 411-422.

Gough, H.G., Fioravanti, M., & Lazzari, R. (1983). Some implications of self versus ideal congruence on the revised Adjective Check List. *Journal of Personality and Social Psychology, 44,* 1214-1220.

Gough, H. & Heilbrun, A. (1980). *The Adjective Check List manual.* Palo Alto: Consulting Psychologists Press.

Guisinger, S. (1984). The first years of the second marriage: Changing parental and couple relations in the remarried family. (Doctoral dissertation, University of California, Berkeley)

Guisinger, S., Cowan, P.A., & Schuldberg, D. (1989). Changing parent and spouse relations in the first years of remarriage of divorced fathers. *Journal of Marriage and the Family, 51,* 445-456.

Hastorf, A.H. & Bender, I.E. (1952). A caution respecting the measurement of empathic ability. *Journal of Abnormal and Social Psychology, 47,* 574-576.

Huntington, D. S. (1982). Attachment, loss and divorce: a reconsideration of the concepts. In L. Messinger (ed.), *Therapy with remarriage families.* Rockville, Md.: Aspen Publications.

Jacobson, N. S., McDonald, D.W., Follette, W.C., & Berley, R.F. (1985). Attributional processes in distressed and nondistressed married couples. *Cognitive Therapy and Research, 9,* 35-50.

Jacobson, N. S., Follette, W.C., & McDonald, D.W. (1982). Reactivity to positive and negative behavior in distressed and nondistressed couples. *Journal of Consulting and Clinical Psychology, 50,* 706-714.

Kernberg, O. (1980). *Internal world and external reality: Object Relations theory applied.* N.Y.: Aronson.

Kitson, G. (1982). Attachment to the spouse and divorce: A scale and its application. *Journal of Marriage and the Family, 44,* 379-393.

Kohut, H. (1984). *How does analysis cure?* Chicago: University of Chicago Press.

Messinger, L. (1985). *Remarriage.* New York: Plenum.

Murray, H.A. (1938). *Explorations in personality.* N.Y.: Oxford University Press.

Murstein, B.I. & Beck, G.D. (1972). Person perception, marriage adjustment, and social desirability. *Journal of Consulting and Clinical Psychology, 39,* 396-403.

Palmer, J. & Byrne, D. (1970). Attraction toward dominant and submissive strangers: similarity vs. complementarity. *Journal of Experimental Research in Personality, 4,* 108-115.

Sager, C. J., Walker, E., Brown, H. S., Crohn, H., & Rodstein, E. (1983). *Treating the remarried family.* N.Y.: Brunner/Mazel.

Spanier, G. R. & Casto, R. (1979). Adjustment to separation and divorce: Analysis of 50 case studies. *Journal of Divorce, 2,* 241-252.

Terman, L. M. & Buttenwieser, P. (1935). Personality factors in marital compatibility: II. *Journal of Social Psychology, 6,* 267-289.

Wald, E. (1981). *The remarried family: Challenge and promise.* New York: Family Service Agency of America.

Wallerstein, J. S., & Blakeslee, S. (1989). *Second chances: Men, women, and children a decade after divorce.* N. Y.: Ticknor and Fields.

Wallerstein, J. & Kelly, J. (1979). *Surviving the breakup: How children and parents cope with divorce.* N.Y.: Brunner/Mazel.

Wallerstein, J. & Kelly, J. (1980). Effects of divorce on the visiting father-child relationship. *American Journal of Psychiatry, 137,* 1534-1539.

Weiss, R. (1975). *Marital Separation.* New York: Basic Books.

Weiss, R. L. (1980). Strategic behavioral marital therapy: Toward a model for assessment and intervention. In S.P. Vincent (ed.), *Advances in family intervention, assessment, and theory (Vol. 1),* pp. 229-271. Greenwich, CT: JAI Press.

Welsh, G. S. (1975). *Creativity and intelligence: A personality approach.* Chapel Hill, N.C.: Institute for Research in Social Science.

Williams, K.B., & Williams, J.E. (1980). The assessment of transactional analysis ego states via the Adjective Check List. *Journal of Personality Assessment, 44,* 120-129.

Appendix 1

Scale means for Husbands' ACL Descriptions of Themselves, Their
Present Wife, and the Former Wife with t-tests of differences
between means

Scale	Mean scale score[a]			Significance of t		
	Self	Present wife	Former wife	self-wife[b]	self-former[c]	present-former[c]
Modus Operandi scales						
1. No. Ckd (number of adjectives checked)	50.8	47.4	40.7	***	***	***
2. Fav (number of favorable adjectives)	53.2	54.4	31.0		***	***
3. Unfav (number of unfavorable adjectives)	46.7	45.8	68.9		***	***
4. Com (communality)	48.7	43.5	25.2	***	***	***

APPENDIX 1 (continued)

Scale	Mean scale score[a]			Significance of t		
	Self	Present wife	Former wife	self–wife[b]	self–former[c]	present–former[c]
Need scales						
5. Ach (achievement)	52.2	52.4	47.1		*	**
6. Dom (dominance)	55.3	54.9	50.3		*	*
7. End (endurance)	49.4	52.8	42.8	*	***	***
8. Ord (order)	50.0	52.8	44.5		***	***
9. Int (intraception)	50.9	51.2	29.1		***	***
10. Nur (nurturance)	52.3	53.0	30.2		***	***
11. Aff (affiliation)	52.5	53.3	32.2		***	***
12. Het (heterosexuality)	58.3	59.2	44.2		***	***
13. Exh (exhibition)	53.7	53.4	55.5			
14. Aut (autonomy)	51.2	50.7	60.6		***	***

Scale						
15. Agg (aggression)	52.8	50.2	62.4		***	***
16. Cha (change)	51.7	46.1	45.6	***	***	***
17. Suc (succorance)	45.6	45.0	55.5		***	***
18. Aba (abasement)	43.1	45.1	45.6			
19. Def (deference)	46.1	47.6	38.7		***	***
Topical scales						
20. Crs (counseling readiness scale)	44.9	48.3	60.9	*	***	***
21. S-Cn (self-control)	46.0	47.9	42.4			*
22. S-Cfd (self-confidence)	54.6	56.7	45.5		***	***
23. P-Adj (personal adjustment)	51.9	51.3	33.3		***	***
24. Iss (ideal self)	53.8	59.7	45.6	***	***	***
25. Cps (creative personality scale)	52.8	55.5	47.6		**	***
26. Mls (military leadership scale)	50.2	48.5	34.5		***	***
27. Mas (masculine attributes scale)	54.5	55.9	55.5		***	***

APPENDIX 1 (continued)

Scale	Mean scale score[a]			Significance of t		
	Self	Present wife	Former wife	self-wife[b]	self-former[c]	present-former[c]
28. Fem (feminine attributes scale)	52.4	48.1	33.7	***		***
Transactional Analysis scales						
29. CP (critical parent)	50.1	48.1	63.3			***
30. NP (nurturing parent)	52.5	54.6	35.7		***	***
31. A (adult)	50.4	53.9	38.5	***	***	***
32. FC (free child)	56.1	55.9	47.6		***	***
33. AC (adapted child)	44.9	44.4	58.0		***	***

Origence-intellectence
scales

34. A-1 (high O, low I)	55.4	58.0	56.6	
35. A-2 (high O, high I)	47.0	46.9	56.5	*** ***
36. A-3 (low O, low I)	50.7	52.0	35.8	*** ***
37. A-4 (low O, high I)	51.2	52.3	44.2	*** ***

[a]Scores are T-scores with a mean of 50 and SD of 10.

[b] DF = 58.

[c] DF = 57.

* p ≤ .05

** p ≤ .01

*** p ≤ .005

Appendix 2

Correlations of Adjective Check List Scales Between Husbands'

Descriptions of Self and Present Wife, Self and Former Wife, and

Present and Former Wives

Scale	Pearson r		
	Self vs. Present Wife[a]	Self vs. Former wife[b]	Present vs. Former Wife[c]
Modus Operandi scales			
1. No. Ckd (number of adjectives checked)	.76***	.57***	.72***
2. Fav (number of favorable adjectives)	.35**	.24	.17
3. Unfav (number of unfavorable adjectives)	.33*	.37***	.17
4. Com (communality)	.27*	.20	.16

Need scales

5. Ach (achievement)	.11	-.25	-.04
6. Dom (dominance)	.27*	-.34**	-.30*
7. End (endurance)	.25	.18	-.03
8. Ord (order)	-.03	.30*	-.08
9. Int (intraception)	.39***	.30*	.20
10. Nur (nurturance)	.19	.36*	.04
11. Aff (affiliation)	.13	.36**	.01
12. Het (heterosexuality)	.34*	-.22	-.23
13. Exh (exhibition)	.05	-.18	-.34**

APPENDIX 2 (continued)

Scale	Pearson r		
	Self vs. Present Wife[a]	Self vs. Former Wife[b]	Present vs. Former Wife[c]
14. Aut (autonomy)	.06	.06	-.39***
15. Agg (aggression)	-.02	.13	-.28*
16. Cha (change)	-.12	.02	-.20
17. Suc (succorance)	.32*	-.21	-.07
18. Aba (abasement)	.10	-.25	-.37***
19. Def (deference)	-.10	.12	-.37***

Topical scales

20. Crs (counseling readiness scale)	.00	.07	-.24
21. S-Cn (self-control)	-.00	-.04	-.37***
22. S-Cfd (self-confidence)	.32*	-.16	-.11
23. P-Adj (personal adjustment)	.39***	.29*	.15
24. Iss (ideal self scale)	.30*	.17	.10
25. Cps (creative personality scale)	.27*	.07	-.02
26. Mls (military leadership scale)	.50***	.20	.31*
27. Mas (masculine attributes scale)	.22	-.14	-.27*

APPENDIX 2 (continued)

Scale	Pearson r		
	Self vs. Present Wife[a]	Self vs. Former Wife[b]	Present vs. Former Wife[c]
28. Fem (feminine attributes scale)	.18	.13	-.06
Transactional Analysis scales			
29. CP (critical parent)	-.06	.19	-.22
30. NP (nurturing parent)	.32≠	.27≠	.09
31. A (adult)	.46≠≠≠	.20	.13
32. FC (free child)	.04	-.14	-.25
33. AC (adapted child)	.39≠≠≠	.21	.18

Origence-intellectence scales

34. A-1 (high O, low I)	.35**	.10
35. A-2 (high O, high I)	.46***	-.07
36. A-3 (low O, low I)	.21	-.13
37. A-4 (low O, high I)	.33**	.18

34. A-1 (high O, low I)	.17	
35. A-2 (high O, high I)	-.02	
36. A-3 (low O, low I)	.25	
37. A-4 (low O, high I)	.35**	

a $\underline{n}$ = 59.
b $\underline{n}$ = 58.
c $\underline{n}$ = 53.

* $p \leq .05$
** $p \leq .01$ Two-tailed tests of significance.
*** $p \leq .005$

<u>Notes</u>. For each column of correlations, less than two correlations out of 37 are expected to be significant at the .05 level or better under chance conditions. Thus, it is unlikely that the patterns of similarity and contrast in this table are due to chance.

Adjustment to Stepfatherhood: The Effects of Marital History and Relations with Children

Bartolomeo J. Palisi
Myron Orleans
David Caddell
Bonnijean Korn

SUMMARY. Marital history and characteristics of stepchildren were viewed as factors which influence adjustment to stepfatherhood. It was hypothesized that marital history affected the amount of conflict present in the relationship between the stepfather and his stepchildren. Characteristics of the stepchildren were viewed as factors which allowed stepfathers to successfully handle potential conflict. Using a sample of stepfathers who were married in 1980-1983 in Orange County, California, it was found that marital history was somewhat related to the stepfathers' involvement with their stepchildren in some activities. Marital history was also somewhat related to the stepfather's feelings about and reactions to his stepchildren. However, the key to the stepfather's adjustment was whether his biological children were present in the household. The effects of this variable were found to be positive. It was concluded that the relationship between marital history and stepfather adjustment is complex and varying.

A modest but developing body of literature which is based on survey research of stepfamily processes and problems has emerged in the last decade (Ganong & Coleman, 1984; Ihinger-Tallman, 1988; Pasley & Ihinger-Tallman, 1987). The clinical and self-help work published in the

---

Bartolomeo J. Palisi, PhD, is Professor of Sociology; Myron Orleans, PhD, is Associate Professor of Sociology; David Caddell and Bonnijean Korn are Research Consultants, Social Science Research Center, California State University-Fullerton, Fullerton, CA 92634.

89

stepfamily field, however, fills many more pages (Capaldi & McRae, 1979; Coleman, Ganong, & Gingrich, 1985; Juroe & Juroe, 1983; Visher & Visher, 1979; 1982). The differences between the survey research findings and clinical writings are substantial as revealed in recent reviews (Ganong & Coleman, 1986; Robinson, 1984). Stepfamilies have been viewed by the clinicians as inevitably posing significant problems of adjustment while most survey researchers have discovered few consequential differences between biologically intact families and stepfamilies.

Survey researchers and clinicians hold sharply contrasting views about the stepfather role. Survey research suggests that stepfathers are not inferior to biological fathers in parental performance (Parish & Taylor, 1979; Raschke & Raschke, 1979; Santrock, Warshak, Lindbergh, & Meadows, 1982). The clinical and particularly the self-help publications contend that the stepfather role is inherently problematical and results in more adjustment problems for family members than does the biological father role (e.g., Capaldi & McRae, 1979; Ganong & Coleman, 1986). An example of the disparity between the survey and clinical approaches is that the survey researchers typically use such terms as "relative success" (Espinoza & Newman, 1979:17) and "competence" (Santrock et al., 1982:472) to describe stepfathering. On the other hand, clinical works such as Visher and Visher (1979:110) emphasize words such as "difficulties" and "distress" which require therapy and insight to be overcome.

These differences may result from contrasting philosophies, definitions, and approaches used in studying stepfathers (Robinson, 1984). However, the disagreements may also reflect a failure to adequately specify the background characteristics and circumstances of stepfathers. Demographic, social, and situational variables may be important for understanding the stepfather's adjustment (Nelson & Nelson, 1982). There have been very few studies of stepfathers which have looked at the relationship between social structural conditions and stepfather adjustment. The few studies of social structural conditions have focused on factors such as whether the stepchild lives at home or not (Ambert, 1986), or on the differences between stepfamilies and first marriage families (Pink & Wampler, 1985; Santrock et al., 1982).

This paper will examine the characteristics of a sample of men who became stepfathers. It will assess how the marital history of stepfathers and their relations with their children and stepchildren are related to their adjustment. The paper will focus on the stepfathers' prior marital status, the number of previous marriages, the length of time apart from the previous spouse, the length of the current marriage, and the decisionmaking structure of the current marriage. Several characteristics of the (step)children, including family of origin, number in the household, and age, will also be examined. These variables will be viewed as indicating a potential for competing demands and divided loyalties between the stepfather's present and previous families.

Specifically, we predict that adjustment to stepfathering will be:

1. greater if the stepfather has not been previously married than if he has been married;
2. inversely related to the number of previous marriages;
3. positively related to the length of separation from the former spouse;
4. positively related to the length of the present marriage;
5. greater if there are no biological children of the husband than if he has his own children in the household;
6. inversely related to the number of stepchildren;
7. inversely related to the age of the oldest stepchild.

We offer these hypotheses to examine some of the understandings of stepfather adjustment implied or explicitly presented in the self-help, clinical and survey research literatures. These various sources of our hypotheses are juxtaposed to provide an opportunity to assess the comparative merits of each approach in accounting for the adjustment of stepfathers.

Hypotheses one and two are based on a reading of some of the clinically-oriented self-help literature (Capaldi & McRae, 1979; Juroe & Juroe, 1983; Rosin, 1988; Visher & Visher, 1979; 1982) which suggests that the greater the number of prior marriages, the greater the range of potential conflicts the stepfather faces and the more complex the task of managing his relationships to former family members. In addition, hypothesis three is based on the logic that the more recently the stepfather has been separated from the former spouse, the greater the likelihood of conflicts over the terms of the divorce agreement and particularly the child custody arrangement. Hypothesis four is based on the reasoning that the longer a stepfather has been married to his present spouse, the more likely it is that the patterns of behavior in the family are stable and that the normative structure is firmly in place.

Survey research offers very limited support for these predictions (hypotheses one through four). White and Booth (1985) found no differences in marital quality between couples in which one partner was remarried as compared with those in which both were remarried. But their data did not enable them to use the number of previous marriages as an independent variable. Clingempeel (1981) found that moderate levels of contact with the former spouse had positive effects on stepfathers' success. In regard to the fourth hypothesis, Rollins and Cannon (1974) found marital satisfaction to be higher in some later stages of marriages than in early periods. Pink and Wampler (1985) found that length of remarriage had no relationship to stepfamily functioning. However, they focused on contrasts between stepfamilies and first marriage families, and only had 28 stepfamilies in their sample. Their study also combined random sampling techniques with non-random techniques.

In the view of some of the clinically-oriented self-help literature (Capaldi & McRae, 1979; Juroe & Juroe, 1983; Rosin, 1988; Visher & Visher, 1979; 1982) the presence of biological children of the husband, along with the stepchildren in the household would generate more conflict because of conditions such as peer rivalries, loyalties of the stepfather to his own children compared to his stepchildren, and jealousies between stepchildren and biological children (Hypothesis five). We also hypothesize following this literature that the larger the number of children in the household, the more problematic the adjustment of the stepfather. Large families have more complex structures, have more difficult economic circumstances, and are more heterogeneous than smaller families.

Again only limited survey research evidence is available to support of the self-help and clinically-based hypotheses focusing on stepfamily composition (hypotheses five and six). Pasley (1987) explored how boundary definition and perceptual problems arise in stepfamilies with ambiguous household composition. The presence of the stepfather's biological children is seen to significantly affect the family, but the impact was not specified as we do in the fifth hypothesis. Some research literature in accord with the self-help and clinical literature has suggested that the presence of both biological children and stepchildren in the family makes the family more complex and therefore less adjusted (Cherlin, 1978; Clingempeel, 1981; Furstenberg and Spanier, 1984). White and Booth (1985) found higher rates of marital instability among complex stepfamilies. Although Ihinger-Tallman (1988) reported that marital quality does not suffer due to complex family structure, she stated that the wife's adjustment to her stepchildren (the husband's biological children) may be even more troublesome than the husband's adjustment to her children. In addition, the wife's problems as a stepmother could affect her relationships with her husband and with her own children. Garbarino et al. (1984) contended that the stepfather may consciously or unconsciously limit the distribution of resources to his stepchildren in order to give his birth children an advantage. Contrary to these findings, other researchers found that live-in children actually facilitate stepfather adjustment (Ambert, 1986; Duberman, 1973).

From some reports of clinical work (Bachrach, 1983; Ganong & Coleman, 1984), we hypothesize (number seven) that older stepchildren in the household inhibit stepfather adjustment more than younger children. This occurs because older children have greater experience with pre-existing family patterns and they are less willing to accept the stepfather as well as stepsiblings. Baptiste (1984) emphasizes the higher likelihood of age-based conflicts in heterogamous remarriages, but some research has suggested that there are adjustment difficulties for older stepchildren in general (Garbarino, Sebes & Schellenbach, 1984; Santrock et al., 1982).

Only indirect survey findings can be offered in support of the hypothesis that older children inhibit stepfather adjustment. Ihinger-Tallman (1988) reports a higher rate of early adolescent emancipation from stepfamilies as compared to first families. This suggests that older stepchildren had significant difficulty in adjustment to stepfamily living. On the other hand, she noted that between 11 and 20 percent of children experience a change of residence after remarriage suggesting substantial adjustment difficulties as well for some children who were too young for emancipation.

METHODS

Sample

The sample was obtained from a random selection of marriage certificates in the Orange County, California Hall of Records in 1984-85. Orange County is among the twenty most populous urban areas in the United States. Over 3,000 marriage certificates from 1980-83 were examined. The names and addresses of men who married women between the ages of 20 and 35 who were remarrying, were selected to maximize the chances that the groom would become a stepfather. The wife was the desired age and was previously married in 20 percent of the certificates. Recent telephone numbers and addresses for these men were obtained from the local phone directory. We found correct telephone numbers for approximately 40 percent of the men whose certificates were selected. All the men who could be reached on the phone were queried as to whether they in fact were stepfathers. A questionnaire was mailed to those who responded affirmatively and who expressed a willingness to participate in the survey. Approximately 60 percent said they were stepfathers and 15 percent who said they were stepfathers refused to participate in the survey.

The return rate of questionnaires sent out was approximately 47 percent. The total number of adequately completed and returned questionnaires where stepchildren were in the household was 60 and these provided the sample for our study. While the N for this study is small, there are few studies of stepfathers which have a larger number of stepfathers as respondents, and very few studies have employed random sampling techniques. Our responses were similar to studies using similar samples (Clingempeel, 1981). None of the previous empirical studies with larger N's have focused on the effects of marital history on stepfather adjustment.

The returns were primarily from non-minority, middle income, well educated stepfathers. Thus, of the total of 60 returned questionnaires which were processed, 87 percent identified themselves as Caucasian, 70 percent reported their own income to be above $30,000 per year, and 80% claimed to have at least some college education. These characteristics are consistent with those of the county from which the sample was derived, although the income and education levels in the sample are a bit higher than those of general county residents. Fifty-five percent of the respondents were in the 30s and the same percentage were in higher prestige occupations. Their wives were typically homogamous with regard to ethnicity, but most had slightly lower education levels and significantly lower incomes.

Measures

The dependent variable (stepfather adjustment) is defined conceptually as the process by which a man who marries a mother with custody of her child(ren) brings himself into accord with the conditions of his domestic relations (Espinoza & Newman, 1979). It is measured both as a behavioral variable and as a subjective one. The behavioral measurement is in terms of the extent of involvement which the respondent had with his stepchildren. It is assumed that stepfathers who interact with their stepchildren and who engage in activities with them have a positive relationship with the stepchildren. Therefore, we asked our respondents how frequently (daily, weekly, monthly, yearly or less) they did the following with their stepchildren: attended spectator events, participated in sports, hobbies or games, celebrated birthdays, had chats or talks, did something that the child appreciated, went for a walk or jog, told the stepchildren they loved them, visited friends or relatives with them, ate home together, participated with the stepchildren's friends, and ran errands with them. We analyzed the relationship between each of these items and the independent variables. Several scales were created from these items (by use of factor analysis) to isolate the possible dimensions of social participation. A companionship scale (COMSCLE) involved participating in games or hobbies, chatting, appreciated acts, walking or jogging and errands. An intimate acts scale (INASCLE) involved eating dinner and telling of love. A friendship scale (FRESCLE) involved taking stepchildren to visit friends, and being involved with the stepchildren's friends.

The subjective aspects of stepfather adjustment are conceptualized as having four dimensions. Stepfathers may hold positive or negative feelings and emotional reactions about their stepchildren. A closely related dimension involves the thoughts and urges which a stepfather has regarding treatment of the stepchildren — desires for action. A third aspect of stepfather adjustment involves how he perceives that other people such as the stepchildren, his wife, or society in general think of the role of stepfather. This is important because a stepfather may adjust more easily to his role if he perceives support from others than if he thinks other people do not appreciate or understand his role. The fourth dimension of stepfather adjustment involves the effects of his relationship with his wife on the stepfather role. Marriage adjustment can be viewed as both affecting the role of stepfather and of being affected by it. Certainly there is no single direction of causality in the relationship between marriage adjustment and stepfather adjustment. However we will emphasize the effects which marriage adjustment has on the stepfather role.

Negative perceptions or feelings and actions of stepfathers toward their children were measured by asking stepfathers how often they experienced a number of feelings or acts (always to rarely) such as feeling remote from stepchildren, arguing with them, wishing the stepchildren did not live with them, wishing the biological father would take the stepchildren away, and thoughts of abandoning the family. These items were selected (based on factor analysis) from a larger group of items. The sum of their scores formed a negative feelings scale (DISSCLE).

To measure the second subjective dimension of stepfather adjustment, desires to act (ESSCLE), a scale was constructed from items selected by using factor analysis. This involved (always to rarely) feeling urges to punish stepchildren in a violent manner, sexual fantasies about the stepchildren, and desires to get drunk or high because of frustrations about the stepchildren.

To measure the third subjective dimension of stepfather adjustment, stepfathers were asked whether they felt stepparents in general are appreciated by stepchildren, spouses, community, and society. Responses were yes or no. A "general appreciation scale" (GENAPP) was constructed which summed the scores for all items. A similar scale was constructed from items which focused on whether the stepfather felt appreciated as a stepparent by his stepchildren, spouse, community, and society. This was called the "self appreciation scale" (SELFAPP).

Marriage adjustment was measured by a scale (MARADJ) composed of seven items taken from Spanier's (1976) Dyadic Satisfaction dimension of the Dyadic Adjustment Scale. These items asked the respondent how often (almost always, most of the time, occasionally, rarely or never) he (a) discussed or considered divorce, separation or termination of the marriage; (b) left the house after a fight; (c) thought things were going well; (d) confided in his mate; (e) quarreled with his partner; (f) regretted being married; and (g) got on each other's nerves. Items a, b, e, f, g in the scale were recoded so that 1 indicated high adjustment and 4 showed low adjustment.

The independent variables which were used to measure marital history were:

1. prior marital status of the stepfather, coded as (1) never married, and (2) married. Fifty three percent of the respondents were previously married.
2. number of times married, coded as (1) never previously married (47 percent), (2) married once previously (42 percent), and (3) married twice previously (11 percent).
3. length of time apart from former (last) spouse, coded from one year to four and more years (60 percent of the previously married were apart four or more years).

Because of the small N in the study, we included all respondents in the measure, "length of time apart from former (last) spouse" by using the following codes: (1) not previously married, (2) apart four or more years, (3) apart three or fewer years. The assumption is that those not previously married have no history of marital conflict, those apart four or more years now experience some conflict from their former marriages, and those apart three or fewer years have the most conflict.

4. length of time married to present spouse, coded as three or fewer years (70 percent) and four or more years.

Stepchildren characteristics were measured as follows:

5. the presence of biological children, coded as none in the household, and one or more. Twenty-three (38 percent) of the stepfathers had at least one biological child in the household.
6. number of stepchildren in the household was coded as the actual number. Thirty-three (55 percent) of the households had one stepchild, 20 (33 percent) had two, 6 (10 percent) had three, and 1 (2 percent) had four.
7. age of the oldest stepchild coded as 0 to 4, 5 to 9, 10 to 14, 15 to 19, etc. All but one of the oldest children were nineteen or younger.

FINDINGS

Correlational Analyses

Table 1 shows that whether or not the stepfather was previously married has a significant relationship to two of the dependent variables, and both relationships are in the predicted direction. Previously unmarried stepfathers were more likely to share companionship than were previously married stepfathers ($r = .310$, $p < .001$). They were also more likely to perceive more marriage adjustment than previously married stepfathers ($r = .301$, $p < .05$).

The number of previous marriages shows much the same relationship to the dependent variables. The correlations are weaker but the two significant correlations involve the companionship and marriage adjustment variables and they are in the predicted direction.

The number of years apart from the former spouse only has a significant relationship to marriage adjustment. As hypothesized, those stepfathers who were apart from their former spouses for longer periods of time perceived more marriage adjustment ($r = -.346$, $p < .01$).

The length of the current marriage appears to have had more impact on stepfather adjustment than any of the other conditions which focused on his previous marital history. It is negatively correlated with the negative feelings scale ($r = -.227$, $p < .01$), which indicates that those with longer marriages had fewer negative feelings about their stepchildren. It is also correlated with the scale which measured desires to escape (ESS-CLE). The correlation is $-.295$, $p < .001$, which indicates that stepfathers with longer marriages had fewer negative desires. There are positive correlations between the number of years married and feeling appreciated by society ($r = .263$, $p < .05$) and feeling appreciated by the wife and stepchildren ($r = .210$, $p < .05$). These findings support hypothesis 4.

The presence of biological children in the household tends to be associ-

Table 1

Relationships Between Stepfather Adjustment and Marital History
and Stepchildren's Characteristics

Marital History	Stepfather Adjustment							
	Comscle	Inascle	Frescle	Disscle	Esscle	Genapp	Selfapp	Maradj
Previous Marriages	.310*** (55)	-.005 (56)	.136 (58)	-.128 (52)	.054 (56)	.251 (54)	.095 (54)	.301* (57)
Number of Marriages	.270*** (58)	-.030 (57)	.112 (59)	-.129 (53)	.063 (58)	.182 (56)	.014 (55)	.220* (59)
Years Since Last Marr.	-.058 (58)	.068 (57)	.003 (59)	.167 (53)	-.013 (58)	-.002 (56)	-.054 (55)	-.346** (59)
Length of Marriage	.033 (56)	-.083 (57)	-.037 (57)	-.227** (51)	-.295*** (56)	.263* (56)	.210* (53)	.185 (59)
Typchld.	-.313** (58)	-.260* (57)	-.319*** (59)	.287* (53)	.302* (58)	.095 (56)	.019 (55)	-.063 (59)
Oldkid.	.184 (58)	.248* (55)	.091 (57)	.108 (51)	.262* (56)	-.063 (55)	.001 (54)	.266* (56)
Nmchld.	.017 (58)	.042 (57)	-.097 (59)	.072 (53)	-.007 (58)	-.215 (56)	-.281* (55)	-.196 (59)

* = significant at the .05 level
** = significant at the .01 level
*** = significant at the .001 level

ated with more adjustment of the stepfather in several ways. Biological children are associated with more companionship of the stepfather with the stepchildren (r = −.313, p < .01), more intimate interaction with stepchildren (r = −.260, p < .05), more involvement with the stepchildren's friends and of the stepchildren with the stepfather's friends (r = −.319, p < .001). In addition, stepfathers with biological children in the household had fewer negative feelings about stepchildren (r = .287, p < .05), and they had fewer desires to escape (r = .302, p < .05). These findings contradict our hypotheses that biological children in the household increase conflict and thus lower adjustment of the stepfather.

Hypothesis 6 is not supported. Only feelings of appreciation by family members is related to the number of stepchildren, and it is in the predicted direction. Those with fewer children perceived more appreciation (r = −.281, p < .05).

Age of the stepchildren has a significant relationship to three measures of stepfather adjustment. As predicted, when the oldest stepchild was relatively young, the stepfathers interact more with their stepchildren in an intimate manner (r = .248, p < .05). However, contrary to our hypothesis those with younger stepchildren had more desire to escape (r = .262, p < .05). In retrospect, this makes sense since younger children require more attention and might cause more stepfather frustration. In addition, stepfathers with younger children had adjusted marriages (r = .266, p < .05), which supports hypothesis 6. Thus, hypothesis 7 is only partially supported.

In summary, only some of the correlations which are significant are generally in the direction we predicted. They show that stepfathers who are most adjusted in their roles had been married to their current spouses for a longer period of time. However stepfathers with no biological children in the household were less adjusted than those with children. In addition, the majority of the correlations are not significant. This indicates very sporadic influence of stepfather history and present family characteristics on the stepfather's role adjustment.

Multiple Regression Analyses

In an effort to introduce controls into the analyses, and to evaluate the relative influence of the independent variable on stepfather adjustment, we conducted eight multiple regression analyses, one for each of the dependent variables (COMSCLE, INASCLE, FRESCLE, DISSCLE, ESSCLE, GENAPP, SELFAPP, MARADJ). For each regression analysis the independent variables were entered in a single step. Because of the study's small N, pairwise deletion of missing data was used. This insures that the largest number of cases are included in each analysis. All of the independent variables for which we reported correlations in Table 1 were used in each analysis. In addition, we added income of the stepfather (coded in five increments beginning with under $10,000 to $50,000 and higher), occupation of stepfather (using codes taken from the National Opinion Research Center's codes of occupational prestige for 1984), age of the stepfather (coded as the age given on the questionnaire by the stepfather), and education of the stepfather (coded as post baccalaureate, bachelor's degree, some college, high school, less).

Three of the regression analyses showed no significant betas between the independent variables and stepfather adjustment. These involved the dependent variables of intimate acts (INASCLE), appreciation by family members (SELFAPP), and marriage adjustment (MARADJ). Therefore, we will not show these in tabular form for purposes of brevity. Table 2 shows the five remaining regression analyses.

One variable stands out as being related to several of the measures of stepfather adjustment in Table 2. The absence of biological children (TYPCHLD) is significantly related to reduced companionship (beta = −.34, p < .05), less friendship involvement (beta = −.33, p < .05), more negative feelings (beta = .36, p < .05), and more desires to escape (beta = .33, p < .05). Of the dependent variables shown in Table 2, only being appreciated by groups in society is unrelated to the presence or absence of biological children in the household. Being appreciated by society is significantly related to the amount of time since the previous marriage (beta = .42, p < .05), and to education (beta = −.46, p < .01). The only other significant relationship found in Table 2 is between length of time married and desires to escape (beta = .35, p < .05). This shows that those married for a short period of time had more desires to escape.

The variables in Table 2 account for between 21 to 38 percent of the variance in stepfather adjustment. However, the variances include the effects of the control variables (occupation, income and age) and none of the single independent variables accounts for a great amount of variance. For example, the presence or absence of biological children accounts for 9 to 10 percent of the variance in the regression analyses where it is significantly related to stepfather adjustment.

DISCUSSION AND CONCLUSIONS

This research began by proposing that marital history of stepfathers and the characteristics of the stepchildren would influence the adjustment of stepfathers by indicating the amount of conflict they would experience. Thus we predicted that adjustment would be greater among those not pre-

Table 2

Multiple Regression Analyses of the Relationships Between
Stepfather Adjustment and the Independent Variables

Betas and Significance Levels

	Comscle	Frescle	Disscle	Esscle	Genapp
Previous Marriages	.508	.368	.067	.056	.507
Typchild	-.347*	-.338*	.360*	.336*	.041
Oldkid	.125	-.103	.028	.283	-.047
Education	.205	-.022	-.155	-.240	-.468**
Income	.095	.090	-.016	.054	-.182
Length of Marriage	-.048	.083	.278	.351*	-.052
Nmchld	.038	.218	-.130	-.090	.200
Age	.113	.269	.062	-.151	-.242
Occupation	-.010	-.067	-.168	-.315	-.259
Years Since Last Marr.	.159	.229	.203	.046	.428*
Number of Marriages	-.181	-.250	-.023	.239	.150
R2	.31	.24	.21	.30	.38

---

*   = significant at the .05 level
** = significant at the .01 level

viously married, or having the fewest former marriages, among those who were separated from the former spouse the longest, and among those whose current marriage had lasted the longest. We also hypothesized that the most adjusted stepfathers would have no biological children in the household, young children, and few stepchildren.

The findings of this study provide only spotty support for our hypotheses. When no controls are introduced it appears that the presence or absence of biological children in the household has significant relationships to the greatest number of measures of interaction with the stepchildren and to two measures of negative subjective reactions to the stepchildren. These findings are supported by the multiple regression analyses, which show the presence of biological children in the household to have a relationship to four of the eight measures of stepfather adjustment — two measures of interaction and two measures of negative reactions.

Biological children may serve to enhance step-father-stepchild relations in several ways. If the biological children and stepchildren are of similar ages they may become playmates and establish friendly relations. They may provide companionship, emotional support and affection for each other. While stepsibling rivalry may also play a role, under certain conditions positive relations are likely to arise. Handel (1985) suggests that deep bonds among siblings can emerge if appropriate family strategies are developed to deal with the central issues of equity, maturity, loyalty, and individuality. Stepsibling bonding may emerge similarly and overcome the rivalry inherent in the complex stepfamily. It would seem possible that the stepfathers in our sample were able to create positive stepsibling arrangements thereby promoting their adjustment to their own role. Duberman's study (1973) supports this possibility. She reported a higher likelihood of positive stepsibling relations if the two sets of children co-reside than if they live apart. Ambert (1986) also found that the stepfather-mother bond to be stronger when step and biological children co-reside.

On the other hand, this finding contrasts sharply with much of the clinical and self-help literature (Capaldi & McRae, 1979; Coleman, Ganong, & Gingrich, 1985; Ganong & Coleman, 1986; Juroe & Juroe, 1983; Visher & Visher, 1979; 82) as well as with some survey research (Cherlin, 1978; Clingempeel, 1981; Furstenberg and Spanier, 1984), but this body of research focused more on the adjustment of stepchildren than of stepfathers.

The claim that adjustment suffers in complex stepfamily systems because of the father-stepfathers' divided loyalties assumes that resolutions are exceedingly difficult. More likely, the stepfathers may be drawn closer to their stepchildren, and they may have fewer negative attitudes toward them because of the strategies they adopt in striving to treat both sets of children in an equitable manner. The presence of their biological children in the household may, in effect, force them to parent to a greater extent than if they had merely been absorbed into a pre-existing family. It becomes incumbent upon them to constitute a viable living pattern and take a more active role with regard to all children in the household. This may lead them to minimize negative thoughts and feelings about their stepchildren and also to exaggerate positive attitudes about stepchildren in the interests of fairness.

Finally, it is possible that fathers who have custody of their own biological children are selectively those who are more likely to view the parental role favorably and act it out with greater commitment. It can be argued that these men might be psychologically predisposed toward this positive perception and commitment or that their commitment is a response to role requirements. In either case, our findings reveal that men adjust more effectively to stepfatherhood when they are fathering their biological children in the same household.

Our correlational findings suggest that length of the current marriage has some effect on feelings which the stepfather has about his stepchildren and on his feelings of appreciation by others. Amato (1987) similarly found that stepfather involvement with stepchildren is higher the longer the stepfamily is in existence. These findings suggest that some of the negative aspects of stepfather adjustment are temporary. They fade insofar as the current marriage endures. Of course, many reconstituted families do not survive the initial stress of negative feelings held by stepfathers and their reluctance or inability to interact appropriately with their stepchildren and to form some sort of parenting relationship (White & Booth, 1985). Our regression findings did suggest, however, that length of marriage is not, in itself, the key to successful stepfather adjustment. Many stepfathers would prefer not to have had stepchildren at all (Ambert, 1986). But once having stepchildren, it appears that adjustment for stepfathers is greater when step and biological children co-reside and for longer term stepfamilies.

Perhaps there is no single profile of high or low risk stepfathers in terms of marital history and characteristics of the stepchild. Many types of stepfathers are able to meet the varying challenges inherent in the role, and go on to participate effectively in stepfamily living. We see the process of adjustment to stepfatherhood as one that is neither as problematical as the image depicted in the clinical literature (Ganong and Coleman, 1986) nor as tractable as some sociological research indicates (Bachrach, 1983). We confirmed Burgoyne and Clark's (1982) finding that different types of stepfathers have different kinds of difficulties in adjusting to the stepfather role. The adjustment to stepfatherhood is clearly a complex and uneven process of accommodation to the constraints and challenges of stepfamily living.

Future research needs to more fully explore the interactions between marital history of the stepfather, demographic variables, and his participation with his stepchildren and biological children with larger data bases than this or any previous studies were able to employ. Further research needs to be done on the relationship between the quality of stepsibling bonds and stepfather adjustment. Studies might also benefit by directly comparing the adjustment process of stepfatherhood to that of biological fatherhood (Espinoza & Newman, 1979). Previous literature has suggested that the nature of stepfather adjustment does not fundamentally differ from adjustment of biological fathers (Parish & Taylor, 1979; Raschke & Raschke, 1979; Santrock et al., 1982). However, these studies did not employ a variety of measures of adjustment such as ours did. Moreover, recent research has suggested that stepfamilies differ from intact families more in terms of levels than patterns of functioning (Peek, Bell, Waldren & Sorell, 1988). Further research into the comparative levels of stepfather functioning might reveal that stepfather adjustment is achievable at a lower level of functioning than for biological fathers. Clearly, stepfather research specifically, and stepfamily research in general is advancing in terms of quality and quantity of work and will continue to do so.

REFERENCES

Amato, P. R. (1987). Family processes in one-parent, stepparent, and intact families: The child's point of view. *Journal of Marriage and the Family*, *49*, 327-337.

Ambert, A. (1986). Being a stepparent: Live-in and visiting stepchildren. *Journal of Marriage and the Family*, *48*, 795-804.

Bachrach, C. A. (1983). Children in families: Characteristics of biological, step-, and adopted children. *Journal of Marriage and the Family*, *45*, 171-179.

Baptiste, D. (1984). Marital and family therapy with racially/culturally intermarried stepfamilies: Issues and guidelines. *Family Relations*, *33*, 373-380.

Burgoyne, J., & Clark, D. (1982). From father to step-father. In L. McKee & M. O'Brien (Eds.), *The father figure* (196-207). New York: Tavistock Publications.

Capaldi, F., & McRae, B. (1979). *Stepfamilies: A cooperative responsibility*. New York: New Viewpoints.

Cherlin, A. (1978). Remarriage as an incomplete institution. *American Journal of Sociology*, *84*, 634-651.

Clingempeel, W. G. (1981). Quasi-kin relationships and marital quality in stepfather families. *Journal of Personality and Social Psychology*, *41*, 890-901.

Coleman, M., Ganong, L. H., & Gingrich, R. (1985). Stepfamily strengths: A review of the popular literature. *Family Relations*, *34*, 583-589.

Duberman, L. (1973). Step-kin relationships. *Journal of Marriage and The Family*, *35*, 283-292.

Espinoza, R., & Newman, Y. (1979). *Stepparenting*. Rockville, Md.: United States Department of Health, Education and Welfare.

Furstenberg, F. F. Jr., & Spanier, G. B. (1984). *Recycling the family: Remarriage after divorce.* Beverly Hills, CA: Sage Publications.

Ganong, L. H., & Coleman, M. (1984). The effects of remarriage on children: A review of the literature. *Family Relations, 33,* 389-406.

Ganong, L. H., & Coleman, M. (1986). A comparison of clinical and empirical literature on children in stepfamilies. *Journal of Marriage and the Family, 48,* 309-318.

Garbino, J., Sebes, J., & Sellenbach, C. (1984). Families at risk for destructive parent-child relations in adolescence. *Child Development, 55,* 174-183.

Handel, G. (1985). Central issues in the construction of sibling relationships. In Handel, G. (Ed.), *The psychosocial interior of the family,* (367-396). New York: Aldine Publishing Company.

Ihinger-Tallman, M. (1988). Research on stepfamilies. In *American review of sociology, 14,* 25-48.

Juroe, D., & Juroe, B. (1983). *Successful stepparenting.* Old Tappan, New Jersey: Fleming H. Revell Company.

Nelson, M. & Nelson, G. K. (1982). Problems of equity in the reconstituted family: A social exchange analysis. *Family Relations, 31,* 223-231.

Parish, T. S., & Taylor, J. C. (1979). The impact of divorce and subsequent father absence on the children's and adolescents' self-concepts. *Journal of Youth and Adolescence, 8,* 427-432.

Pasley, K. (1987). Family boundary ambiguity: Perceptions of adult stepfamily members. In K. Pasley & M. Ihinger-Tallman (Eds.) *Remarriage and stepparenting: Current research and theory* (206-224). New York: The Guilford Press.

Peek, C. W., Bell, N., Waldren, T., & Sorell, G. T. (1988). Patterns of functioning in families of remarried and first-married couples. *Journal of Marriage and the Family, 50,* 699-708.

Pink, J. E. T., & Wampler, K. S. (1985). Problem areas in stepfamilies: Cohesion, adaptability, and the stepfather-adolescent relationship. *Family Relations, 34,* 327-335.

Raschke, H. J., & Raschke, V. J. (1979). Family conflict and children's self concepts: A comparison of intact and single parent families. *Journal of Marriage and the Family, 41,* 364-367.

Robinson, B. E. (1984). The contemporary American stepfather. *Family Relations, 33,* 381-388.

Rollins, B., & Cannon K. (1974). Marital satisfaction over the family life cycle. *Journal of Marriage and the Family, 36,* 271-284.

Rosin, M. (1988). Stepfathering: Advice on creating new families. New York: Random House.

Santrock, J. W., Warshak, R., Lindberg, C., & Meadows, L. (1982). Children's and parent's observed social behavior in stepfather families. *Child Development, 53,* 472-480.

Spanier, G. (1976). Measuring dyadic adjustment: New scales for assessing the quality of marriage and similar dyads. *Journal of Marriage and the Family,* *38*, 13-26.

Visher, E. B., & Visher, J. (1979). Stepfamilies: A guide to working with stepparents and stepchildren. New York: Bruner/Mazel.

Visher, E. B., & Visher, J. (1982). How to win as a stepfamily. New York: Dembner Books.

White, L. K., & Booth, A. (1985). The quality and stability of remarriages: The role of stepchildren. *American Sociological Review, 50,* 689-698.

Child Support Noncompliance and Divorced Fathers: Rethinking the Role of Paternal Involvement

Joyce A. Arditti

SUMMARY. Despite the wide citation of the number of children not receiving child support, not enough is known about the characteristics and conditions that might be related to fathers' child support payments. The purpose of this discussion is to explore the issue of child support compliance with the larger scope of post-divorce paternal involvement. Three areas of concern, fathers' visitation, the coparental relationship, and custodial arrangement, are examined as they relate to child support compliance and overall postdivorce paternal involvement. Points of intervention and policy recommendations which would facilitate child support payment and father involvement in general are discussed.

Concern about the divorce experience often revolves around the financial adequacy of custodial mothers and their children. Figures vary with regard to how many children actually receive child support, and as to what the financial situations of their custodial mothers and noncustodial fathers may be. Weitzman (1985) reports that 71% of custodial mothers experience a downward financial spiral after divorce while 43% of divorced fathers experience an improved financial situation. An investigation sponsored by the Office of Child Support Enforcement reports that of the 8.7

Joyce A. Arditti, PhD, is Assistant Professor, Department of Family and Child Development, Virginia Polytechnic Institute and State University, Blacksburg, VA 24061-0416.

The author would like to thank Deborah Godwin and Carol MacKinnon for their comments on earlier drafts of this paper.

107

million single mothers living with children under the age of 21, 58% were awarded or had an agreement to receive child support payments and 46% were due payments in 1983. Of those due payments, one-half received the full amount due, one-quarter received partial payment, and one-quarter received no payments (U.S. Bureau of the Census, 1985). Another report indicated that in 1985, approximately half of the women with ordered support awards received the full payment (U.S. Bureau of the Census, 1986). Clearly, for many women following divorce, the high noncompliance rate contributes to an insecure and unstable financial situation (Buehler 1989).

The problem of child support noncompliance has become so serious in terms of its economic implications for custodial mothers and children that Congress has passed Child Support Enforcement Amendments which require states to institute programs to deduct support from fathers' paychecks and tax returns. The underlying argument for enforcement legislation is that lax child support enforcement is the root cause of fathers' nonpayment and that implementing stronger enforcement procedures is the only way to insure that men will fulfill their support obligations (Weitzman, 1988). This perspective, while receiving support among some researchers and policymakers, ignores underlying social, emotional, and interpersonal factors that may contribute to men's resistance to pay child support.

Chambers (1983), in contrast to Weitzman's perspective, believes that an absence of financial responsibility on the part of many divorced fathers is rooted in the typically devitalized or distant relations between noncustodial fathers and their children, rather than in weak enforcement policies. He asserts that a sense of responsibility grows from a sense of attachment and that attachment is nurtured by quality interaction. Generally it is very difficult for noncustodial fathers to develop and sustain vital relationships with children and they begin to feel less and less a part of their children's lives. Subsequently, child support orders are often experienced as a form of "taxation without representation" for many divorced fathers (Chambers, 1983, p. 287).

In a similar vein, Haskins (1988) comments that the popular view of all noncustodial fathers as "brazen" and "unconcerned" is too simplistic. He found that in his sample of fathers only two reasons — unemployment and mother's failure to spend money on children — were cited as justification for not paying support (1988). In a study on single fathers, Grief (1985) explores the issue of child support noncompliance noting a number of reasons fathers give for not paying support (p. 124): (a) Harsh economic conditions and unemployment; (b) Fathers believe the judge has been biased toward the mother and has set an unreasonably high amount to be paid—especially when the ex-wife works and is making a decent salary; and (c) Fathers frequently claim they are not paying child support because their visitation rights have been withheld or made difficult to arrange.

In sum then, despite the wide citation of the number of children not receiving child support, not enough is known about the characteristics and conditions that might be related to fathers' child support payments. This gap in the literature can partially be attributed to an overemphasis on the financial or economic aspects of child support and a relative absence of psychosocial analysis. Salkind (1983) observes that noneconomic factors have been the least well studied and child support continues to be the province of economists and lawyers. Furthermore, research documenting the experience of divorced fathers in general is relatively scarce in comparison to the wealth of literature about mothers and children. Such information is crucial for effective policy recommendations and legislative action. Enforcement programs are often ineffective, costly, and may have unintended consequences. For example, in a study examining the impact of current child support reform, Nichols-Casebolt (1986) found that such reform, while improving the financial conditions for custodial families, had the unanticipated effect of actually increasing poverty for noncustodial families.

The purpose of this discussion is to explore the issue of child support compliance within the context of the fathers' divorce experience by considering the broader issue of post-divorce paternal involvement. A more comprehensive explanation of why many noncustodial fathers fail to pay support may lie in a broader pattern of distancing and increasing noninvolvement. Longitudinal studies by both Hetherington, Cox, and Cox (1976) and Wallerstein and Kelly (1980) document this pattern of withdrawal after divorce, especially with regard to visitation. Grief (1979) also substantiates increasing noninvolvement on the part of fathers and concludes that the father's loss of influence over the child is self-reinforcing and negative which in turn contributes to greater paternal withdrawal from the child. Koch & Lowery (1985), summarizing the available research on noncustodial fathers, state that many fathers withdraw from their families physically, emotionally, and financially, often at considerable emotional cost to most men.

In considering explanations other than poor enforcement for many men's failure to pay child support, it is important to acknowledge evidence that a discrepancy may exist between mothers' reports of fathers' involvement and fathers' own report of their activities. Weitzman (1985) found that in her sample, the median report by fathers was that they saw their children weekly, whereas mothers reported those same fathers as seeing their children less than monthly. Another study by Goldsmith (1980) found that fathers reported significantly more involvement with their children than custodial mothers corroborated. This included the overall frequency of reported contact and paternal involvement with various activities. Some of the research suggests that child support payment may also be underestimated in some cases due to the heavy reliance on mothers' reports. Fathers tended to report paying more child support than mothers reported receiving. For example, 79% of the men surveyed in Tropf's (1980) study reported never missing one payment of support. Wright and Price (1986) also report a parallel discrepancy between ex-spouses' reports of child support payment. Seventy-two percent of the fathers they surveyed reported that they always paid their child support on time, while less than half of the mothers (41%) reported that they received their support on time.

The above discrepancies are important because nearly all the Census Bureau statistics on divorce and child support are based on interviews with mothers (Haskins et al., 1987, unpublished manuscript). Subsequently, most of the statistics used by researchers, policymakers, and the media may be inaccurate or at least reinforce a particularly dim picture of child support compliance and visitation patterns. It is possible that divorced fathers are more involved than previously believed based on the heavy reliance on mothers' reports and the absence of information about divorced fathers' participation in parenting.

In the following discussion, three areas of concern, father's visitation, the coparental relationship, and custodial arrangement, are considered as they relate to child support compliance and overall paternal involvement. Current research suggests that these factors are interrelated and have direct and indirect effects on compliance. In the applied realm, the consideration of these factors are significant in that they give professionals various points of intervention to encourage father involvement and postdivorce adjustment for all family members. In the policy realm, the consideration of factors associated with child support compliance within the context of father involvement may lead to more effective and informed decisions with respect to child support legislation, enforcement policy, and divorce laws in general.

VISITATION

Information regarding visitation may be the most important link to understanding the dynamics of child support compliance. It is relatively well known that fathers tend to decrease the frequency and duration of their visits over time (Furstenburg et al., 1983; Hetherington, Cox, & Cox, 1976; Wallerstein and Kelly, 1980). Moreover, contact with the noncustodial parent is crucial for children's psychological adjustment and emotional well-being (Hetherington et al., 1976; Wallerstein and Kelly, 1980; Emery, Hetherington, & Dilalla, 1984). What remains relatively unexplored is the relationship between visitation and children's economic well-being. Although intuitively it seems that visitation and child support would be related, given that paternal involvement is multifaceted, empirical validation of this potential association is scanty. There is some evidence that suggests a link between frequent or satisfying visitation patterns and child support payment (Chambers, 1979; Furstenburg et al., 1983). The direction of influence is unclear — that is it is unknown as to whether fathers who support their children financially feel more obligated to attend to their "investment" or whether fathers who have more frequent contact with their children somehow are "reminded" to financially support them. Wallerstein and Huntington (1983) emphasize the importance of visitation with respect to child support compliance. Although there may be many confounding factors, in their sample of 55 families, they found that over time, the link between visitation and child support payment becomes more profound. Furthermore, the frequency was discovered to be less important than the pattern and duration of each visit — child support was found to be highly correlated with weekend and overnight visits. However, it should be recognized that frequent or regular visitation may not necessarily reflect a loving or concerned father. It is possible that the impact of visitation on child support may be mitigated by the quality of the father-child relationship. Wallerstein and Huntington note that the significant link between a loving father-child relationship and good child support over the years was striking. Thus it may be that visitation — to the extent that it is associated with loving father-child relations — is related to good support.

COPARENTAL RELATIONSHIP

Much of the concern regarding noncustodial fathers' involvement centers on the quality of the relationship between former spouses and this has bearing on the issue of child support compliance. Koch and Lowery (1984) suggest that the coparental relationship between ex-spouses is a key determinant in the level of overall postdivorce paternal involvement. Wright and Price (1986) offer some evidence supporting a direct link between good relations between ex-spouses and child support compliance. They examined the relation of attachment between former spouses, the quality of their coparental communication, and compliance with court-ordered payment of child support. Results suggested that divorced persons who continue to have some level of attachment to their former spouse and who view their current relationship with the ex-spouse as being of good quality, reflect a family pattern in which the father has a stronger desire to fulfill his responsibility to maintain financial support of his children even if he does not have custody. Koch and Lowery (1984) and Kurdek (1986) also suggest that the coparental relationship has a direct effect on child support compliance finding that the level of parental conflict is related negatively to the regularity of payments. Wallerstein and Huntington (1983) however, were unable to find a significant link between child support payment and relations between former spouses.

Perhaps the impact of coparental relations may be better understood in terms of its indirect influence. Other research points to the fact that coparental relations have an important role in determining visitation patterns and fathers' feelings of warmth for their children. Recall in the previous section the positive association noted between visitation, warm father-child relations, and child support payment. Burke (1985) reported that the most important predictor of noncustodial fathers' warmth for and involvement with their children was the relations between ex-spouses. In general, hostile relations between ex-spouses and little discussion regarding childrearing are negatively associated with father involvement and contact with children (Ahrons, 1983; Hetherington, Cox, & Cox, 1976; Lund, 1987). Furstenburg (1988) however, found that the quality of relations between former spouses had only a modest effect on the level of participation by the noncustodial parent. In fact, he attributes situational factors such as geographical distance between fathers' residence and children's residence as being more important in determining the level of postdivorce involvement between fathers and children.

It may be then that coparental relations (as mitigated by situational factors such as geographic distance) are important in two ways. First, fathers may directly associate payment with what they are feeling for their ex-spouses. For although it is "child support" it is paid to the mother—the former spouse—and negative feelings could arouse a resistance to pay that spouse and an inability to separate children's needs from personal animosity. Conversely, positive or cooperative sentiments would arouse no such hostility or resistance to pay a former spouse and perhaps serve as an incentive to continue to provide support. Second, coparental relations may be important to the extent they facilitate or restrict visitation. Given the linkage that exists between frequent and/or satisfying visitation and good father-child relations, good coparental relations may serve to foster physical and emotional paternal involvement which in turn is associated with child support payment.

CUSTODY

Another variable which may have significance in terms of child support compliance and to paternal involvement in general is legal custody status and subsequent satisfaction with that status. Although an increasing number of fathers are awarded joint-legal custody and a small number of fathers are awarded sole custody, in the overwhelming majority of cases custody of children is awarded to the mother (Buehler, 1989; Furstenburg, 1988; Grief, 1979). This may contribute to stressful postdivorce relationships and a lack of incentives for fathers to pay child support. Salkind (1983) notes a paradox with respect to modern expectations about fathering. There is a conflict between the encouragement and social pressure for fathers to participate fully in childrearing and yet the "denial" of equal parenting in the event of marital dissolution. He sees an arrangement that gives one parent (usually the mother) total control over visitation as placing the custodial parent in a position of control and power. This places the other parent (usually the father) in a position of powerlessness leading to stress and emotional withdrawal. Salkind emphasizes that it is important to remember that father absence for the child is also child absence for the father. Current custody practices tend to be insensitive to this notion of "child absence" and the emotional well-being of fathers—especially those fathers who were active and involved in parenting before the divorce. Salkind believes that if fathers are emotionally supported following divorce, it is more likely they will provide financial support.

There is some evidence that joint custody status can be positively and significantly related to overall paternal involvement (Bowman, 1983;

Grief 1979; D'Andrea, 1983). Generally, joint custody is an arrangement whereby both parents are vested with equal legal authority for making important decisions pertaining to the welfare of their child(ren) and stipulates greater parity with regard to child care than sole custody. Sole custody restricts the noncustodial parent's legal right of child access to that visitation set out by the court (Hyde, 1984; Roman and Haddad, 1978). Overall, joint custody fathers tend to be more satisfied with their custody status than noncustodial/visitation fathers and more frequent contact with children is found to be associated with satisfaction of custody status (D'Andrea, 1983; Grief, 1979). Furthermore, joint custody fathers report greater perceptions of being close with and having greater influence on their children than visitation fathers (D'Andrea, 1983; Grief, 1979). However, it is important to recognize that when joint custody is entered into under duress, satisfaction levels may be even lower than for sole-custody families (Felner and Terre, 1987).

It seems then, that a different kind of psychological involvement may grow out of the opportunity to take care of or parent one's children rather than "visiting" them. Recall that Wallerstein and Huntington (1983) note the significance of the emotional quality of the father-child relationship in terms of contact and financial support. Greater psychological involvement stemming out of joint custody arrangements may facilitate emotional closeness between divorced fathers and their children and thus more frequent and compliant child support payments.

CONCLUSIONS AND POLICY IMPLICATIONS

It is clear that we need to learn more about the conditions and situational factors that may facilitate different facets of postdivorce paternal involvement. More research is needed which examines the divorce experience from the perspective of the father in order to better understand the dynamics of postdivorce paternal involvement and further explore the linkages between custody, the coparental relationship, visitation, and child support compliance. The existing evidence concerning these factors is somewhat fragmented in that research generally conceptualizes child support payment apart from visitation and emotional issues. What evidence does exist in the literature regarding these phenomena seems to point to a more comprehensive approach.

The importance of linkages between financial support and other kinds of involvement lies in the ability to intervene at one level and influence other positive outcomes. For example, it is possible that a more positive approach (and one that will be more welcomed on the part of divorced men) would be to legally facilitate father-child contact through more explicitly liberal visitation policies or varied custodial arrangements. There is evidence that suggests divorced men are generally unsatisfied with their visitation schedule, would like to see their children more frequently, and often believe that their visitation is interfered with by their ex-spouses (Haskins et al., 1987). If child support from fathers is in part contingent on the quality of the postdivorce relationship they have with their children, to advise anything other than a policy that facilitates father-child contact would be self-defeating and destructive to the postdivorce adjustment for all members of the family.

Joint custody may be an effective policy for insuring that child support payments are made. Although there is some controversy as to the appropriateness of this kind of arrangement and its impact on the psychological adjustment of children, there are several studies that seem to support the viability of joint custody awards (Ahrons, 1980; Grief, 1979). Buehler (1989) notes a pervasive, but unsubstantiated, idea in the literature is that joint custody only works well if former spouses have a positive coparental relationship. For example, Luepnitz (1982) found that even when parental conflict was high, children in joint custody families reported higher levels of self-esteem than children in either paternal or maternal custody families. Beuhler speculates that based on the available research, it may be that an active relationship with both parents serves to mitigate the harmful effects of parental conflict on children's well-being. For many families, joint custody is an arrangement that will facilitate the healthy development of children without sacrificing the integrity of the noncustodial parent. It also allows both parents to seek a fuller life outside of parenting because major childrearing responsibilities (including financial) would be shared.

The literature also suggests other points of intervention in terms of the influence of the coparental relationship on both visitation (Ahrons, 1983; Hetherington et al., 1976; Koch and Lowery, 1985; Lund, 1987); and child support payment (Wright & Price, 1986). In many cases, the adversary system may promote or exacerbate conflict and hostility between parents. And to the extent that the adversary process promotes conflict and poor coparental relations, it seems to be detrimental to children in divorce (Scott & Emery, 1987). Because of increasing dissatisfaction with the adversary system, there has been increased interest in alternative methods of resolving child custody disputes, visitation problems, and developing equitable settlements. Divorce mediation has emerged as the major alternative to either litigation or out-of-court negotiation between attorneys (Scott & Emery, 1987). In divorce mediation, divorcing parties meet with an impartial third party to identify, discuss, and hopefully settle the disputes that result from marital dissolution (Scott & Emery, 1987). At this time, the states of California, Delaware, and Maine have enacted mandatory mediation legislation requiring that all parties requesting a custody or visitation hearing first attempt to settle the dispute in mediation. Several other states have mediation services available to couples who voluntarily wish to use them (Freed & Foster, 1984). Divorce mediation reduces the adversarial nature of the divorce process, encourages cooperativeness, and promotes the subsequent exploration of options other than traditional custody and visitation arrangements. Bahr (1980) found that the use of divorce mediation as opposed to litigation led to more satisfaction with respect to custody arrangements, financial settlement and the decision to divorce in general. Divorce mediation could be central to a package of policies aimed at promoting postdivorce paternal involvement and financial responsibility.

A system of divorce in which professionals attempted to facilitate a cooperative coparental relationship could prove to be very cost-effective not only in terms of the positive effect such cooperation could have on child support compliance but also in reducing court costs and legal fees. Scott & Emery (1984) point out that in evaluating the cost effectiveness of mediation, it is important to distinguish between the private costs for the divorcing spouses and public costs as calculated in terms of court time. In terms of the private cost of mediation, the overall expense is not much different from the cost of litigation (Bahr, 1981b). However in terms of whether mediation is effective in reducing public costs, evidence does suggest that divorce mediation can successfully divert a large percentage of cases from the more expensive custody hearing. Furthermore, agreements are reached more quickly in mediation and mediated agreements tend to last longer (McIsaac, 1982). Fiscal analyses of several court-based programs project that mediation reduces costs (as a function of court time) by 10%-50% (Bahr, 1981a).

Facilitating and encouraging parental involvement on the part of divorced fathers may be an easier, more effective approach to insuring that children receive their child support than enforcement. Enforcement may actually have a negative effect in terms of further alienating fathers from their children. Perhaps the place of enforcement should be a last ditch effort for those divorced fathers who do not respond to other types of legislation. Of course, this kind of philosophy is in contrast to the underlying argument of universal enforcement whereby all noncustodial parents who are ordered to pay child support automatically have that amount of money deducted from their paycheck — similar to the Social-Security system. However, such a system, while perhaps benefiting those children whose fathers would not pay child support otherwise, overlooks those fathers who voluntarily comply and poses risks for individual privacy. Furthermore, universal enforcement does not address the problem of psychological disengagement over time of most divorced fathers from their children.

If, as a society, we embrace more severe enforcement policies, we also need to temper this change with policies addressing other aspects of the postdivorce situation. This includes considering more than simply the child's and custodial mother's financial needs and recognizing fathers' needs. As a society, we should be alarmed hy the downward financial spiral of custodial mothers and their children. But a secondary issue which has remained relatively unexplored, is the almost inevitable disengagement of divorced fathers from their children and the utilization of policies which seem to promote and reinforce fathering from the periphery. The widespread noninvolvement of divorced fathers in parenting may have direct and indirect consequences in terms of children's emotional and financial well-being. Rather than simply focusing on financial responsibility, it is important to recognize that father involvement is multifaceted — financial (child support), physical (visitation), and emotional (feelings of closeness with children) — and that these different aspects of involvement are most likely interrelated. Policies and interventions promoting more liberal visitation rights, divorce mediation, and joint custody may be instrumental in fostering father involvement, represent viable alternatives to the majority of current postdivorce arrangements, and challenge the underlying philosophy of enforcement policy.

REFERENCES

Ahrons, C. (1980). Joint custody arrangements in the postdivorce family. *Journal of Divorce, 3*, 189-205.

Ahrons, C. (1983). Predictors of paternal involvement postdivorce: Mothers' & fathers' perceptions. *Journal of Divorce, 6*, 55-69.

Bahr, S.J. (1980). *Divorce Mediation: An evaluation of an alternative divorce policy*. Unpublished manuscript, University of Utah.

Bahr, S.J. (1981a). An evaluation of court mediation: A comparison in divorce cases with children. *Journal of Family Issues, 2*, 39-60.

Bahr, S.J. (1981b). Mediation is the answer. *Family Advocate*, 32-35.

Bowman, M. (1983). Parenting after divorce: A comparative study of mother custody and joint custody families. *Dissertation Abstracts International, 44*, 578A.

Buehler, C. (1989). Influential factors and equity issues in divorce settlements. *Family Relations, 38*, 76-82.

Burke, M. (1985). *Factors affecting the relationship of the non-custodial father and his children.* Paper presented to the annual meeting of the National Council on Family Relations, Dallas, Texas.

Chambers, D. (1979). *Making Fathers Pay: The enforcement of child support.* Chicago: University of Chicago Press.

Chambers, D. (1983). Child support in the twenty-first century. In J. Cassetty (Ed.), *The Parental Child-Support Obligation* (pp. 283-298). Lexington, MA: Lexington Books.

D'Andrea, Ann (1983). Joint custody as related to paternal involvement and paternal self-esteem. *Conciliation Courts Review, 21*, 81-87.

Emery, R., Hetherington, M., and Dilalla, L. (1984). Divorce, children, and social policy. In H. Stevenson and A. Siegal (Eds.), *Child Development Research and Social Policy* (pp. 189-266). Chicago: University of Chicago Press.

Felner, R.D., & Terre, Lisa (1987). Child custody dispositions and children's adaptation following divorce. In Lois Weithorn, (Ed.), *Psychology and Child Custody Determinations.* University of Nebraska Press: Lincoln.

Freed, D.J., & Foster, H.H. (1984). Divorce in the fifty states: An overview. *Family Law Quarterly, 17*, 365-447.

Furstenburg, F.F., J.L. Peterson, C.W. Nord, and Zill, N. (1983). The life course of children of divorce: Marital disruption and parental contact. *American Sociological Review, 48*, 656-658.

Furstenburg, F. (1988). Marital disruptions, child custody, and visitation. In S. Kamerman & A. Kahn (Eds.), *Child Support: From Debt Collection to Social Policy* (pp. 277-305). Beverly Hills: Sage.

Goldsmith, Jean (1981). Relationships between former spouses: Descriptive findings. *Journal of Divorce, 4*, 1-20.

Grief, G. (1985). *Single Fathers.* Lexington, MA: Lexington Books.

Grief, Judith (1979). Fathers, children, and joint custody. *American Journal of Orthopsychiatry, 49*, 311-319.

Haskins, R. (1988). Child Support: A fathers view. In S. Kamerman & A. Kahn (Eds.), *Child Support: From Debt Collection to Social Policy* (pp. 306-327). Beverly Hills: Sage.

Haskins, R., Richey, T., Wicker, F. (1987). *Paying and visiting: Child support enforcement and fathering from afar.* Unpublished Manuscript.

Hetherington, M., Cox, M., & Cox, R. (1976). Divorced Fathers. *The Family Coordinator, 25*, 417-428.

Hyde, L. (1984). Child custody in divorce. *Juvenile and Family Court Journal, 35*, (1).

Koch, M. & Lowery, C. (1984). Visitation & the noncustodial father. *Journal of Divorce, 8*, 47-65.

Kurdek, L. (1986). Custodial mothers' perceptions of visitation and payment of child support by noncustodial fathers in families with low and high levels of preseparation interparent conflict. *Journal of Applied Developmental Psychology, 1,* 307-323.

Luepnitz, D. (1982). *Child Custody.* Lexington, MA: D.C. Heath.

Lund, M. (1987). The noncustodial father: Common challenges in parenting after divorce. In C. Lewis & M. O'Brien (Eds.), *Reassessing Fatherhood* (pp. 212-224). Beverly Hills: Sage.

McIsaac, H. (1982). Court-connected mediation. *Conciliation Courts Review, 21,* 49-56.

Nichols-Casebolt, A. (1986). The economic impact of child support reform on the poverty status of custodial and non-custodial families. *Journal of Marriage and The Family, 48,* 875-880.

Roman, M., & Haddad, W. (1978). *The disposable parent.* New York: Holt, Rinehart and Winston.

Salkind, N.J. (1983). The father-child postdivorce relationship and child support. In J. Cassetty (Ed.), *The Parental Child-Support Obligation* (pp. 173-192). Lexington, MA: Lexington Books.

Scott, E.S. & Emery, R.E. (1987). Child custody dispute resolution: The adversarial system and divorce mediation. In Lois Weithorn (Ed.), *Psychology and Child Custody Determinations* (pp. 23-56). University of Nebraska Press: Lincoln.

Tropf, W.D. (1980). The nature of relationships divorced men maintain with their first families. (Doctoral Dissertation, University of Florida, 1980). *Dissertation Abstracts International,* 42, 875A.

U.S. Bureau of the Census (1985). Child Support & Alimony: 1983. *Current Population Reports,* Special Studies, Series P. 23, No. 141. Washington D.C.: U.S. Government Printing Office.

U.S. Bureau of the Census (1986). Child support and alimony; 1985. *Current Population Reports,* Series P. 23, No. 152. Washington D.C.: U.S. Government Printing Office.

Wallerstein, J.S. & Huntington, D.S. (1983). Bread and roses: Nonfinancial issues related to fathers' economic support of their children following divorce. In J. Cassetty (Ed.), *The Parental Child-Support Obligation* (pp. 135-155). Lexington, MA: Lexington Books.

Wallerstein, J.S & Kelly, J. (1980). *Surviving the breakup: How children and parents cope with divorce.* New York: Basic Books.

Weitzman, L. (1985). *The divorce revolution: The Unexpected Social and Economic Consequences for Women and Children in America.* New York: Free Press.

Weitzman, L. (1988). Child support myths and reality. In S. Kamerman & A. Kahn (Eds.) *Child Support: From Debt Collection to Social Policy* (pp. 251-276). Beverly Hills: Sage.

Wright, David, & Price, Sharon (1986). Court-ordered child support payment: The effect of the former spouse relationship on compliance. *Journal of Marriage & The Family,* 48, 869-874.

Exploring Ways to Get Divorced Fathers to Comply Willingly with Child Support Agreements

James R. Dudley

SUMMARY. Most public policy attention given to the child support issue has focused on the impact of involuntary measures rather than the factors that may encourage fathers to comply willingly with their child support agreements. In this study of 255 divorced fathers, the researcher examines several possible predictor variables of child support compliance, including the divorce proceedings, type of child support agreement, custody arrangements, and frequency of the father's contact with his children. Fathers with shared physical and shared legal custody, and fathers having more frequent contact with their children, were more likely to be in compliance. The results strongly suggest that more attention should be given in divorce agreements to provisions that will enhance the father's involvement in the physical and decision-making aspects of his children's lives so as to increase the likelihood of his involvement in the financial aspects.

Getting divorced fathers to contribute to the financial needs of their children is one of the more critical and complicated problems facing American society. In 1984, four million women were supposed to receive child support for their children. Only about half received the full amount they were due, 26% received partial payments, and 24% received no payment (U.S. Census, 1986). Of the 2.9 million women below the poverty level with children of an absent father, only 43% were awarded child

James R. Dudley, PhD, is Associate Professor in the School of Social Administration, Temple University, Philadelphia, PA 19122.

This study was supported by a grant from Temple University. The author wishes to thank Dr. John Franklin for his support and encouragement in the writing of this article.

121

support. The impact of this loss of income has disastrous effects on these mothers and children, particularly those in poverty (Albrecht, 1980; Bane, 1979; Weitzman, 1986).

Most of the public policy attention devoted to the child support issue has focused on the enforcement of child support by governmental agencies. It is often presumed that divorced fathers will pay support; and when they do not, the remedy is to apply involuntary measures to make them pay (Cassetty, 1978; Chambers, 1979). While child support enforcement efforts are necessary to hold non-custodial fathers accountable for their financial obligations to their children, these efforts should be seen as a last resort measure, not the first and primary means of addressing this issue. It is the author's view that prior steps which are preventive in nature and encourage the father's voluntary participation should be given much more serious consideration. Everyone will benefit if divorced fathers willingly contribute to their children's financial well-being. Mothers and children will likely be more financially secure, fathers will feel more committed to their children financially and in other ways, and collection agencies will be less necessary.

More serious attention needs to be given to numerous factors that may play a role in influencing whether or not a father willingly pays child support. Several such factors are considered in this article, including how divorce agreements are negotiated, variations in the ways in which child support agreements are structured, custody arrangements, the degree to which fathers continue to be actively involved in their children's lives, and selected personal characteristics of the fathers and the families.

First, the nature of the legal proceedings used to work out divorce agreements may be an important context for exploration in determining whether divorced fathers will pay support, particularly over time. Even when a child support agreement is worked out separately from the divorce agreement, the divorce proceedings often set a norm for how the parents will continue to work out their issues over time. Also, child support resolution is directly related to the resolution of the other aspects of divorce, including property, alimony, and custody.

Divorce proceedings vary considerably in the extent to which they foster cooperative or adversarial relationships between a father and his former spouse (Clingempeel & Reppucci, 1982). Litigated proceedings could result in delinquent child support payments if they have precipitated greater conflict between the spouses, with the father feeling that he is being coerced into contributing. Conversely, one could argue that the strict legal penalties for non-payment of support from court-ordered measures could increase the likelihood that a father will pay support (Weitz-man, 1988).

Professional mediation, in contrast to litigation, places emphasis on the parents' playing a major role in working out their agreement together, in a cooperative manner (Bahr, 1981; Ebel, 1980; Girdner, 1985). Using this approach, several studies have found that mediation in child support resulted in improved compliance by parents who pay support because both parents agreed to the arrangements (Chambers, 1979; Irving, Benjamin, & Trocme, 1984; Pearson & Thoennes, 1983).

The way in which a child support agreement is structured also could have an impact on whether a non-custodial parent continues to pay. Often, child support is court-ordered and must be sent to an agency of the court. In other cases, payments are sent directly to the custodial parent. In regard to these two options, Young (1975) found higher compliance with court-ordered arrangements.

Also, child support agreements sometimes have provisions for the father to pay directly for some of his children's expenses (for example, their clothes or day camp fees). Sometimes the arrangement is informal rather than part of the agreement. Studies could not be found that have focused on the impact of this type of arrangement on child support compliance. While it is recognized that this arrangement would not work for all divorced parents, it may increase the likelihood of long-term financial participation by many non-custodial parents because they become directly involved in spending some of the child support money and in seeing the benefits that accrue to their children. This type of arrangement may also strengthen the bonds between a father and his children, particularly if associated directly with specific child-parent activities.

The custody arrangement may also influence whether a divorced father will be reliable in paying child support, as this arrangement normally defines the extent to which he has responsibility for the physical care and major decisions of his children, areas that are interrelated with the financial aspects. It would seem most likely that fathers with shared physical custody and sole custody would be more prone than other fathers to comply with their child support agreements. The influence of shared legal custody (fathers sharing the major decisions of their children with their former spouse but not having shared physical custody) on complying with a child support agreement is not as apparent, and no studies could be found that have focused on this relationship.

Related to the custody arrangement, the degree to which a father remains physically in contact with his children may be another predictor of whether he will willingly pay child support. Two studies have found that

fathers who had little or no contact with their children were less committed to paying support than more involved fathers because their children
were not active in their lives (Chambers, 1979; Furstenberg, Nord, Peterson, & Zill, 1983). A related finding revealed that when non-custodial
fathers or their former spouses moved a long distance away, they were
less likely to pay regular support, presumably because they were unable to
stay involved in their children's lives (Cassetty, 1978; Chambers, 1979).

Personal characteristics of the father and the family may also predict
whether a father is more likely to pay support. While these variables
should not condone fathers for not assuming their financial obligations,
they may provide helpful insights into understanding their behavior. One
explanation pertains to the father's income. Fathers who have low incomes or are unemployed have been found to be a poor risk for support
collection (Cassetty, 1978; Young, 1975). However, income alone does
not predict whether support is paid, as fathers with higher incomes have
been reported to be just as likely to be delinquent as lower income fathers
(Weitzman, 1985). Young (1975) found that fathers with average incomes
rather than low or high incomes were more likely to respond to public
child support collection.

Numerous other variables may be predictors of whether a father pays
support. The length of the marriage before separation has been reported to
be a predictor, with fathers married ten years or more being more likely to
comply (Chambers, 1979). Whether or not a father has remarried may
also be a predictor because assuming responsibility to a second family
often means withdrawing from the first family (Furstenberg, Nord, Peterson, & Zill, 1983). Whether the father's former spouse has remarried also
has been reported to be a predictor of compliance with child support (Cassetty, 1978). Finally, women with only a high school education were less
likely to receive support than women with four or more years of college
(U.S. Census, 1986).

The study presented in this article focused on the following research
questions:

1. Are any of the following variables predictors of whether or not a
   father continues to comply with his child support agreement after a
   divorce?

   A. Type of divorce proceedings.
   B. Type of child support agreement (payments sent through the
      court, payments directly to the former spouse, combination of
      payments to the former spouse and direct payment for some chil-

dren's expenses, or sharing all of the children's expenses with the former spouse).
C. Custody agreement.
D. Amount of direct contact that the father has with his children.
E. Selected personal and family characteristics.

2. What explanations are provided by fathers for being delinquent in paying their child support obligations?

METHOD

Research Participants

The research participants were 255 divorced fathers. All had at least one child under 19 years of age and resided in the Philadelphia area. Eighty-eight percent (222) were white, 10% (26) were black, and 2% were other minorities. These fathers had a mean age of 40.7 years; the mean age of their former spouses was 38.2 years. Most of them were middle income wage earners, with 60% having incomes over $30,000, and only 12.5% having incomes of $20,000 or less. Also, their educational levels were relatively high, with only 17% having a high school diploma or less and 59% having at least a college degree.

These 255 fathers had been divorced for an average of 5 years. Forty-two percent had been divorced from one to three years, 24% from four to six years, 15% from seven to nine years, and 19% for ten years or more. The majority (55%) had only one child, and 34% had two children. Most of the children were between the ages of five and 18 years, with only 7% of the fathers having younger children. Thirty-nine percent of the fathers and 36% of their former spouses had remarried.

The intent of this study was to generate a relatively large sample of divorced fathers representing, as much as possible, the demographic characteristics and the range of custody and child support arrangements of divorced fathers in the Philadelphia area. Three criteria were required: being divorced, having at least one child under 19 years, and residing in Philadelphia or one of its four Pennsylvania suburban counties. Fathers meeting these criteria were identified from a range of sources, including fathers' groups, Parents Without Partners, day care and school programs, churches, a police league, divorce mediators, human service professionals, fathers who were already identified as participants of the study, and numerous media announcements. The response rate was 64%, based on fathers who were sent questionnaires.

This purposive sampling approach was successful in obtaining the range of custody and child support arrangements. However, black and other minority fathers are underrepresented even though special efforts were made to involve them. Also, fathers with less formal education and low to moderate incomes were underrepresented.

Procedure

A mailed questionnaire was used. Questions were asked about divorce proceedings, child support arrangements, custody, and the frequency of the fathers' contact with their children at the time of divorce and presently. Also, they were asked whether they regularly paid child support; if they did not, they were asked, in an open-ended question, why not?

One limitation of the study was that it totally relied on the self-reporting of the fathers. Even though the fathers were assured of confidentiality, it may have been difficult for some of them to admit that they were not paying child support, for example. Also, the views of the former spouses were not elicited, and studies have shown that divorced fathers and mothers often differ in their reporting on many topics (Goldsmith, 1980).

RESULTS

Twenty (7.8%) of the 255 respondents reported that they did not comply with their child support agreements at the present time. Of these 20 fathers, 13 paid no support and seven paid less than what was ordered. The remaining 207 fathers who answered this question reported that they either closely followed their child support agreement or contributed more than was required. Twenty-eight fathers did not respond to the question. Twenty-two of the non-respondents had sole custody, shared physical custody, or their children had moved in with them, while no explanation was given as to why the other six fathers did not respond to this question.

In most cases, failure to comply with a child support agreement did not occur consistently from the time of divorce to the present time. Only seven of the 20 fathers who reported that they did not presently comply were also out of compliance at the time of divorce. The other 13 fathers reported that they were in compliance at the time of divorce. An additional 15 fathers were out of compliance with their support agreements at the time of divorce but were presently in compliance. For this last group, the reasons given for becoming compliant included renegotiating visitation, custody, or child support, and changes in employment.

Divorce Proceedings

The fathers were involved in divorce proceedings in four distinct ways: 18% involved a court settlement by a judge, 50% involved an out of court settlement by two attorneys, 21% used mediation, and 11% were decided without outside assistance except for the filing procedures. However, the type of divorce proceeding that was used was not significantly related to whether the respondent was in compliance with his child support agreement either at the time of divorce (Chi-Square = 6.59, df = 3, n.s.) or presently (Chi-Square = 3.80, df = 3, n.s.). Also, non-compliant fathers did not return to court at a later time significantly more often than compliant fathers to negotiate changes in child support, custody, or visitation.

Child Support Agreements

The types of child support agreements that were worked out around the time of divorce varied in four distinct ways. One hundred and thirteen fathers (49.6%) were required to make child support payments through the courts, and 57 (25%) made payments directly to their former spouses. Thirty-one of the fathers (13.6%) indicated that they had a combined arrangement of sending support payments to their former spouses and directly paying for some of their children's expenses beyond medical insurance (for example, clothes and day care). It is not known how many of these direct payment arrangements were formalized in child support agreements and how many were informal. Finally, 27 fathers (11.8%) indicated that they shared all child care expenses with their former spouses rather than sending a fixed amount of money to them each month. This arrangement was not necessarily shared equally between the former spouses. Twenty-seven fathers did not respond to this question or did not fit into one of these categories.

Seventeen of the non-compliant fathers had one of the two traditional arrangements (payments sent through the court or directly to the former spouse), one had a combined arrangement, and two did not indicate the type of child support agreement that they had. However, the type of child support agreement was not statistically significantly related to whether or not he paid child support (Chi-Square = 4.48, df = 3, n.s.).

Custody

The custody arrangements of the total group of respondents is presented in Table 1. In 17 (85%) of the 20 non-compliant cases, the mothers had sole custody. Only two non-compliant fathers (10%) had shared legal cus-

Table 1

NON-COMPLIANCE WITH CHILD SUPPORT AGREEMENT BY CUSTODY (%)

COMPLIANCE STATUS	MOTHER SOLE	MO. PHYSICAL SHARED LEGAL	SHARED LEGAL/PHY.	FATHER PHYSICAL
1. Compliant Group	84 (83.2)	56 (96.6)	51 (98.1)	10 (100)
2. Non-Compliant Group	17 (16.8)	2 (3.4)	1 (1.9)	0 (0)
Total Group*	101 (100)	58 (100)	52 (100)	10 (100)

Chi-Square = 12.00, df = 1, p < .001. (Custody categories collapsed to mother custody and all others.)

* Six of the fathers did not indicate a custody arrangement and twenty-eight additional fathers did not respond to the question of whether or not they complied with their support agreements.

tody with their former spouses, and one non-compliant father had shared physical and legal custody. When the mother custody category was compared to all other custody arrangements in terms of whether or not fathers were in compliance, a significant relationship was found (see Table 1).

Father's Contact with His Children

The frequency of the father's contact with his children was measured in terms of overnights that his children normally stayed with him. As Table 2 indicates, the frequency of the father's present contact with his children was significantly related to whether or not he was presently complying with his child support agreement, with fathers having more frequent contact more likely being compliant. Similarly, the frequency of the father's contact with his children at the time of divorce was related to compliance at divorce, with the more active fathers again being more likely to be compliant.

Characteristics of the Fathers

Table 3 indicates how the 20 non-compliant fathers were different from the remaining respondents based on personal and family characteristics. The non-compliant fathers were divorced for significantly more years, and their former spouses were more likely to be remarried. Also, this subgroup had significantly lower incomes and less formal education than the remaining fathers. Otherwise, differences were not evident between the two groups based on their race, geographic distance from their former spouse, number of years married, whether the father was remarried, and characteristics of their children (number, age, sex).

Explanations for Not Paying Child Support

In an open-ended question, the fathers who reported being out of compliance with their child support agreements were asked why this was so. Three fathers cited employment-related problems. All three said that they could not find full-time work, with one of them indicating that a felony conviction added to his difficulty.

Three fathers indicated that they did not pay support because they did not have contact with their children. In all three cases they had not seen their children for at least ten years. One had been a substance abuser for over 20 years and was wanting to re-enter his son's life but did not know how to do it. In addition to these cases, another father attributed his non-payment of child support to his current drug addiction, even though he had occasional contact with his children.

Table 2

NON-COMPLIANCE WITH CHILD SUPPORT AGREEMENT BY FREQUENCY OF
FATHER'S CONTACT WITH HIS CHILDREN PRESENTLY

COMPLIANCE STATUS OF FATHER	FREQUENCY OF FATHER'S CONTACT PRESENTLY*		
	Mean	S.D.	n
1. Compliant Fathers	4.55	2.19	207
2. Non-compliant Fathers**	2.90	2.56	19

$t = 3.11$, $df = 224$, $p = .002$

* Frequency of contact is measured on an 8 point scale with
  1 = no contact, 2 = no overnights but some contact, 3 =
  occasional overnights, 4 = one overnight/month, 5 = two to
  three overnights/month, 6 = one to two overnights/week, 7 =
  three to six overnights/week, and 8 = every overnight.

** One of the non-compliant fathers did not indicate the
   frequency of his contact with his children.

130

Table 3

OTHER CORRELATES OF NON-COMPLIANCE WITH CHILD SUPPORT AGREEMENT

CORRELATES	COMPLIANT GROUP	NON-COMPLIANT GROUP
Years Divorced (mean)**	4.58 years	7.35 years
Father's Income $30,000 or Less***	38.4%	68.4%
Father's Education High School Diploma or Less*	15.5%	45.0%
Former Spouse Remarried*	32.4%	60.0%

*   p < .05

**   p < .01

*** p < .0001

131

Four fathers attributed their non-compliance to their children's changing circumstances. Two said that their children primarily lived with them, even though the child support agreement had not been renegotiated. In the other two instances, their children were 17 and 18 years of age respectively, and these fathers did not feel financially responsible any longer. In one case, the son was reported to be earning almost as much money as the father, and in the other case the father said that the agreement was no longer in force even though his child was still in high school.

Two fathers blamed their non-compliance on their former spouse's interference with their visitation arrangement. Two others also focused on their former spouses, with one claiming that she was financially secure, and the other explaining that he had agreed not to see his children if the new stepfather would agree to pay for their expenses.

Two other fathers attributed their non-compliance to other issues in their divorce agreements. In particular, both thought that their former spouses had received a financial advantage in their property settlements.

Only one father simply admitted that paying support was not a priority and that he often procrastinated about making payments. The final two fathers did not provide an explanation.

DISCUSSION

A very low percentage of the fathers in this sample reported being out of compliance with their child support agreements. Several other studies also have reported that most of their subjects regularly paid support (Berkman, 1986; Dominic & Schlesinger, 1980; Grief, 1979; Haskins, 1988; Koch & Lowery, 1984). Since these findings do not reflect U.S. Census data, these samples may include fathers who reported that they were compliant when they were not. Unfortunately, there was no cross-check on their responses. Also, these samples probably underrepresent particular groups of non-compliant fathers. Nevertheless, much can be learned from studying fathers who regularly pay support as well as those who do not.

According to the findings, divorced fathers who have some type of custody responsibility are more likely to comply with their child support agreement. The most predictive custody categories were instances in which the father had shared physical/legal custody or sole custody. Probably the most interesting finding was that fathers who did not share physical custody but shared in the major decisions of their children (shared legal custody) were more likely to comply than fathers without any custody. This suggests that both types of shared custody (legal and physical) may need to be given serious consideration to increase the likelihood of voluntary compliance with child support. Shared legal custody without shared physical custody may, for example, be most suited to the divorced family in which the father wants to have input but where frequent exchange of the children is problematic.

Other findings also strongly suggest that divorced fathers who are more involved with their children will be more likely to comply. This was evident in the considerably higher frequency of a father's contact with his children among compliant fathers.

While the type of support agreement was not found to be a predictor statistically, only one of the 20 non-compliant fathers had a combined arrangement in which they directly paid for some of their children's expenses. This may suggest that a partial direct payment of child support is another form of father involvement to consider. More research is needed to determine the impact of the father's involvement in directly paying for *some* of his children's expenses, and whether it works for particular groups but not others. This arrangement occurred fairly equally among the fathers in three custody categories: mother custody, shared legal/mother physical, and shared legal/shared physical. Almost all of the fathers who shared all of their children's expenses with their former spouses were either sole or shared legal/shared physical custodians, suggesting that this arrangement may only be appropriate for these two custodial groups.

More attention should also be given to the variety of explanations that non-compliant fathers report for not paying child support (for example, if the father is unemployed or complains that his former spouse is interfering with the visitation agreement). While the resolution of such problems of the father cannot be settled in a child support hearing, to ignore them altogether may only further alienate the father from his financial obligations to his children.

Instituting legal measures to enforce the collection of child support (e.g., using wage attachments, tax refund offsets, liens on property) should be supported if fathers are not willing to voluntarily contribute. However, we should first be asking whether we are taking all of the preventive steps that are necessary to encourage the voluntary participation of fathers in complying with child support agreements. If we emphasize the involuntary measures without the voluntary ones, we may be inadvertently pushing countless fathers even further out of their children's lives and creating even greater hardship for the children and their mothers. Based on American values, we are likely to have more effective results by helping fathers to choose to do something rather than by forcing them to do it. Among the important ways that we can encourage divorced fathers to choose to comply with child support agreements is to take them more seriously as family members during divorce proceedings. More specifically, we should ensure that there are optimum provisions in divorce agreements for a father's involvement in the physical and decision-making aspects of his children's lives a well as the financial aspects.

REFERENCES

Albrecht, S. L. (1980). Reactions and adjustments to divorce: Differences in the experiences of males and females. *Family Relations, 29,* 59-68.

Bahr, S. J. (1981). An evaluation of court mediation for divorce cases with children. *Journal of Family Issues, 2,* 39-60.

Bane, M. J. (1979). Marital disruption and the lives of children. In G. Levinger & O.C. Moles (Eds.), *Divorce and separation.* New York: Basic Books.

Berkman, B. G. (1986). Father involvement and regularity of child support in post-divorce families. *Journal of Divorce, 9,* 67-74.

Cassetty, J. (1978). *Child support and public policy: Securing support from absent fathers.* Lexington, MA: Lexington Books.

Chambers, D. L. (1979). *Making fathers pay: The enforcement of child support.* Chicago: University of Chicago Press.

Clingempeel, W.G. & Reppucci, N.D. (1982). Joint custody after divorce: Major issues and goals for research. *Psychological Bulletin, 91,* 102-127.

Dominic, K.T. & Schlesinger, B. (1980). Weekend fathers: Family shadows. *Journal of Divorce, 3,* 241-247.

Ebel, D. M. (1980). Bar programs — other ways to resolve disputes. *Litigation, 6,* 25-28.

Furstenberg, F. F., Jr., Nord, C. W., Peterson, J. L., & Zill, N. (1983). The life course of children of divorce: Marital disruption and parental contact. *American Sociological Review, 48,* 656-668.

Girdner, L. (1985). Adjudication and mediation: A comparison of custody decision-making processes involving third parties. *Journal of Divorce, 9,* 33-47.

Grief, J.B. (1979). Fathers, children, and joint custody. *American Journal of Orthopsychiatry, 49,* 311-319.

Haskins, R. (1988). Child support: A father's view. In A. J. Kahn & S. B. Kamerman (Eds.), *Child support: From debt collection to social policy.* Beverly Hills, CA: Sage.

Irving, H. H., Benjamin, M. & Trocme, N. (1984). Shared parenting: An empirical analysis utilizing a large data base. *Family Process, 23,* 561-569.

Koch, M. A. & Lowery, C. R. (1984). Visitation and the noncustodial father. *Journal of Divorce, 8,* 47-65.

Pearson, J., & Thoennes, N. (1983). A preliminary portrait of client reactions to three court mediation programs. In J. A. Lemmon (Ed.), *Reaching effective agreements. Mediation Quarterly,* no. 3. San Francisco: Jossey-Bass.

U. S. Bureau of Census (1986). Current Population Reports, Series P-23, No. 148. Child support and alimony: 1983 (Supplemental Report). Washington, DC: U. S. Government Printing Office.

Weitzman, L. (1986). *The divorce revolution: The unexpected social and economic consequences for women and children in America*. New York: Free Press.

Weitzman, L. (1988). Child support myths and reality. In A. J. Kahn & S. B. Kamerman (Eds.), *Child support: From debt collection to social policy*. Beverly Hills, CA: Sage.

Young, A. (1975). Absent parent child support: Cost-benefit analysis. Washington DC: Department of Health, Education, and Welfare, Social and Rehabilitation Service.

WOMEN
AND DIVORCE

Correlates of Women's Adjustment
During the Separation and Divorce Process

Krisanne Bursik

SUMMARY. This study sought to clarify those factors related to successful adjustment at different times during the divorce process. A longitudinal research design was used to study three diverse samples of women in the process of adaptation. Certain variables previously found to predict adjustment, such as the woman's age and the presence of children, were not significantly associated with the multiple indicators of adjustment used in this study. Sex role attitudes, social isolation, and inter-spouse acrimony emerged as stronger correlates of adjustment. The predictive power of several variables changed over time, emphasizing the importance of controlling the length of separation for a given sample.

Over the last twenty years numerous studies have sought to clarify those factors which are related to women's postseparation and postdivorce adjustment. This research emphasis on women's adjustment is due largely to

Krisanne Bursik, PhD, is Assistant Professor in the Psychology Department, Suffolk University, 41 Temple Street, Boston, MA 02114.

The author wishes to thank Nicole Barenbaum and Janet Malley for their assistance with the data collection.

137

the fact that in the majority of cases women obtain custody of minor children, and the children's adjustment to separation and divorce is often studied concurrently. The focus of this research has generally been the causes and correlates of divorce, with the dissolution of the marriage often treated as a simple and readily identifiable event. Although divorce as a transition has been alluded to by various researchers, little emphasis has been placed on understanding or operationalizing the process involved in making a successful or unsuccessful transition from the married to the single status. The scarcity of such studies is, of course, in part explained by the great difficulty in obtaining longitudinal data, especially at a time of turbulence in the lives of those we wish to study.

It is often the case that marital separation and divorce is a disruptive and emotionally draining process for those who must experience it. As one of the most stressful life changes a person can experience (Holmes & Rahe, 1967), divorce demands personal reorganization and adjustment to new roles and lifestyles. Many studies in recent years have documented the increased incidence of emotional and physical health problems for those in the process of divorce (Bloom, Asher, & White, 1978; Chiriboga, Roberts, & Stein, 1978; Hetherington, Cox, & Cox, 1978; Weiss, 1975).

On the other hand, crisis theorists such as Caplan (1974) assert that a mastery of major life crises can have positive, growth producing effects. Marital separation and subsequent divorce may involve relief if the marriage being terminated was stressful or involved violence. It is possible that this life change may even provide opportunities for increased growth and development (Bloom, White, & Asher, 1979; Chiriboga & Cutler, 1977). If the divorce allows an individual to gain new skills for coping more effectively in the future, the process may not be totally negative in the long term (Brown & Manela, 1978; Salts, 1979). Conceptualizing the divorce process in this manner, the purpose of this longitudinal study was to identify the correlates of successful or unsuccessful adjustment to marital separation and divorce as seen in three different samples of women.

PREDICTORS OF POSTSEPARATION ADJUSTMENT

Recent research into women's postseparation and postdivorce adjustment has yielded an equivocal set of findings. Many of the discrepancies regarding key predictors of adjustment appear to be the result of methodological differences. Variables that are predictive of postseparation adjustment may not be predictive of postdivorce adjustment as there may be many months or even years between these two events. Despite this lack of

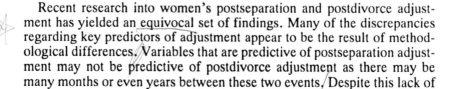

uniformity, the following variables have been identified as having predictive power.

Often cited as key predictors of women's adaptation to separation and divorce are age, and the related factor, length of marriage. Although these represent two separate variables, it is also the case that they are highly correlated in most samples (Kitson & Raschke, 1981). Many studies have shown that the termination of longer marriages produces more traumatic effects and more problematic adjustment (Goode, 1956; Hetherington, Cox, & Cox, 1978) and that older women experience a more difficult period of adjustment than do younger women (Chiriboga, Roberts, & Stein, 1978; Hetherington, Cox, & Cox, 1978; Nelson, 1981). However, in contradiction to these findings, Granvold, Pedler, and Schellie (1979) found that it was older women and those who had been married longer who showed significantly *higher* levels of adjustment. Still other studies have found *neither* age nor length of marriage to be significant predictors of postseparation adjustment (Pett, 1982). Therefore, although it appears that in some cases older women and those married for longer periods of time experience more distress and have a more difficult process of adjustment following separation and/or divorce, the findings are not conclusive.

Family structure variables such as the presence or absence of children, as well as the number and age of children, have also been indicated as important predictors of women's adaptation to separation and divorce. In particular, divorced women with two or more children have been found to be at risk for maladjustment (Goode, 1956), and the presence of younger children has been associated with feelings of depression among divorced women (Price-Bonham & Balswick, 1980). However, some authors suggest that having to be responsible for custodial children may indeed provide the impetus to maintain the daily routine of the family (Weiss, 1975). Little is known, however, about the specific types of support children may provide, and how this support may be a function of the child's age and sex. At this juncture, the majority of studies indicate that the added burden of financial pressures, as well as the loss of one adult to perform parenting functions, serve to hamper the process of adaptation for women who have young children.

Several studies have explored the hypothesis that an individual's sex role attitudes may be important predictors of their adjustment to separation and divorce. It has been shown that women with traditional sex role attitudes, who are in the process of separation and divorce, experience less positive adjustment and report higher levels of psychological distress (Brown & Manela, 1978; Granvold, Pedler, & Schellie, 1979). Regardless of their age, race, education, or working status, these women were more vulnerable to low self-esteem during the process of the divorce (Brown & Manela, 1978). On the other hand, nontraditional sex role attitudes appear to serve an adaptive function during the divorce process.

The emotional support and social integration gained from interactions with friends, family, and other members of the social support network are seen as important predictors of adaptation to many types of life stress. Extended family members and friends may give support in the form of direct financial assistance, childcare, temporary living space, and companionship (McLanahan, Wedemeyer, & Adelberg, 1981; Spanier & Casto, 1979; Weiss, 1975). This emotional and practical support, or the perception that it is available, may help reduce the stresses of the initial separation period and contribute to enhanced postdivorce adjustment (Pett, 1982; Raschke, 1977; Stokes, 1983).

The relationship between former spouses also appears to be a key predictor of divorce adjustment, especially when the former spouses continue to share childrearing responsibilities. Several studies have found that a relationship with the spouse (ex-spouse) which is hostile or strained is predictive of various types of maladjustment (Goetting, 1980; Nelson, 1981). However, other studies have shown that it is the presence of positive feelings for the ex-spouse, indicative of a persisting attachment, which relate to maladjustment (Berman, 1988; Brown, Felton, Whiteman, & Manela, 1980).

Objectives

This brief review of the literature indicates that studies of postseparation and postdivorce adjustment have yielded conflicting results. For this reason, these variables were viewed as potential predictors of women's adjustment to separation and divorce. As many of these studies have not adequately controlled for the length of time which has elapsed since the separation, it is not clear whether these variables are related to adjustment throughout the separation and divorce process. Therefore, the current study sought to clarify the importance of these variables as predictors of adjustment to marital separation at different times during the divorce process. The specific hypotheses were as follows:

1. Women who were younger would show higher levels of postseparation adjustment.
2. Women who were married shorter periods of time would show higher levels of postseparation adjustment.

3. Women with fewer children would show higher levels of postseparation adjustment.
4. Women with older children would show higher levels of postseparation adjustment than those women with younger children.
5. Women with nontraditional sex role attitudes would show higher levels of postseparation adjustment than those with traditional sex role attitudes.
6. Women who have and utilize a social support network would show higher levels of postseparation adjustment than those women who are socially isolated.
7. Women who maintain a civil or amicable relationship with the ex-spouse would show higher levels of adjustment than those whose relationships with the ex-spouse are hostile or strained.

METHOD

Subjects

The participants in this study were 104 women in the early stages of the separation and divorce process, all physically separated from their husbands for less than eight months. These women were recruited through a search of the public divorce dockets of two counties in the greater Boston area (Middlesex and Norfolk). The overall Time 1 sample consisted of three subsamples: 36 women without children, 35 women with young children, and 33 women with adult children. Those women in the sample with young children each had at least one child between the ages of six and twelve, and no children over the age of fourteen. The women in the sample with adult children each had at least one child 18 years of age or older, and no children younger than 18.

All three samples included: (1) women sampled directly from public court records; (2) women married at least five years; (3) women physically separated from their husbands less than eight months at the time of the Time 1 interview; (4) women from roughly the same geographic area; and (5) women with at least a tenth grade education (to insure adequate literacy).

Procedures

Those individuals who met the sampling criteria for one of the three samples were sent a letter briefly describing the research project. Each woman who agreed to participate was then interviewed regarding her own perspectives on the separation and divorce. The interviews lasted between one and two hours in most cases. The participants also completed a number of self-report questionnaires and projective measures.

Within a year of the initial interview, all participants were re-contacted to arrange a follow-up interview. At Time 2, 95 women (91% of the original sample) participated in the follow-up: 32 women without children, 35 women with young children, and 28 women with adult children. The procedures for the follow-up were essentially the same as for the initial data collection. The Time 1 interview was modified slightly in some sections for use at Time 2. Those questionnaires administered at Time 1 were given again at Time 2 with only slight modifications as needed in certain cases.

Predictor Variables

The "predictor" variables in this study have been selected from those previously found to be associated with adjustment to this specific life change, as well as from those related to adaptation to change in situations other than that of separation and divorce. Although these variables are referred to as "predictor" variables, the term is being used in a theoretical sense only; the data are synchronous, and causality cannot be inferred.

Age, Length of Marriage, and Family Structure

These variables, which define the three subsamples, were coded from a demographic questionnaire given at Time 1. The specific family structure variables included number of children and age of children.

Sex Role Attitudes

The traditionality/nontraditionality of the women's sex role attitudes was assessed at Time 1 and Time 2 using the Personal Attributes Questionnaire (Spence, Helmreich, & Stapp, 1974). This instrument consists of 24 items which were agreed upon by college students as being typical of one sex or the other. Eight items were rated as being typical of females, although socially desirable for both sexes (feminine); eight were considered as typical of males, although socially desirable for both sexes (masculine); and eight items were considered typical of one sex or the other and more desirable for that sex (sex-typed). Subjects are asked to rate each item on a five-point scale ranging from "not at all" to "very" characteristic of themselves. A total score was obtained for each scale by summing across items.

Social Support

Social support was assessed at Time 1 and Time 2 by measuring levels of social participation and social isolation as reported during the interview. A detailed codebook was developed to code the Time 1 and Time 2 interviews for information regarding social support. The scoring was done by a trained coder who had demonstrated .94 reliability with expert coding.

The level of social participation with friends, relatives, and members of the spouse's family was coded from the interview. The maximum amount of contact with individuals from each group was coded, with scores ranging from "rarely" (less than once a month) to frequently (more than once a week). The mean of these scores was then used as an aggregate indicator of social participation.

A social isolation score was formed by combining the coding of three different topics from the interview. First, subjects were coded for loss of contact with friends, relatives, or members of the spouse's family which was due to the separation. Second, loneliness was coded if expressed anywhere in the interview. Last, expressions of a desire for increased intimacy in interpersonal relationships were coded. These different codes were standard scored, an the mean of the three scores was used as an indicator of social isolation.

Relationship with Spouse

Two variables assessing the nature of the relationship with the husband were used. First, an adaptation of the Conflict Tactics Scales (Straus, 1979) was used to assess the level of acrimony in the pre-separation marital relationship. The women reported the frequency with which they and their husbands used various strategies for handling conflict with each other. A 5-point scale, ranging from "never" to "more than once a month," was used to rate the frequency of these various strategies. A violence scale was created from this measure; it included such items as "pushed, grabbed, or shoved the other person."

The nature of the woman's current relationship with her husband, or exhusband, was coded from the Time 1 and Time 2 interviews. In particular, the following interview questions were used: "What would you say is the state of your relationship with your husband right now?" "Do you talk with him?" "How do these conversations go?" Responses were coded to assess the level of conflict or hostility using a six-point scale with codes ranging from "very hostile" to "friendly."

Variables Assessing Adjustment

Adjustment was assessed from a variety of perspectives using a range of measures in order to provide as comprehensive, rich and accurate information as possible regarding the effects of divorce. The following variables were considered useful as indicators of adjustment: self-esteem, life satisfaction, mood disturbance, stress symptoms, and physical health. Measures of each construct were obtained at both Time 1 and Time 2.

Self-esteem

It is obviously important to examine the effects of the divorce experience on the woman's attitudes and feelings about herself. The extensive literature on self-esteem makes it clear that this variable is an important indicator of mental health (Jahoda, 1958; Rosenberg, 1965, 1979; Wylie, 1974), and therefore of general adjustment. The woman's level of self-esteem was measured using the Self-Esteem Scale (Rosenberg, 1965), a ten-item scale with each item rated on a four-point scale from "strongly agree" to "strongly disagree."

Life Satisfaction

An overall assessment of global feelings of life satisfaction was obtained from a single item: "In general, how satisfied are you with the way you are spending your life these days?" Responses range from "very satisfied" to "not at all satisfied." This type of item is similar to that used by Gurin, Veroff, and Feld (1960) and Bradburn and Caplovitz (1965). Life satisfaction has been found to be greater among people who are better socially adjusted, who demonstrate more trust in people, who feel less alienated, and who suffer less from anxiety, worry, and psychosomatic symptoms (see Robinson & Shaver, 1973, for a review).

Mood Disturbance

Level of negative affect was measured by the Profile of Mood States (McNair, Lorr, & Droppleman, 1971), an adjective self-rating scale which measures six dimensions of mood: tension-anxiety, depression-dejection, anger-hostility, fatigue-inertia, confusion-bewilderment, and vigor-activity. Numerous studies have demonstrated that the POMS significantly differentiates a variety of emotionally distraught clinical samples from samples of adults not experiencing emotional distress, and that it is sensitive to efforts to either arouse or ameliorate emotional disturbance (see McNair, Lorr, & Droppleman, 1971, for a review of validity studies).

Stress Symptoms

An adaptation of the stress symptomatology measure employed by Gurin, Veroff, and Feld (1960) in their national survey of mental health was used (see also Veroff, Kulka, & Douvan, 1981). This self-report measure consists of 23 items reflecting a range of psychological and physical symptoms (e.g., excessive drinking, nightmares, sleep disturbances). The frequency of each symptom is rated on a four-point scale. An overall index of stress symptomatology was generated by summing across items.

Physical Health

A self-report questionnaire concerning the woman's health during the previous three months, as well as over the past year, was administered. The items for this questionnaire were drawn from the many available illness questionnaires (e.g., Abramson, Terespolsky, Brook, & Kark, 1965; Wahler, 1973). The presence/absence of 35 physical disorders (e.g., allergy, colitis, bad headaches) is rated first, followed by a rating of the frequency of acute disorders on a six-point scale ranging from "once or twice" to "daily."

Factor analyses of the Time 1 and Time 2 data drawn from the various measures of adjustment (i.e., the symptom checklist, the self-esteem scale, the mood profile, and the health questionnaire) yielded three independent indicators of adjustment accounting for nearly 75 percent of the variance in scores. These indicators were: *emotional health* (the four POMS scales assessing anger-hostility, confusion-bewilderment, tension-anxiety, and depression-dejection), *well-being* (self-esteem, life satisfaction, and the vigor-activity scale from the POMS), and *physical health* (including stress symptoms and recent illnesses). Since these factors replicated in the two years, account for considerable variance in the various measures, and make intuitive sense, these three separate indicators of adjustment were used.

RESULTS

The results are presented in several sections. First, sample differences on the Time 1 predictor and adjustment variables are presented, followed by an examination of the subsample correlations between these variables.

The next section examines the sample differences on these variables and their relationships at Time 2. Sample differences on change scores measuring adaptation over time are then addressed.

Comparison of the Samples at Time 1

Analyses of variance were conducted on the Time 1 predictor variables. The means for each subsample on each of these variables are presented in Table 1. Of course, a number of significant differences were found for those variables that define the three samples. The samples were significantly different in age, length of marriage, number of children, age of oldest child, and age of youngest child.

However, when considering those Time 1 predictor variables that were not preselected to distinguish the samples, additional sample differences were found. In terms of the social support variables, the samples were significantly different in perceived level of social isolation. The subsample of women without children reported a significantly higher level of social isolation than the two samples of women with children. In terms of the variables assessing the nature of the relationship with the husband (ex-husband), the samples were again significantly different. Women with young children reported the poorest relationships with their husbands, while the sample of women without children reported more amicable relationships. No significant differences were found between the samples for the remaining predictor variables assessed at Time 1.

To rule out the possibility that the significant age differences accounted for the sample differences on the remaining predictor variables, the ANOVAs were performed again with age as a covariate. The results of these analyses remained essentially the same; in some cases significance levels varied slightly, but in no case did previously significant sample differences disappear nor nonsignificant differences become significant. In the cases of length of marriage and number of children, the effect of the covariate was also significant.

Analyses of variance were then conducted on the Time 1 variables assessing adjustment. Despite the number of significant sample differences found for the Time 1 predictor variables, *no* sample differences were found when comparing the three samples on any of the Time 1 indicators of adjustment. As Table 2 indicates, the samples did not significantly differ in terms of emotional health, well-being, or physical health.

TABLE 1

Sample Differences on Time 1 Predictor Variables

Variable	No children sample(n=36) mean (s.d.)	Young children sample(n=35) mean (s.d.)	Adult children sample(n=33) mean (s.d.)	F	p
Age in years	32.44 (5.23)	33.34 (4.08)	50.73 (5.20)	147.65	<.001
Years married	8.81 (4.33)	11.65 (3.06)	24.58 (8.02)	75.91	<.001
Number of children	0.00 (0.00)	2.11 (.82)	3.15 (1.76)	72.09	<.001
Age of oldest child	0.00 (0.00)	9.46 (2.71)	27.27 (5.25)	150.36	<.001
Age of youngest child	0.00 (0.00)	6.11 (2.79)	21.09 (2.39)	269.01	<.001

147

TABLE 1 (continued)

Masculinity scale 1	28.42 (5.28)	*	27.64 (5.12)	t = .61 n.s.
Femininity scale 1	33.64 (4.01)	*	34.21 (4.79)	t =-.53 n.s.
Social participation 1	2.36 (.45)	2.35 (.55)	2.29 (.49)	.14 n.s.
Social isolation 1	1.51 (.21)	1.35 (.26)	1.40 (.30)	3.23 <.05
Violence scale 1	3.39 (3.92)	4.43 (6.33)	4.04 (6.03)	.29 n.s.
Relationship with spouse 1	4.11 (1.65)	2.85 (1.65)	3.43 (1.76)	4.70 <.05

* Note: Data not available for this subsample at Time 1

TABLE 2

Sample Differences on Time 1 Adjustment Variables

Variable	No children sample (n=36) mean (s.d.)	Young children sample (n=35) mean (s.d.)	Adult children sample (n=33) mean (s.d.)	F	p
Emotional health 1	57.17 (27.51)	51.80 (28.64)	49.91 (38.36)	.48	n.s.
Well-being 1	50.86 (6.70)	49.67 (8.24)	49.57 (8.90)	.28	n.s.
Physical health 1	49.51 (8.46)	49.09 (8.57)	51.51 (10.15)	.67	n.s.

Predictors of Adjustment at Time 1

Pearson correlation coefficients were used to assess the relationship between the predictor variables and the Time 1 indicators of adjustment. These analyses indicate the correlates of women's adjustment at the presumably stressful time immediately following the separation. Since the three subsamples differed significantly on many of the Time 1 predictor variables, correlations were computed individually for each subsample. In that the sample sizes for these subsample analyses were relatively small, those correlations which approached significance (p < .10) are also included in the appropriate tables so that trends may be seen.

Table 3 presents the Time 1 correlations for the three subsamples. The masculinity scale was a consistently strong predictor of adjustment for both the women without children and the women with adult children. The femininity scale, on the other hand, was not significantly related to any indicator of adjustment at Time 1. Unfortunately, masculinity and femininity scores from the PAQ were not available at Time 1 for the sample of women with young children.

In terms of the Time 1 measures of social support, neither social participation nor social isolation was significantly associated with adjustment in any subsample. In fact, the only other variable which was significantly related to Time 1 adjustment was the violence scale. This measure was negatively related to well-being for the women with young children (r = −.36, p < .05) and negatively related to physical health for both the women without children (r = −.47, p < .01) and the women with adult children (r = −.58, p < .01).

Comparison of the Samples at Time 2

The means for the three subsamples on those predictor variables assessed at Time 2 are presented in Table 4. As was the case at Time 1, the subsamples again differed significantly in regard to the nature of the relationship with the ex-husband. Women without children were more likely to be maintaining relationships with the ex-spouse that were neutral or civil while both the women with adult children and the women with young children were more likely to describe the relationship with the ex-spouse as strained. Overall, the subsamples were significantly different on only one of the five predictor variables measured at Time 2. Of course, the samples were again significantly different on those variables which define the three groups (age, length of marriage, number of children, and age of children). Again, the pattern of significant and nonsignificant sample dif-

TABLE 3

Predictors of Adjustment at Time 1 for Each Subsample

Adjustment Variables

Predictor Variables	Emotional health			Well-being			Physical health		
	S1[a]	S2	S3	S1	S2	S3	S1	S2	S3
Masculinity scale 1	.44**	b	.54***	.53***	b	.61***	.17	b	.42*
Femininity scale 1	-.24	b	-.06	-.16	b	.24	-.02	b	.02
Social participation 1	.12	.22	.34¬	-.06	.18	.23	.14	.27	.15

151

TABLE 3 (continued)

Social isolation 1	-.11	-.12	-.11	-.12	.07	.01	-.13	-.14	-.12
Violence scale 1	-.29⌐	-.32⌐	-.27	-.32⌐	-.36*	-.20	-.47**	-.18	-.58**
Relationship with spouse 1	-.03	.00	.32⌐	-.05	-.07	.09	.10	-.25	.33⌐

⌐ $p<.10$, * $p<.05$, ** $p<.01$, *** $p<.001$, two-tailed

a S1 = Subsample 1, women without children (n=36)
  S2 = Subsample 2, women with young children (n=35)
  S3 = Subsample 3, women with adult children (n=33)

b Masculinity and femininity scores not available for this subsample at Time 1.

TABLE 4

Sample Differences on Time 2 Predictor Variables

Variable	No children sample (n=32) mean (s.d.)	Young children sample (n=35) mean (s.d.)	Adult children sample (n=28) mean (s.d.)	F	p
Masculinity scale 2	28.44 (6.30)	29.57 (4.29)	28.46 (4.81)	.49	n.s.
Femininity scale 2	32.69 (3.85)	34.77 (2.71)	33.89 (4.30)	2.69	n.s.
Social participation 2	2.29 (.49)	2.29 (.69)	2.18 (.39)	.38	n.s.
Social isolation 2	1.50 (.30)	1.41 (.28)	1.38 (.24)	1.60	n.s.
Relationship with spouse 2	4.19 (1.47)	2.80 (1.67)	2.93 (1.39)	7.79	<.001

ferences were not altered when the ANOVAs were performed with age as a covariate.

The means for each sample on each of the Time 2 adjustment variables are presented in Table 5. Once again, *no* significant differences were found when comparing the three samples in terms of adjustment at Time 2. The three groups were equivalent, as they were at Time 1, in emotional health, well-being, and physical health. This equivalence remained when age was used as a covariate.

Predictors of Adjustment at Time 2

When examining the relationships between the predictor and adjustment variables at Time 2, some commonalities with the Time 1 findings may be seen, although new patterns also emerge. The correlations between the Time 2 predictor variables and adjustment indicators for the three subsamples are presented in Table 6. Again at Time 2, higher scores on the masculinity scale were significantly associated with enhanced adjustment for all three subsamples. For the women without children, masculinity scores were significantly related to well-being ($r = .53$, $p < .01$). A similar pattern can be seen for the sample of women with young children; masculinity scores were related to well-being ($r = .54$, $p < .001$) as well as emotional health ($r = .34$, $p < .05$). This variable was also significantly correlated with emotional health for the sample of women with adult children ($r = .39$, $p < .05$).

In terms of the Time 2 measures of social support, social participation was not significantly associated with adjustment. But unlike the pattern of relationships at Time 1, social isolation was negatively associated with adjustment at Time 2. For the women with young children, social isolation was negatively correlated with emotional health ($r = -.42$, $p < .05$) and well-being ($r = -.44$, $p < .01$). It was also negatively associated with these indicators of adjustment for the sample of women with adult children.

Finally, a relationship with the ex-spouse at Time 2 which was characterized by a low level of acrimony was related to enhanced adjustment. A civil relationship with the spouse was significantly associated with physical health for the women without children ($r = .47$, $p < .05$). This variable was also significantly related to emotional health for the sample of women with young children ($r = .50$, $p < .01$). Trends in the expected direction were also present for the sample of women with adult children.

TABLE 5

Sample Differences on Time 2 Adjustment Variables

Variable	No children sample (n=32) mean (s.d.)	Young children sample (n=35) mean (s.d.)	Adult children sample (n=28) mean (s.d.)	F	p
Emotional health 2	61.50 (31.15)	64.63 (24.66)	67.18 (27.13)	.31	n.s.
Well-being 2	50.41 (7.72)	49.09 (7.45)	50.67 (7.79)	.39	n.s.
Physical health 2	49.28 (6.82)	50.00 (8.61)	50.82 (11.21)	.21	n.s.

155

TABLE 6

Predictors of Adjustment at Time 2 for Each Subsample

Adjustment Variables

Predictor Variables	Emotional health			Well-being			Physical health		
	S1[a]	S2	S3	S1	S2	S3	S1	S2	S3
Masculinity scale 2	.28	.34*	.39*	.53**	.54***	.34¬	.09	.08	-.12
Femininity scale 2	-.10	-.19	.08	.11	-.27	.17	-.28	-.31¬	-.26

Social participation 2	.18	.15	.13	-.04	.01	.08	-.02	.19	-.07
Social isolation 2	-.21	-.42*	-.49**	-.29⌐	-.44**	-.41*	-.18	.17	-.03
Relationship with spouse 2	.34⌐	.50**	.27	.25	.13	.32⌐	.47**	.20	.31

⌐ p<.10, * p<.05, ** p<.01, *** p<.001, two-tailed

a S1 = Subsample 1, women without children (n=32)
   S2 = Subsample 2, women with young children (n=35)
   S3 = Subsample 3, women with adult children (n=28)

Sample Differences in Adaptation
Between Time 1 and Time 2

The three samples were also compared in terms of the change in adjustment, or adaptation, between Time 1 and Time 2. Sample by time repeated measures ANOVAs were conducted for each of the adjustment indicators. For all women, emotional health ratings substantially improved by Time 2 ($F = 16.19$, $p < .001$). A significant sample by time interaction was also found; the subsamples of women with young children and women with adult children improved significantly more in emotional health than did the subsample of women without children. It is interesting to note that although highest in emotional health at Time 1, the women without children showed very little adaptation over time, and, in fact, reported the lowest overall emotional ratings at Time 2. On the other hand, the women with adult children had the lowest overall emotional health ratings at Time 1, yet exceeded the two other samples in emotional health at Time 2. These significant effects remained when age was used as a covariate.

The sample by time repeated measures ANOVAs for well-being and physical health yielded different results. There were no significant effects for sample or time, nor were there any significant sample by time interactions. These indicators of adjustment appear to be measuring more stable attributes rather than capturing fluctuations in adaptation over time. Performing these ANOVAs with age as a covariate did not alter the nonsignificant effects.

DISCUSSION

The results replicate some of the previous findings regarding factors which are significantly associated with adjustment to marital separation and divorce. In some cases, however, variables previously found to predict adjustment were not associated with the indicators of adjustment used in this study. While some factors were associated with adjustment at Time 1, sometimes different variables emerged as strong predictors at Time 2, highlighting the importance of controlling the length of separation for a given sample and studying the adaptation process over time.

Although it has generally been found that older women, and those married for longer periods of time, experience a more difficult adjustment to marital disruption, this was not the case in the present study. The women with adult children, although significantly older and married significantly longer than the women in the other samples, were *not* significantly lower in adjustment on any of the Time 1 or Time 2 indicators of adjustment.

Based on the results of several previously mentioned studies, it was also predicted that the number of children as well as the age of the children would be significantly related to postseparation adjustment. Specifically, it was hypothesized that those women with more children and those with younger children would be at risk. These hypotheses were not supported. The samples with children did not differ significantly from the sample without children on any of the indicators of adjustment. Further, the women with young children and the women with older children were equivalent on all Time 1 and Time 2 adjustment measures.

Nontraditional sex role attitudes were predicted to serve an adaptive role during the divorce process, and this hypothesis was confirmed in the subsample analyses at both Time 1 and Time 2. In fact, the masculinity scale of the Personal Attributes Questionnaire was among the strongest predictors of the women's emotional health, well-being, and physical health. The femininity scale, on the other hand, had little predictive power. These results replicate studies such as those by Brown and Manela (1978) and Granvold, Pedler, and Schellie (1979), highlighting the importance of nontraditional sex roles for enhanced postseparation adjustment.

The emotional support and social integration gained from interactions with family and friends did not appear to lessen distress during the postseparation period. However, social isolation was a much stronger predictor, especially at Time 2. Those women who reported a loss of contact with friends and family as a result of the separation, or who expressed a need for greater intimacy in their interpersonal relationships, were lower in emotional health, well-being, and physical health. Disruption of the social network was often not experienced until Time 2, roughly one and a half years after the physical separation. By this time, some women reported that interactions with married friends were strained, or had in some cases ceased altogether. Others reported that they continued to experience disapproval from extended family members regarding their decision to initiate and/or pursue the divorce. These losses of contact or support were reported as particularly painful consequences of the divorce process. These findings support the conclusions drawn by Pett (1982): The perception that support and resources are available from the network, rather than the actual use of such resources, enhances adjustment to stressful life events.

Among the most significant predictors of emotional and physical health were those variables reflecting the nature of the woman's relationship with her spouse at various points in time. An indicator of preseparation acrimony, the measure of physical violence was a strong predictor of emotional distress and physical health problems at Time 1. Although the women's report of the nature of the relationship with the spouse at Time 1 was not related to Time 1 adjustment, the quality of this relationship at Time 2 was clearly related to their health and well-being at that stage of the divorce process. The Time 2 findings correspond to those from other studies in which adjustment was assessed even later in the divorce process (e.g., Hetherington, Cox, & Cox, 1978; Nelson, 1981; Weiss, 1975). It is interesting to note that this same relationship was found for the subsample of women without children. Although contact with the spouse was much less frequent due to the lack of children, strained or acrimonious relationships were problematic nonetheless.

CONCLUSIONS

A 1977 article describing women's experience of the divorce process made the following statements:

> When they divorce, American women seldom find the freedom to which they aspire. On the contrary, to put it colloquially, the majority find themselves trapped between a rock and a hard place. The more violently they struggle, the more tightly they are gripped by the trap — the walls literally close in, and they seek escape by drastic means. (Herman, 1977, p. 107)

Although this response is a possibility, it is only one of several possibilities. In this study, a wide range of adjustment levels and adaptation patterns was found. In general, the women reported significantly greater levels of emotional health at Time 2 than at Time 1. Although their overall well-being and physical health ratings did not show significant change over time, most women did express the view that things were generally better after a year had passed.

A number of factors significantly associated with adjustment to marital separation and divorce were found. In general, unchangeable factors generally considered outside the individual's control (e.g., age, number of children, age of children) were *not* strongly associated with adjustment, while those factors which are at least potentially modifiable (e.g., social isolation or the relationship with the ex-spouse) were significantly related to several measures of adjustment at both years. Although beyond the scope of the present study, these potentially modifiable factors need further investigation so that relevant clinical, legal, and community interventions can be designed and implemented.

REFERENCES

Abramson, J.H., Terespolsky, L., Brook, J.G., & Kark, S.L. (1965). Cornell Medical Index as a health measure in epidemiological studies: A test of the validity of a health questionnaire. *British Journal of Preventive Medicine, 19*, 102-110.

Berman, W.H. (1988). The role of attachment in the post-divorce experience. *Journal of Personality and Social Psychology, 54*, 496-503.

Bloom, B.L., Asher, S.J., & White, S.W. (1978). Marital disruption as a stressor: A review and analysis. *Psychological Bulletin, 85*, 867-894.

Bloom, B.L., White, S.W., & Asher, S.J. (1979). Marital disruption as a stressful life event. In G. Levinger and O.C. Moles (Eds.), *Divorce and separation: Contexts, causes, and consequences.* New York: Basic Books.

Bradburn, N., & Caplovitz, D. (1965). *Reports on happiness.* Chicago: Aldine.

Brown, P., Felton, B.J., Whiteman, V., & Manela, R. (1980). Attachment and distress following marital separation. *Journal of Divorce, 3*, 303-317.

Brown, P., & Manela, R. (1978). Changing family roles: women and divorce. *Journal of Divorce, 1*, 315-328.

Caplan, G. (1974). *Support systems and community mental health.* New York: Behavioral Publications.

Chiriboga, D.A., & Cutler, L. (1977). Stress responses among divorcing men and women. *Journal of Divorce, 1*, 95-106.

Chiriboga, D.A., Roberts, J., & Stein, J. (1978). Psychological well-being during marital separation. *Journal of Divorce, 2*, 21-36.

Goetting, A. (1980). Divorce outcome research: Issues and perspectives. *Journal of Family Issues, 2*, 350-378.

Goode, W. (1956). *After divorce.* New York: Free Press.

Granvold, D., Pedler, L., & Schellie, S. (1979). A study of sex-role expectancy and female postdivorce adjustment. *Journal of Divorce, 2*, 383-393.

Gurin, G., Veroff, J., & Feld, S. (1960). *Americans view their mental health.* New York: Basic Books.

Herman, S. (1977). Women, divorce, and suicide. *Journal of Divorce, 1*, 107-117.

Hetherington, E.M., Cox, M., & Cox, R. (1978). The aftermath of divorce. In J.H. Stevens, Jr. & M. Matthews (Eds.), *Mother-child, father-child relations* (pp. 149-176). Washington, D.C.: National Association for the Education of Young Children.

Holmes, R., & Rahe, R. (1967). The social readjustment rating scale. *Journal of Psychosomatic Research, 11*, 213-218.

Jahoda, M. (1958). *Current concepts of positive mental health.* New York: Basic Books.

Kitson, G., & Raschke, H. (1981). Divorce research: What we know, what we need to know. *Journal of Divorce, 4*, 1-37.

McLanahan, S., Wedemeyer, N., & Adelberg, T. (1981). Network structure, social support, and psychological well-being in the single-parent family. *Journal of Marriage and the Family, 43*, 601-612.

McNair, D., Lorr, M., & Droppleman, L. (1971). *Profile of mood states.* San Diego: Educational and Industrial Testing Service.

Nelson, G. (1981). Moderators of women's and children's adjustment following parental divorce. *Journal of Divorce, 4*, 71-83.

Pett, M.G. (1982). Predictors of satisfactory social adjustment of divorced single parents. *Journal of Divorce, 5*, 1-17.

Price-Bonham, S., & Balswick, J. (1980). The noninstitutions: Divorce, desertion, and remarriage. *Journal of Marriage and the Family, 42*, 959-972.

Raschke, H. (1977). The role of social participation in post-separation and post-divorce adjustment. *Journal of Divorce, 1*, 129-140.

Robinson, J., & Shaver, P. (1973). *Measures of social psychological attitudes.* Ann Arbor, MI: Institute for Social Research.

Rosenberg, M. (1965). *Society and the adolescent self-image.* Princeton, N.J.: Princeton University Press.

Rosenberg, M. (1979). *Conceiving the self.* New York: Basic Books.

Salts, C.J. (1979). Divorce process: integration of theory. *Journal of Divorce, 2*, 233-240.

Spanier, G., & Casto, R. (1979). Adjustment to separation and divorce: An analysis of 50 case studies. *Journal of Divorce, 2*, 263-269.

Spence, J., & Helmreich, R. (1980). Masculine instrumentality and feminine expressiveness: Their relationship with sex role attitudes and behaviors. *Psychology of Women Quarterly, 5*, 147-163.

Spence, J., Helmreich, R., & Stapp, J. (1974). The Personal Attributes Questionnaire: A measure of sex-role stereotypes and masculinity-femininity. *Journal Supplement Abstract Service Catalog of Selected Documents in Psychology, 4*, 43.

Stokes, J.P. (1983). Predicting satisfaction with social support from social network structure. *American Journal of Community Psychology, 11*, 141-151.

Straus, M.A. (1979). Measuring intrafamily conflict and violence: The conflict tactics (CT) scales. *Journal of Marriage and the Family, 41*, 75-88.

Veroff, J., Kulka, R., & Douvan, E. (1981). *Mental Health in America.* New York: Basic Books.

Wahler, J.J. (1973). *Wahler physical symptoms inventory.* Western Psychological Services.

Weiss, R.S. (1975). *Marital Separation.* New York: Basic Books.

Wylie, R. (1974). *The self-concept: A review of methodological considerations and measuring instruments* (Vol. 1). Lincoln, NE: University of Nebraska Press.

Economic Consequences of Divorce
or Separation Among Women in Poverty

Teresa A. Mauldin

SUMMARY. This study, using data from the National Longitudinal Survey's Young Women Cohort, looked at characteristics of low-income women following divorce or separation. Resources and characteristics that would help explain a woman's ability to move out of poverty in the year following divorce or separation were analyzed. Discriminant analysis results indicated that the most important discriminators of whether or not women would move out of poverty immediately following marital disruption were current employment status, job training, education, race, and presence of a child under six years old.

Since the 1960's there has been a rapid increase in the rate of marital disruption through separation and divorce. During this same time period numerous studies have found that divorce has detrimental economic effects on women (Bane & Weiss, 1980; Cherlin, 1981; Corcoran, 1981; Duncan & Morgan, 1981; Espenshade, 1979; Hoffman, 1977; Hoffman & Holmes, 1979; Pearce, 1978; Weiss, 1984; Weitzman, 1985). The 1986 census data documented that poverty rates for female headed households are substantially higher than those for male headed households. Female headed families accounted for one-half of all poor families and one-half of these were headed by a woman who was divorced or separated (U.S. Bureau of Census, 1987).

The rapid rise in the divorce rate experienced during the late 1960's and early 1970's has leveled off. The number of divorces actually declined in 1982 and 1983 (U.S. Department of Health and Human Services, 1984a; 1984b). However, the divorce rate is likely to remain high and informa-

Teresa A. Mauldin, PhD, is Assistant Professor, University of Georgia, Department of Housing, Home Management and Consumer Economics, Dawson Hall, Athens, GA 30602.

tion is needed regarding alternative strategies for improving the financial status of women following marital disruption. Unfortunately, little research exists which identifies means by which women can improve their economic situation following marital disruption. The purpose of this research was to examine resources and characteristics of low income women that might enhance their financial situation following divorce or separation.

LITERATURE REVIEW

It is well-documented that women are more likely to experience large financial losses following divorce than their husbands (Duncan & Morgan, 1981; Mott & Moore, 1978; Spanier & Casto, 1979; Weitzman, 1985). Duncan and Morgan (1981), using data from the Panel Study of Income Dynamics, found that one-third of the women living in families with incomes above the poverty line prior to marital disruption lived in poverty after divorce. The financial status of the men in the study was affected far less by this change in family structure.

Mott (1979) found that the poverty rate for mature white women increased from 10 to 35 percent as a result of marital disruption while the rate for black women increased from 38 to 51 percent. Young women experienced similar transitions into poverty. Mott suggested that this movement into poverty was the result of the female householder's inability to earn enough to compensate for the loss of her husband's earnings.

While many studies have found a reduction in the level of living for the majority of women and their families, only a few studies have analyzed the effects of marital disruption on families at various income levels. Weitzman (1985) found that wives from low-income families experienced less reduction in income than those in middle and higher income families. Also, discrepancies between husbands' and wives' post-divorce per capita income was smallest among low and middle income families. Weiss (1984) reported similar results. Women in the upper income level experienced the greatest reduction in income while women in the lower income level experienced the least reduction in income.

Unlike the previously mentioned studies, Kohn, Brown and Feldberg (1979) found that a small portion of its sample actually experienced an increase in its level of living. This study found that the former spouse contributed little or nothing to the families' pre-disruption economic well-being.

Researchers have identified various factors which might augment or diminish the negative effects of marital disruption on the financial well-being of women after divorce or separation. Among these factors are the fact that, on average, women earn less than men, children typically live with their mothers following disruption, and child and spousal support payments are low and received infrequently (Duncan, 1984). Other factors include the loss of economies of scale, greater prevalence of disruption among poor families, and loss of spouse's income (Bane, 1976; Masnick & Bane, 1980; Seal, 1979; Weitzman, 1985). Lack of career commitment in women, inappropriate work plans of young women and lack of investment in work-related human capital (human resources) have also been cited as factors that may affect the economic well-being of women after marital disruption (Rudd & Sanik, 1983).

These factors suggest that several resources and characteristics might enhance a woman's ability to provide financially for her family following marital disruption. In order to develop appropriate public policy it is important to know which resources and characteristics prove helpful in improving financial well-being of women following divorce or separation.

For most divorced women the major source of income is their own earnings. Mott and Moore (1978) indicated that the most effective way for divorced women to maintain their income at a satisfactory level was to be employed year round at an adequate wage rate. Shaw (1978) found that without their own earnings female householders were likely to be below or near the poverty threshold. Thus, employment may be a major factor in improving financial well-being following marital disruption.

Another factor which may affect a woman's ability to improve her situation following marital disruption is the presence of young children. Young children have been found to deter mothers' labor force participation. Census data indicated that labor force participation was lower among divorced women with children under 6 years of age than other divorced women (Hayghe, 1984).

Race may also be an important factor. Previous research has found that blacks have a higher separation and divorce rate than whites (Norton & Glick, 1979). But when income was controlled, this difference disappears (Bahr & Galligan, 1984; Hampton, 1975). Previous research has also indicated that black women are more likely to experience poverty than white women (Mott & Moore, 1978; Shaw, 1978). White divorced women are more likely to be employed after disruption than black divorced women (Mott & Moore, 1978).

Another variable which may be important in determining a woman's ability to provide for her family following marital disruption is assets from the marriage. Little is known about the affect of assets on the economic well-being of women following divorce. In many cases, few assets are brought from the marriage and what assets exist are usually of low economic value (Weitzman, 1985).

Several studies (Hauserman, 1983; Rudd & Sanik, 1983; Seal, 1979; Smith & Beninger, 1982) suggested that a woman's stock of work-related human capital (human resources) may affect her ability to provide for her family following marital disruption. However, little empirical evidence related to these factors is available. Education has been found to be important (Day & Bahr, 1986; Larson, 1984; Mott & Moore, 1979). Other human capital variables that might be important include job training, work experience and health. Previous work experience and job training would increase a woman's productivity thereby increasing her potential earnings. Poor health is likely to reduce a woman's labor force participation and in turn her earnings potential.

This study sought to identify resources and characteristics of women and their families which would help improve their economic situation immediately following divorce or separation. Specifically this study sought to determine: (1) whether or not the stock of work-related human capital (human resources) possessed by women who remained in poverty following disruption and that of women who moved out of poverty following disruption was different; (2) whether or not other characteristics of women and their families who remained in poverty and of those who moved out of poverty following disruption are different; and (3) which factors are the best predictors of whether a woman remains in poverty following marital disruption or moves out of poverty following marital disruption.

SAMPLE

This analysis is based on a subsample of women from the National Longitudinal Survey of Work Experience of Young Women (NLS). The NLS contains data on a nationally representative sample of young women who were interviewed by the U.S. Bureau of the Census eleven times between 1968 and 1982. The original sample consisted of 5,159 women aged 14 to 24 in 1968. Of this group, 768 young women experienced marital disruption through divorce or separation for the first time between the years 1969 and 1980. Only 620 cases had complete data. It was required that no previous disruption had been indicated and that the women were still separated or divorced in the survey following first report of disruption.

The sample for this study consisted of 101 young women (from the 620) who either remained in poverty following marital disruption or who moved above the poverty level following marital disruption. Thirty percent of this group moved out of poverty while 70 percent remained in poverty following marital disruption. Poverty status was determined by comparing pre-disruption and post-disruption family income to the relevant Bureau of Census poverty line.

The poverty line is an arbitrarily defined standard. It is a ratio of actual income to Bureau of Census established minimal income for a certain number of family members. This absolute poverty threshold cutoff was used to categorize respondents. Women whose income was $1 above the poverty threshold either before or following disruption were considered nonpoor in the relevant time period. This arbitrary distinction possibly overlooks the fact that the economic situation of women closest to their relevant poverty line might be similar. Also, since the poverty line is affected by family size, movement out of poverty may be due to either a loss of a family member or an increase in income in the year following marital disruption.

In order to get a clearer idea of how respondents' income changed following marital disruption, the distance from the poverty line (in dollars) was calculated for pre- and post-disruption periods. Table 1 shows that for women who moved out of poverty, the distance below the poverty line

TABLE 1.
DISTANCE FROM THE POVERTY LINE
PRE-DISRUPTION (IN DOLLARS)

WOMEN WHO	AVERAGE	RANGE
MOVED OUT OF POVERTY	$4530 BELOW Poverty Line	$224 to $10995 BELOW Poverty Line
REMAINED IN POVERTY	$5747 BELOW Poverty Line	$23 to $15278 BELOW Poverty Line

before disruption ranged from $224 to $10,995 (changes between pre- and post-disruption incomes are stated in 1985 dollars). Following divorce or separation the distance above the poverty line for these women ranged from $219 to $30,192 (Table 2). For women who remained in poverty distance below the poverty line ranged from $23 to $15,278 before disruption and $371 to $17,797 following disruption.

Table 3 shows that for those families who moved out of poverty, only three experienced a decrease in total dollar income. Since the poverty line is a ratio of actual income to a minimal standard, this would suggest movement out of poverty due to a decrease in needs as reflected by household size. The other families who moved out of poverty experienced an income gain. For those families who remained in poverty following disruption about 30 percent experienced an income increase while approximately 70 percent experienced a decrease in income. The increases and decreases in actual income for these two groups suggest that some families experienced changes due to loss of husbands' income, changes in labor force participation by the woman (either entering the labor force, increas-

TABLE 2.

DISTANCE FROM THE POVERTY LINE POST-DISRUPTION (IN DOLLARS)

WOMEN WHO	AVERAGE	RANGE
MOVED OUT OF POVERTY	$7414 ABOVE Poverty Line	$219 to $30192 ABOVE Poverty Line
REMAINED IN POVERTY	$6550 BELOW Poverty Line	$371 to $17797 BELOW Poverty Line

TABLE 3.
CHANGE IN TOTAL DOLLAR INCOME
FOLLOWING MARITAL DISRUPTION

WOMEN WHO	INCOME	AVERAGE	RANGE
MOVED OUT OF POVERTY	DECREASE (n=3)	$1106	$369 - $1930
	INCREASE (n=27)	$9912	$2350 - $36229
REMAINED IN POVERTY	DECREASE (n=50)	$2417	$246 - 15945
	INCREASE (n=21)	$3879	$220 - $11350

ing hours worked, or changing occupation), or changes in source of income.

MEASUREMENT OF VARIABLES

Variables for analysis were divided into two groups. Human capital variables included education, job training, health and occupational status. Education was reported as a continuous variable in the initial analyses and later categorized for the discriminant analysis procedure. The following categories were used: 8 years or less, 9 to 11 years, 12 years, and some college or college degree. Job training was coded one (1) if the woman had received any form of job training prior to marital disruption; zero otherwise. Health was coded one (1) if the woman had a health limitation; zero otherwise. Occupational status, a proxy for work experience, was measured by the Duncan Index.[1]

Non-human capital variables included current employment status, presence of a child under six, race and pre-disruption husband's income. Current employment status was coded one (1) if the woman was currently employed; zero otherwise. If a woman had a child under six years old, the variable was coded one (1); if not it was coded zero (0). If a woman was

black, race was coded one (1); if she was white, race was coded zero (0).
Pre-disruption husband's income was measured by husband's income in
the year prior to marital disruption and was used as a proxy for assets.

ANALYSIS

The analysis consisted of two parts. First, in order to determine whether
or not the level of human capital stock possessed by women who remained
in poverty and women who moved out of poverty following marital disruption differed, a t-statistic for testing the hypothesis that the means of
the two groups were equal was computed. A t-test was performed to determine differences in the non-human capital variables as well.

In the second part of the analysis, discriminant analysis was used to
determine which variables were the best predictors of whether a respondent remained in poverty or moved out of poverty following marital disruption. Discriminant analysis will identify those variables which distinguish between two or more groups with respect to several variables
simultaneously. The criterion variable was coded one (1) if the woman
moved out of poverty following marital disruption and zero (0) if the
woman remained in poverty following marital disruption. The human capital and non-human capital variables were used as the predictor variables.
Discriminant analysis was conducted with prior probabilities adjusted to
the proportion of cases actually residing in each of the two groups.

RESULTS

Differences between the two groups of women and the potentially discriminating variables are summarized in Table 4. The t-test procedure
indicated statistically significant differences on all human capital variables. Women who moved out of poverty had attained a higher level of
education than women who remained in poverty (11.9 and 10.18 years
respectively). Women who moved out of poverty were more likely to have
had some job training. As would be expected with a sample of young
women, neither group was very likely to have had a health problem; however those women who remained in poverty were more likely to have a
health problem (28 percent) than woman who moved out of poverty (10
percent).

Table 4 also includes univariate results for the non-human capital variables. T-tests indicated statistically significant differences on current employment status and race. Seventy-three percent of the women who moved
out of poverty were currently employed compared to only 23 percent of

TABLE 4.

T-TEST RESULTS

VARIABLES	WOMEN WHO REMAINED IN POVERTY	WOMEN WHO MOVED OUT OF POVERTY
HUMAN CAPITAL		
Education	10.18* (2.31)	11.9* (2.23)
Job Training	0.23* (.42)	0.63* (.49)
Health	0.28* (.45)	0.10* (.31)
Occupational Status	18.72* (16.33)	38.23* (19.71)
NON-HUMAN CAPITAL		
Current Employment Status	0.25* (.44)	0.73* (.45)
Presence of a Child Under Six	0.89 (.32)	0.77 (.43)
Race	0.69* (.47)	0.40* (.50)
Pre-Disruption Husband's Income	5488.57 (5299.24)	3954.84 (3211.60)

Note. Means with standard deviations in parentheses. *Significantly different at p <.05.

the women who remained in poverty. Women who remained in poverty were more likely to be black than women who moved out of poverty.

Results of the discriminant analysis are summarized in Table 5. The discriminant analysis indicated that current employment status was the most useful variable in discriminating between women who moved out of poverty and women who remained in poverty following marital disruption. Job training, education, race, and presence of a child under six (in

TABLE 5.

DISCRIMINANT ANALYSIS: STANDARDIZED COEFFICIENTS OF CANONICAL FUNCTION

VARIABLE	STANDARDIZED COEFFICIENTS	RANK
Current Employment Status	0.62988	1
Job Training	0.51502	2
Education	0.34374	3
Race	-0.33378	4
Presence of a Child Under Six	-0.20266	5

Note, Eigenvalue = 0.60131
Canonical Correlation = 0.6127
Squared Canonical Correlation = .3754
Wilks' Lambda = 0.624
Chi-Squared = 45.434
D.F. = 5
Prob < 0.0000

that order) added to the ability to discriminate between the two groups. Health and pre-disruption husbands' income did not contribute to the ability to distinguish between the two groups of women.

The results of the discriminant analysis are not completely consistent with the results of the univariate analysis. Presence of a child under six was not found to be significant in the t-test analysis but was found to be a distinguishing factor in the discriminant analysis. The reason that a situation like this may occur is because discriminant analysis takes into account intercorrelations among variables whereas it is not in individual t-tests.

The discriminant function predicted group membership fairly well as indicated by the canonical correlation of .6127. Or, interpreted somewhat differently, the canonical correlation squared indicated that the two groups explained .37 of the variance in the discriminant function. Wilks' lambda of 0.624 indicated that the groups are only somewhat distinct relative to the amount of dispersion within the group. In other words, the group centroids are not greatly separated.

The somewhat high Wilks' lambda, though significant, is of concern. It indicates that there is not a great distinction between the two groups. A plot of the predictor variables indicated some overlap in the two groups. One of the reasons for this result is probably the use of the absolute poverty threshold cutoff to define the two groups of women. It is likely that fewer differences exist among women closest to their relevant poverty line. In fact, follow-up analyses support this conclusion.[2]

CONCLUSIONS

Investment in work-related human capital does distinguish women who moved out of poverty from women who remained in poverty following marital disruption. Also, univariated results indicated that women who moved out of poverty following marital disruption had higher levels of human capital stock. However, discriminant analysis results indicated that the most important discriminator was current employment status.

The canonical correlation squared (.37) indicated that the variables studied accounted for much of the variation in the discriminant function. However, the study has several limitations. It is a study of the economic situation of women in their first year of marital disruption; given more time to adjust, the relationships observed may not apply. Particularly relevant is the effect of remarriage on economic well-being (Day & Bahr, 1986; Duncan & Hoffman, 1985). Remarriage was specifically eliminated from this study in order to study how a woman's own resources and characteristics might affect her ability to improve her family's financial situation following marital disruption.

Besides this time or adjustment limitation, duration of poverty before marital disruption has not been considered. Recent research (Bane & Ellwood, 1986) has found that the longer a person has been poor, the lower the probability of escaping poverty. Because of this omission, caution should be taken in interpreting the results of this study. In addition, because of the small sample size and as a result the inability to check the adequacy of classification, caution should also be exercised in generalizing from these results to other divorced women.

At least three conclusions can be drawn from this study. First, for low-income women, investment in human capital does appear to diminish the negative economic effects of marital disruption. While investment in human capital is an obvious answer to improving economic well-being, the analyses reported here further stress its importance. More research is needed particularly in the area of job training. Unfortunately the NLS does not contain data on the type of job training attempted or attained by the women in the surveys, only on the fact that they had job training. Many of the women who experience economic hardship following divorce are eligible for training programs targeted for single parents. Also, many women are likely to be awarded support for training and education as a part of the divorce settlement. Careful study needs to be undertaken to determine what types of programs are the most beneficial.

Second, employment alone makes a tremendous difference in whether or not these women can adequately provide for their family immediately following marital disruption. Further research is needed to determine if differences continue to exist while controlling for employment status prior to disruption and whether changes in employment, such as a better job or longer hours, was necessary to bring about improvements in their financial situation following marital disruption.

The significance of the current employment variable suggests that consideration needs to be given to building in work incentives in the various social programs for single parents. However, since presence of young children may prevent women from working, consideration must be given to adequate, inexpensive child care.

Third, while the results of this study are consistent (for the most part) with previous research findings, the analyses indicated that pre-disruption husbands' income does not distinguish between women who remained in poverty and women who moved out of poverty following marital disruption. T-test results indicated no significant difference in pre-disruption husband's income among the two groups of women studied. If pre-disruption husband's income is any indication of assets brought from the marriage, human capital appears to be more important to a woman and her family than non-human assets.

Much of the previous research on the economic consequences of divorce found that marital disruption is an event which leads to economic hardship. This study on low-income women found that marital disruption can result in both economic hardship and economic gain. For most women already in poverty their situation becomes worse, but some experience a gain in income following marital disruption. In the future researchers need to more carefully analyze changes in economic status of women following marital disruption. These changes may not always be negative. Postive changes in economic well-being following divorce or separation do occur and can provide direction for public policy.

NOTES

1. A possible measure of weeks worked for this study was the sum of weeks worked from the 1968 survey until disruption. Because actual weeks worked in the NLS was limited by lack of data prior to 1968 and every-other year surveys after 1973, measurement error with the variable would be high. An alternative,

predicted-weeks-worked, was estimated but found to be highly correlated with occupational status. As a result, occupational status was utilized as a proxy for work experience. Because of collinearity between education and occupational status, occupational status was dropped from the final analysis.

2. For copies of results contact author.

REFERENCES

Bahr, S.J., & Galligan, R. (1984). Teenage marriage and marital stability. *Youth and Society*, 15, 387-400.

Bane, M.J. (1976). *Here to stay: American families in the twentieth century*. New York: Basic Books, Inc., Publishers.

Bane, M.J., & Ellwood, D.T. (1986). Slipping into and out of poverty: The dynamics of spells. *Journal of Human Resources*, 21, 1-23.

Bane, M.J., & Weiss, R.S. (1980). Alone together: The world of single-parent families. *American Demographics*, 2, 11-14,48.

Cherlin, A.J. (1981). *Marriage divorce remarriage*. Cambridge, MA: Harvard University Press.

Corcoran, M.E. (1981). Work experience, labor force withdrawals, and women's wages: Empirical results using the 1976 panel of income dynamics. In M.S. Hill, D.H. Hill and J.N. Morgan (Eds.), *Five thousand American families — patterns of economics progress – Volume IX* (pp. 1-41). Ann Arbor: Survey Research Center.

Day, R.D., & Bahr, S.J. (1986). Income changes following divorce and remarriage. *Journal of Divorce*, 9, 75-88.

Duncan, G.J. (1984). *Years of poverty years of plenty: The changing economic fortunes of American workers and families*. Ann Arbor: Survey Research Center, Institute for Social Research.

Duncan, G.J., & Hoffman, S.D. (1985). A reconsideration of the economic consequences of marital dissolution. *Demography*, 22, 485-497.

Duncan, G.J., & Morgan, J.N. (1981). Persistence and change in economic status and the role of changing families composition. In M.S. Hill, D.H. Hill & J.N. Morgan (Eds.), *Five thousand American families – patterns of economic progress – Vol. IX* (pp. 1-41). Ann Arbor: Survey Research Center, Institute for Social Research.

Espendshade, T.J. (1979). The economic consequences of divorce. *Journal of Marriage and the Family*, 41, 615-625.

Hampton, R. (1975). Marital disruption: Some social and economic consequences. In G.J. Duncan & J.N. Morgan (Eds.), *Five thousand American families – patterns of economic progress – Vol. III* (pp. 163-188). Ann Arbor: Survey Research Center, Institute for Social Research.

Hauserman, N.R. (1983). Homemakers and divorce: Problems of the invisible occupation. *Family Law Quarterly*, 17, 41-63.

Hayghe, H. (1984). Working mothers reach record number in 1984. *Monthly Labor Review*, 107(12), 31-34.

Hoffman, S. (1977). Marital instability and the economic status of women. *Demography*, 14, 67-76.

Hoffman, S., & Holmes, J. (1976). Husbands, Wives, and Divorce. In G.J. Duncan & J.N. Morgan (Eds.), *Five thousand American families – patterns of economic progress – Volume IV* (pp. 23-75). Ann Arbor: Survey Research Center.

Kohen, J.A., Brown, C.A., & Feldberg, R. (1979). Divorced mothers: The costs and benefits of female control. In G. Levinger & O.C. Moles (Eds.), *Divorce and separation: Context, causes and consequences* (pp. 228-245). New York: Basic Books, Inc., Publishers.

Larson, J.M. (1984). *The relationship of human capital to income sources of recently divorced or separated female heads of household.* Unpublished master's thesis, University of Wisconsin-Madison.

Maddala, G.S. (1977). *Econometrics.* New York: McGraw-Hill Book Company.

Masnick, G., & Bane, M.J. (1980). *The nation's families: 1960-1990.* Mass.: Auburn House Publishing Company.

Mott, F.L. (1979). *The socioeconomic status of households headed by women* (R & D Monograph 72). Washington, D.C.: Employment and Training Administration.

Mott, F.L., & Moore, S.F. (1978). The causes and consequences of marital disruption. In F.L. Mott (Ed.), *Women, work and family* (pp. 113-132). Lexington, MA: D.C. Heath & Company.

Mott, F.L., & Moore, S.F. (1979). The causes of marital disruption among young American women: An interdisciplinary perspective. *Journal of Marriage and the Family*, 41, 355-365.

Norton, A.J., & Glick, P.C. (1979). Marital instability in America: Past, present, and future. In G. Levinger & O. C. Moles (Eds.), *Divorce and separation: Context, causes and consequences* (pp.1-19). New York: Basic Books, Inc., Publishers.

Pearce, D. (1978). The feminization of poverty: women, work and welfare. *The Urban and Social Change Review*, 11, 28-36.

Rudd, N.M., & Sanik, M.M. (1983). Inappropriate work plans of young women: Causes and consequences. In K.D. Rettig & M. Abdel-Ghany (Eds.), *Economic decisions of families: Security for the elderly and labor force participation of women* (pp. 197-211). Washington, D.C.: American Home Economics Association.

Seal, K. (1979). A decade of no-fault divorce: What it has meant financially for women in California. *Family Advocate*, 4, 10-15.

Shaw, L.B. (1978). Economic consequences of marital disruption. In *Women's changing roles at home and on the job* (pp. 181-191). Proceedings of a Conference on the National Longitudinal Survey of Mature Women. Special Report No. 26.

Smith, J.W., & Beninger, E.S. (1982). Women's nonmarket labor: Dissolution of marriage and opportunity cost. *Journal of Family Issues*, 3, 251-265.

Spanier, G.B., & Casto, R.F. (1979). Adjustment to separation and divorce: A qualtitative analysis. In G. Levinger & O.C. Moles (Eds.), *Divorce and sepa-*

ration: Context, causes and consequences (pp. 211-227). New York: Basic Books, Inc., Publishers.

U.S. Bureau of Census. (1987). *Current population reports*, P-60, No. 157. Washington, D.C.: U.S. Government Printing Office.

U.S. Department of Health and Human Services. (1984a). *Advanced report of final divorce statistics, 1981*. (Monthly Vital Statistics Report, 32, January 17). Washington, D.C.: U.S. Government Printing Office.

U.S. Department of Health and Human Services. (1984b). *Annual summary of births, deaths, marriages, and divorces: United States, 1983*. (Monthly Vital Statistics Report, 32, September 21). Washington, D.C.: U.S. Government Printing Office.

Weiss, R.S. (1984). The impact of marital dissolution on income and consumption in single-parent households. *Journal of Marriage and the Family*, 46, 115-127.

Weitzman, L.J. (1985). *The divorce revolution: The unexpected social and economic consequences for women and children in America*. New York: The Free Press.

Child-Rearing Effectiveness
of Divorced Mothers:
Relationship to Coping Strategies
and Social Support

Susan D. Holloway
Sandra Machida

SUMMARY. The association of coping strategies and social support to maternal distress and parenting style was investigated. Interviews were conducted with 58 divorced mothers of preschool children. Results indicated that use of active behavioral and cognitive coping strategies was associated with feelings of control in child-rearing situations and with authoritative parenting. Reliance on coping strategies that involved distancing, escape/avoidance, and social support was associated with symptoms of distress. Availability of family members for social support was generally associated with less authoritative parenting behavior, but also with less distress. Availability of friends was related to more authoritative behavior, but more distress. Coping and social support by friends contributed significantly to authoritativeness and distress beyond the variance

Susan D. Holloway, PhD, is Associate Professor, Department of Human Development, University of Maryland, College Park, MD 20742. Sandra Machida, PhD, is affiliated with the Center for Policy Studies on Youth and the Family, California State University at Chico.

This work was supported by a grant to the first author from the Center for Educational Research and Development at the University of Maryland and by funds from the Professional Development Office at the California State University at Chico. Funding for data analysis was provided by the Computer Science Center at the University of Maryland and the Computer Center at the California State University at Chico. We thank Robin Allison, Patricia Black, Kathy Dahlgren, Kristi Ivosevich, Pam Kidgell, Yong Kim, Joan Mayer, Karen Olsen, and Judith Steele for their able assistance in collecting and coding the data. Bruce Fuller and John Guthrie provided insightful comments throughout the project.

179

contributed by mothers' education, financial stability, time since separation, and geographical region.

When a married couple with children decides to separate, the parenting skills of each partner often deteriorate, at least temporarily. Following divorce or separation, parents may offer less intellectual stimulation (MacKinnon, Brody, & Stoneman, 1987), and be more rejecting of their children (Felner, Farber, Ginter, Boike, & Cowen, 1980). They are more likely than parents from intact families to report feeling angry at their children and are more likely to report having little tolerance of misbehavior (Crossman & Adam, 1980).

While these findings reflect the stressful nature of parental divorce on the family, it is also true that the impact of divorce depends on the personal and financial resources available to help parents cope with stressful events. Divorcing parents who are able to maintain warmth, availability, and authoritative control facilitate the successful adjustment of their children to the new family structure (Brody, Pellegrini, & Sigel, 1986; Guidubaldi, Cleminshaw, Perry, & Nastasi, 1984; Hetherington, Cox, & Cox, 1978; Hodges, Buschbaum, & Tierney, 1983). Psychological characteristics of mothers — including emotional distress and child-rearing values — have been found to offset the stressful circumstances, including divorce, on the positive and negative behaviors of mothers (Conger, McCarty, Yang, Lahey, & Kropp, 1984).

Little is known about the personal and environmental factors which enable a parent to maintain appropriate child-rearing behavior under the strain of marital separation or divorce. In this study, we examined two factors which may be related to parenting effectiveness: social support and coping strategies. Our goal was to investigate the relationship between these factors and to determine their association to various indicators of child-rearing effectiveness and to general perceived distress.

EFFECTS OF SOCIAL SUPPORT

Social support appears to play an important part in reducing stressful effects of difficult situations such as divorce. Participation in adult social activities in the second six months after divorce appears to reduce stress experienced by men and women (Nelson, 1981; Raschke, 1977). Predictors of satisfactory social adjustment of divorced mothers included the quality of relationship with significant others, as well as perceived size of and satisfaction with social network support (Pett, 1982). Greater adjustment to divorce is reported by women who have relationships in which more needs (e.g., companionship, information, aid) are met by fewer persons (Daniels-Mohring & Berger, 1984). Assistance with housework and child care is also related to less depression on the part of single parent women (Keith & Schafer, 1982).

Most studies cited above use global measures of depression or psychiatric symptoms as outcomes. There is also evidence that availability of social support affects divorced womens' parenting behavior. Mothers' sense of pleasure and competence in negotiation with children appears to be related to their satisfaction with their relationships with friends and family (Bowen, 1982).

The concept of social support is differentiated and needs to be analyzed in terms of various component dimensions. Early work focused on extensiveness of social support, with later conceptualizations focusing more on the structure, nature, and quality of the support (House, 1987). In the current study, we examined social support in terms of *number* of relatives and friends available to offer assistance, information, and companionship, and the *satisfaction* of the sample of divorced mothers with the support available. Maternal distress and child-rearing effectiveness was expected to be related to number of friends available, and satisfaction with friends' support. There is some evidence that social support by family members may often increase rather than decrease feelings of stress or depression (Beal, 1979; Rook, 1987). Therefore, we expected support by family members to be negatively related to maternal distress and child-rearing effectiveness.

EFFECTS OF COPING STRATEGIES

Individuals may offset the negative effects of a stressful situation by using effective coping strategies. The efficacy of various types of coping strategies in reducing stress has been studied extensively. Most studies find that coping by avoidance is not an effective strategy (Holahan & Moos, 1985, 1987). Attempts to deal with a problem by actively managing or changing the situation is generally an effective way to lessen stress in many situations (e.g., Billings & Moos, 1984; Pearlin & Schooler, 1978). However, in the situation of divorce, the individual often has little opportunity to actively change or control circumstances. To the extent that the situation is uncontrollable, emotion-focused coping — in which the individual manages his or her emotional response to the stressor rather than trying to change the situation — may be more effective than active problem-focused strategies. Propst, Pardington, Ostrom, & Watkins (1986) examined coping style as one of several predictors of depression, anxiety,

and perceived stress in divorced women. Both emotion-focused and problem-focused coping strategies were negatively related to anxiety, depression, and perception of stress, but emotion-focused coping was a stronger
predictor. Other studies have also indicated that direct attempts to change
a situation or solve a problem may not be effective in less controllable
situations (Elman and Gilbert, 1984).

Divorced mothers may have little control over some aspects of their
current situation — such as their income or the behavior of their ex-
spouse — and hence would be better off using emotion-focused coping. On
the other hand, with their children they have not only an opportunity but
in fact a responsibility to maintain control. It may be that women who
engage in problem-focused coping maintain appropriate control of their
children during the stressful period following divorce. Therefore, we expected that problem-focused coping would also be associated with greater
feelings of control and with less distress. Women who used avoidance
strategies were expected to have less feeling of control, be less authoritative, and feel more distress.

The relationship between coping strategies and social support has been
examined in several studies. It appears that individuals who have effective
social support are less likely to use avoidance coping strategies and more
likely to use active-cognitive or active-behavioral strategies (Holahan &
Moos, 1987). Similar findings emerged in a study by Dunkel-Schetter,
Folkman, and Lazarus (1987), who found that social support was associated with problem-focused coping, but not with emotion-focused coping.
No studies have investigated the relationship between coping and social
support in the situation of divorce; however, based on the literature examining reaction to general life stress, we expected that social support would
be associated with behavioral and active cognitive strategies, but not with
avoidance strategies.

INCOME AND TIME SINCE SEPARATION

The financial problems experienced by divorced women and their children have been the subject of much investigation. Low income increases
the stress experienced by divorced mothers (Colletta, 1979; Hodges, Tierney, & Buchsbaum, 1984; Pett & Vaughan-Cole, 1986), and predicts
maladjustment in children from divorced families (Hodges, Wechsler, &
Ballantine, 1979). Colletta (1983) found that, while some stresses are
higher in divorced families than in intact families even when income is not
an issue, low income divorced mothers report greater levels of stress than
moderate income divorced mothers, and that high levels of stress were

found to be significantly related to the mothers being more demanding and restrictive with their children. This evidence suggests that financial circumstances should be taken into account. Women's educational background influences their career options and hence also their financial stability. In this study, therefore, mother's education and financial stability were included as control variables.

The amount of time that has elapsed since separation also affects the amount of stress experienced by the family, the type of coping strategies used, and the effectiveness of different strategies (Folkman & Lazarus, 1985; Hetherington, Cox, & Cox, 1978). Therefore, time since separation was also used as a control variable in this study.

SUMMARY

Evidence is strong that characteristics of the environment such as social support and characteristics of individuals such as coping style may attenuate the effects of stressful situations. Yet several important questions remain to be addressed. First, most of the studies have focused on a variety of life strains; little is known about the dynamics of social support, coping, and stress in the specific situation of divorce. Second, even among those studies focusing on the stress created by divorce, few have examined parenting behavior. Third, few studies have examined the association of the interaction between social support and coping on adjustment and parenting. In this study we address these issues by examining the independent and interactive association of coping and social support on the level of distress experienced by recently divorced mothers of preschool children, on their ability to behave authoritatively and on their feelings of control in dealing with their children.

METHOD

Subjects

The sample included 58 divorced, single mothers and their preschool-age children ($M = 4.5$ years, $SD = 4.5$ months). Three of the mothers were black; the remaining participants were white. There were 35 boys and 23 girls in the sample. About two-thirds of the mothers lived in a university community in Northern California while the remaining one-third were drawn from a suburban community in Maryland.

All mothers worked or were attending school. Average monthly income was $1200. Mean occupational score on the Hollingshead Index of Social

Status (1975) was 5.2, indicating that most of the mothers were working in clerical, service, or sales jobs. The average level of schooling was approximately one year of post-secondary education ($SD = 1.57$ years).

On average, mothers had been separated from their ex-husbands for 31 months ($SD = 15.56$ months) and had been legally divorced for about ten months ($SD = 13.89$ months). Fifty-nine percent of the mothers had sole custody while the remaining mothers either had joint legal or physical custody of their children. Fifty-five percent of the children were cared for in day-care centers while their mothers were working or attending class; the remaining children were cared for in family day-care homes or by babysitters.

Procedure

Day-care centers and family day-care homes were approached for cooperation in identifying single, divorced mothers with preschool-aged children. In addition, single parent groups and residents of single-parent housing developments were contacted, and advertisements were placed in local newspapers. Letters of invitation was sent out to all women identified through these sources. Mothers returned a consent form if they were interested in participating. Once the form was returned, the interviewer set up an appointment for an interview. The Family Inventory of Resources for Management was sent ahead so that the mothers could complete it before the interviewer arrived at her home.

Measures

A family's level of financial resources was determined by summing the items on the Financial Well-being and Sources of Financial Support subscales of the Family Inventory of Resources for Management (McCubbin, Comeau & Harkins, 1980). These subscales assess a family's financial resources, stability, and security; the subscales contain statements such as "I seem to have little or no problem paying my bills on time," "I would have no problem getting a loan at a bank if I wanted one," and "I feel I am able to make financial contributions to a good cause." Mothers responded on a four point Likert response scale ranging from "does not at all describe my family" to "describes my family very well." Three items judged less relevant for single parents were dropped. Scores on the resulting 21 items were totalled; coefficient alpha for the total score was .73.

Social support was assessed by asking mothers about ten situations in which they may have needed information, assistance, or companionship. Mothers were told, "Below are listed some situations you may have encountered in which you wished to have the help or participation of another person. For each situation please write the first name of each person you contacted, and indicate whether they were a friend or family member." Regarding assistance three situations were given: needing to borrow money, needing to borrow a car, and needing to leave a sick child with someone for a few hours. Regarding information, two situations were used: needing information regarding a planned purchase and needing advice concerning an important decision. For companionship there were four situations: wanting to talk on the phone, wanting to go shopping, wanting to visit someone, and wanting to go out to dinner.

Composites were created for each type of situation. Coefficient alpha was calculated for composites containing more than two variables. Composites were created for number of friends available for assistance (alpha = .78), companionship (alpha = .82), and information (two items), as well as for number of relatives available for assistance (alpha = .68), companionship (alpha = .75), and information (two items). Two totals were also computed: number of different friends mentioned across the ten situations (alpha = .89), and number of family members mentioned across the situations (alpha = .85).

Mothers also indicated their satisfaction with the help received on a six point scale ranging from "not at all satisfied" to "very satisfied." However, these ratings were correlated very highly with the variables indicating availability of the individuals, and so were not used in further analyses.

Maternal coping. Maternal coping was assessed using the Ways of Coping (Revised) (Folkman & Lazarus, 1985). This 66-item questionnaire contains a wide range of thoughts and actions that may be used to deal with specific stressful encounters. The subject responds on a 4-point Likert scale (0 = does not apply and/or not used; 3 = used a great deal). In the present study, mothers were asked to indicate which of the 66 behaviors or thoughts they had used since separating from their former husbands. Item scores were summed to create a single index representing frequency of using various coping strategies (coefficient alpha = .84). Additionally, items were grouped in eight subscales identified by the authors of the scale (Folkman, Lazarus, Dunkel-Schetter, DeLongis, & Gruen, 1986). These subscales and their coefficient alphas in the present sample were the following: confrontative coping (alpha = .57), distancing (alpha = .72), self-control (alpha = .49), seeking social support (alpha = .74), accepting responsibility (alpha = .34), escape-avoidance (alpha = .68), planful problem-solving (alpha = .68), and positive reappraisal (alpha = .66). The three subscales with coefficient alpha less than .60 (confrontative coping, self-control, and accepting responsibility) were judged insufficiently reliable and were omitted from subsequent analyses. Table 1 contains subscale means and sample items for those subscales that were retained.

Mother belief variables. To assess mothers' beliefs about control over child-rearing outcomes, mothers were asked to recall their child being involved in five recent positive events (playing well with another child, helping with chores, giving a gift, taking on a challenging task, behaving affectionately) and five negative events (refusing to share, refusing to go to bed, becoming very angry, not telling the truth, refusing to clean up). Then they were asked to indicate on a 6 point scale "how much can you control your child's [cleaning up]?" The response scale ranged from "not at all" to "entirely." Ratings were summed over the ten events, forming an index of mothers' perceptions of control over their children (coefficient alpha = .73). This variable is subsequently referred to as *perceived control*.

Maternal Authoritativeness and Perceived Distress. To ascertain their firmness in supervising and controlling their children's behavior, mothers were asked to respond to seven statements about rule-setting and household responsibility (see Appendix A for instrument). Mothers indicated on a five point scale how well each statement described her family (1 = "not at all"; 5 = "very well"). Scores on these items were summed to create an index of *mother authoritativeness* (coefficient alpha = .66).

To assess mothers' symptoms of *perceived distress*, the SCL-90-R was administered (Derogatis, 1975). The SCL-90-R reflects psychopathology in terms of 9 primary symptom dimensions. Respondents are asked to indicate how much discomfort each of 90 problems has caused them during the past week. They indicate their response on a five point scale ranking from "not at all" to "extremely." Several studies have found that the SCL-90-R is highly sensitive to stress-related changes (Derogatis, 1982). In our study, item scores were summed to create a total score for perceived distress (coefficient alpha = .97).

RESULTS

Preliminary Tests

For each dependent and independent variable, the significance of differences between the East and West Coast samples was tested. Two areas of difference emerged. First, families on the East coast had more financial

Table 1. Description of Coping Subscales

Coping scale	Mean	SD	Sample items
Distancing	1.03	.60	I went on as if nothing had happened.
			I tried to forget the whole thing.
Social support	1.58	.65	I talked to someone to find out more about the situation.
			I talked to someone about how I was feeling.
Escape/avoid	.96	.53	I hoped a miracle would happen.
			I avoided being with people in general.

TABLE 1 (continued)

Coping scale	Mean	SD	Sample items
Problem solving	1.73	.56	I made a plan of action and followed it.
			I just concentrated on what I had to do next.
Positive reappraisal	1.84	.58	I changed or grew as a person in a good way.
			I found new faith.
Total score	93.29	20.93	[Sum of all items]

resources than those on the West coast (t (56) $= 2.95, p < .01$). Second, mothers on the East Coast appeared to have more friends. The regional difference was significant for total number of friends ($t(28) = 3.11, p < .01$), and for friends available for assistance ($t(26) = 3.47, p < .01$), information ($t(56) = 2.71, p < .01$) and companionship ($t(27) = 2.17, p < .05$). All subsequent analyses controlled on region.

Partial correlations (controlling on region) were computed among the outcome measures (distress, control in child rearing, authoritativeness). None was significant. Partial correlations were also obtained among the demographic measures (mother's education, financial stability, and time since separation). Mothers with higher education had greater financial stability ($r = .32, p < .01$), and those with greater financial stability had been separated longer ($r = .29, p < .05$). Partial correlations computed between the demographic variables and the outcomes revealed only one significant correlation: mothers who were more educated felt more control over child rearing ($r = .30, p < .05$).

Coping Strategies

Partial correlations (controlling for region) were calculated between the coping subscales and the demographic and outcome measures. As Table 2 indicates, mothers who were more highly educated were more likely to cope by using social support, problem solving, and positive reappraisal. Mothers who had been separated longer were less likely to cope by using social support.

Regarding the measures of adjustment and parenting, mothers who reported more distress were more likely to cope by distancing, social support, and escape/avoidance. Women who felt that they were able to control their children's behavior, and women who were more authoritative in their interactions with children, were more likely to cope using problem solving and positive appraisal. Distress, perceptions of control, and authoritativeness were also associated with total coping score.

Partial correlations were also computed between the social support indicators and the demographic and outcome measures. No significant correlations were found between social support and mother's education, financial stability, or time since separation. Correlations between social support and the outcome measures are reported in Table 3. Distress was associated with less reliance on relatives for companionship and more reliance on friends for companionship. Authoritativeness was positively associated with reliance on friends for aid and companionship, and was negatively associated with reliance on friends for these same functions. Perceived control was not significantly associated with any of the social support measures.

Table 2. Association of coping strategies to demographic and adjustment measures

	Demographics			Adjustment Measures		
	Ed level	Finance	Time Seprtd	Dis-tress	Control	Authori-tative
Coping Scales						
Distance	11	-01	14	26*	22	03
Social support	26*	01	-26*	29*	21	01
Escape/avoid	-11	-07	13	46***	-05	07
Problem solving	35**	-05	10	22	32**	38**
Positive apprsl	29*	-07	-03	18	37***	29*
Total Coping	21	-01	07	50***	39**	32**

Note. Pearson product moment correlations reported; n = 56-58; decimal points omitted.

* p < .05   ** p < .01   *** p < .001

Table 3. Association of social support to adjustment measures

| | Adjustment Measures | | |
Social Support	Distress	Control	Authoritative
Aid - friend	09	14	35**
Aid - relative	-17	-20	-34***
Info - friend	-01	02	16
Info - relative	-20	-15	-05
Companion - friend	27*	-08	41**
Companion - relative	-26*	-09	-30*
Total - friend	19	05	44***
Total - relative	-24	-18	-33**

Note. Pearson product moment correlations reported; n = 56-58; decimal points omitted.

* p < .05   ** p < .01   *** p < .001

The association of social support and coping was also examined using partial correlations. Relationships tended to be weak, but indicated that reliance on relatives was generally associated with less use of coping active cognitive and behavioral strategies. Women who relied on relatives for assistance were less likely to cope by using distancing ($r = -.26, p < .05$) and problem solving ($r = -.43, p < .001$). Overall reliance on relatives was associated with less use of problem solving ($r = -.35, p < .01$) and lower scores on the total coping scale ($r = -.25, p < .05$).

A series of multiple regression runs was performed in order to determine whether coping and social support were significant predictors of adjustment after accounting for educational background of the mother, time since separation, and region. Independent variables included mother's education, time since separation, region, total coping score, total number of friends available, and the interaction between coping and total number of friends. Dependent variables included score on the distress scale, perceived control, and authoritativeness. First a simultaneous multiple regression was conducted in which all independent variables were entered. A second set of regressions was computed with only mother's education, region, and time since separation as predictors. The significance of the R-square change between the restricted model (education, region, time since separation) and the full model (education, region, time since separation, coping, social support from friends, and the interaction term) was tested for each of the three independent variables.

Region, total coping, and social support from friends were significant predictors of authoritativeness (Table 4). The R-square increased from .07 to .34 when the coping and support items were included; this change was significant ($F(3,50 = 6.82, p < .01$). For perceived control, mother's education and total coping were significant predictors. The R-square increased from .09 to .21 when the coping and support items were included; this change bordered on significance ($F(3,50) = 2.58$, ns).

For perceived distress, significant predictors included coping and the interaction between coping and social support. The R-square increased from .05 to .33 when the coping and social support items were added. This increment was significant ($F(3,50) = 7.09, p < .01$).

The relation of the interaction between coping and social support to perceived distress is graphically depicted in Figure 1. Four groups were created by computing median splits on the coping and social support variables. Mean score on the distress scale are graphed for each of the groups. It is apparent that the difference between high and low social support by friends is larger for those individuals who make frequent use of various coping strategies. The group who used many coping strategies frequently

Table 4. Association of demographic, coping, and social support variables to adjustment

Dependent var	F	Adjusted R^2	Independent var	Beta
Authoritativeness	4.39***	.26	Education	-.07
			Time separated	.06
			Region	.39**
			Total coping	.29*
			Number friends	.46***
			Coping X Friends	-.05
Control	2.27*	.12	Education	.22+
			Time separated	.06
			Region	-.06
			Total coping	.32**
			Number friends	.02
			Coping X Friends	.17

TABLE 4 (continued)

Dependent var	F	Adjusted R^2	Independent var	Beta
Distress	4.27**	.26	Education	-.06
			Time separated	-.12
			Region	-.18
			Total coping	.49***
			Number friends	.18
			Coping X Friends	.19+

<u>Note</u>. N = 56-58.

+ p < .15   * p < .05   ** p < .01   *** p < .001

FIGURE 1. Mean distress score for groups formed by coping and social support by friends.

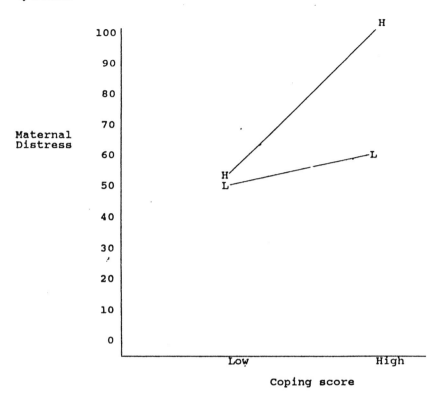

Legend:
    H: High social support
    L: Low social support

and who had many friends was much more likely to cite distress than were any of the other groups.

DISCUSSION

Impressive evidence of an association between coping strategies and maternal beliefs and behavior emerged in this study. Women who reported greater distress tended to rely more heavily on the coping strategies of escape/avoidance and distancing than did women reporting less distress. These findings are in accord with the literature finding avoidance to be an ineffective coping strategy (e.g., Holahan & Moos, 1987). Distancing also contains items which can be seen as escape strategies (e.g., I went on as if nothing had happened). Therefore, it is not surprising that it was related to perceived distress. Women who reported more distress also made somewhat more use of social support. This finding is a bit more surprising; in past literature use of social support has usually been categorized as a positive way of coping (Dunkel-Schetter, Folkman & Lazarus, 1987; Holahan & Moos, 1987). However, the literature on social support — as well as findings from the more detailed social support questions in the current study — clearly suggests that some types of social support are effective and some are detrimental. The social support subscale on the Ways of Coping scale refer to support in a general way, including that provided by friends and family; a more precise assessment of the use of social support for coping might have presented a clearer picture.

Feelings of control regarding child-rearing and authoritative behavior towards children were associated with coping strategies that reflected active problem solving and positive reappraisal. These findings are in accord with many studies finding that active behavioral strategies are associated with positive adjustment (e.g., Holahan & Moos, 1985; Pearlin & Schooler, 1978).

The relation of social support (as measured with the more detailed instrument devised for this study) to the measures of parenting effectiveness was modest. The most powerful association was between social support and authoritativeness. It appears that women who relied on their own family for assistance or companionship were less able to maintain authoritative relations with their children than were women who relied on friends. Social support by relatives was also associated with less use of coping strategies and particularly with less use of problem solving. These findings are supported by other studies finding that the assistance or companionship of relatives may not always have a positive impact (Beal, 1979; Rook, 1987). On the other hand, reliance on relatives for companionship was associated with less distress, while reliance on friends for companionship was associated with more distress. This finding bears further investigation. It may be that friends provide the type of resources that help mothers deal effectively with their children, but do not provide the basic emotional support needed to offset feelings of distress.

It should also be noted that the sample was fairly homogeneous in terms of social class background. For other groups, such as professional women, the relationships among coping, social support, and adjustment may be different than those found for this sample of largely working class mothers. Homogeneity of the sample may also explain why mothers' financial stability was not a stronger predictor of adjustment. Another reason for the lack of relationship between parental effectiveness and education level is that well-educated women may experience a sudden drop in financial resources and lifestyle subsequent to divorce. Some respondents in this study were experiencing severe financial pressures; one interviewer noted that one family appeared to have no food at all in the house. The mother reported that her ex-husband was habitually delinquent on child support payments and she often had no money even for essentials such as food, so the interviewer initiated a community effort to raise money for the family's groceries.

A number of suggestions for future research can be raised based on the findings from this study. First, the process of divorce calls for coping with changes in multiple domains — work, children, and adult relationships. Our measure tapped coping without distinguishing this more micro-level of situation. As Pearlin & Schooler note (1978), however, different types of coping may be effective for each of the domains, so future studies should maintain these fine-grained distinctions. Second, a process account of coping in divorce is needed; a coping strategy that is effective during the period of separation may not be effective ten or twelve months later. Third, the association between social structure and coping bears further investigation. Social structural indicators in addition to social support and financial situation should be considered. For example, the age of children might influence the effects of coping; women with preschool children may perceive less opportunity to attend night school in order to develop professional skills, for example. In uncontrollable situations, managing their emotional response to financial pressure might be more effective than attempting to actively change their situation (Howard, 1974; Lykes, 1983; Weisz, Rothbaum, & Blackburn, 1984). Sensitivity to contextual features such as social support should help mental health professionals and their clients identify strategies for coping with divorce that are most likely to result in positive adjustment for parents and children.

REFERENCES

Billings, A. G., & Moos, R. H. (1981). The role of coping responses and social resources in attenuating the stress of life events. *Journal of Behavioral Medicine, 4,* 139-157.

Billings, A. G., & Moos, R. H. (1984). Coping, stress, and social resources among adults with unipolar depression. *Journal of Personality and Social Psychology*, *46*, 877-891.

Beal, E. W. (1979). Children of divorce: A family systems perspective. *Journal of Social Issues*, *35*, 140-154.

Bowen, G. L. (1982). Social network and the maternal role satisfaction of formerly-married mothers. *Journal of Divorce*, *5*, 77-83.

Brody, G. H., Pellegrini, A. D., & Sigel, I. E. (1986). Marital quality and mother-child and father-child interactions with school-aged children. *Developmental Psychology*, *22*, 291-296.

Colletta, N. D. (1979). The impact of divorce: Father absence of poverty? *Journal of Divorce*, *3*, 27-35.

Colletta, N. D. (1983). Stressful lives: The situations of divorced mothers and their children. *Journal of Divorce*, *6*, 19-31.

Conger, R. D., McCarty, J. A., Yang, R. K., Lahey, B. B., & Kropp, J. P. (1984). Perception of child, child-rearing values, and emotional distress as mediating links between environmental stressors and observed maternal behavior. *Child Development*, *55*, 2234-2247.

Crossman, S. M., & Adam, G. R. (1980). Divorce, single parenting, and child development. *The Journal of Psychology*, *105*, 205-217.

Daniels-Mohring, D., & Berger, M. (1984). Social network changes and the adjustment to divorce. *Journal of Divorce*, *8*, 17-31.

Derogatis, L. R. (1975). *The SCL-90-R*. Clinical Psychometrics Research, Baltimore, MD.

Dunkel-Schetter, C., Folkman, S., & Lazarus, R. S. (1987). Correlates of social support receipt. *Journal of Personality and Social Psychology*, *53*, 71-80.

Elman, M. R., & Gilbert, L. A. (1984). Coping strategies for role conflict in married professional women with children. *Family Relations*, *33*, 317-327.

Felner, R. D., Farber, S. S., Ginter, M. A., Boike, M. F., & Cowen, E. L. (1980). Family stress and organization following parental divorce or death. *Journal of Divorce*, *4*, 67-76.

Folkman, S., & Lazarus, R. (1985). If it changes it must be a process: Study of emotion and coping during three stages of a college examination. *Journal of Personality and Social Psychology*, *48*, 150-170.

Folkman, S., Lazarus, R. S., Dunkel-Schetter, C., DeLongis, A., & Gruen, R. (1986). Dynamics of a stressful encounter: Cognitive appraisal, coping, and encounter outcomes. *Journal of Personality and Social Psychology*, *50*, 992-1003.

Guidubaldi, J., Cleminshaw, H. K., Perry, J. D., & Nastasi, B. K. (1984, April). Factors related to academic and social adjustment of elementary grade divorced-family children. Paper presented at the annual meeting of the American Educational Research Association, New Orleans.

Hetherington, E. M., Cox, M. & Cox, R. (1978). Long-term effects of divorce and remarriage on the adjustment of children. *Journal of the American Academy of Child Psychiatry*, *24*, 518-530.

Hodges, W. F., Buschbaum, H. K., & Tierney, C. W. (1983). Parent-child relationships and adjustment in preschool children in divorced and intact families. *Journal of Divorce, 7*, 43-58.

Hodges, W. F., Tierney, C. W., & Buschbaum, H. K. (1984). The cumulative effect of stress on preschool children of divorced and intact families. *Journal of Marriage and the Family*, 46, 611-617.

Holahan, C. J., & Moos, R. H. (1985). Life stress and health: Personality, coping, and family support in stress resistance. *Journal of Personality and Social Psychology, 49*, 739-747.

Holahan, C. J., & Moos, R. H. (1987). Personal and contextual determinants of coping strategies. *Journal of Personality and Social Psychology, 52*, 946-955.

Hollingshead, A. (1975). *The Four-Factor Index of Social Status*. Unpublished manuscript.

House, J. S. (1987). Social support and social structure. *Sociological Forum, 2*, 135-146.

Howard, A. (1974). *Ain't no big thing: Coping strategies in a Hawaiian-American community*. Honolulu: University Press of Hawaii.

Lazarus, R. S., & Folkman, S. (1984). *Stress, appraisal, and coping*. New York: Springer.

Lykes, M. B. (1983). Discrimination and coping in the lives of black women: Analysis of oral history data. *Journal of Social Issues, 39*, 79-100.

Keith, P. M., & Schafer, R. B. (1982). Correlates of depression among single parent, employed mothers. *Journal of Divorce, 5*, 49-59.

MacKinnon, C. E., Brody, G. H., & Stoneman, Z. (1987). The longitudinal effects of divorce and maternal employment on the home environments of preschool children. *Journal of Divorce, 9*, 65-78.

McCubbin, H., Comeau, J., Harkins, J. (1980). *Family Inventory of Resources for Management (FIRM)*. St. Paul MN: Family Social Science, University of Minnesota.

Nelson, G. (1981). Moderators of women's and children's adjustment following divorce. *Journal of Divorce, 4*, 71-83.

Pearlin, L. I., & Schooler, C. (1978). The structure of coping. *Journal of Health and Social Behavior, 19*, 2-21.

Pett, M. G. (1982). Predictors of satisfactory social adjustment of divorced single parents. *Journal of Divorce, 5*, 1-17.

Pett, M. A., & Vaughan-Cole, B. (1986). The impact of income issues and social status on post-divorce adjustment of custodial parents. *Family Relations, 35*, 103-111.

Propst, L. R., Pardington, A., Ostrom, R., & Watkins, P. (1986). Predictors of coping in divorced single mothers. *Journal of Divorce, 9*, 33-53.

Raschke, H. J. (1977). The role of social participation in postseparation and post-divorce adjustment. *Journal of Divorce, 1*, 129-140.

Rook, K. S. (1987). Social support versus companionship: Effects of life stress, loneliness, and evaluations by others. *Journal of Personality and Social Psychology, 52,* 1132-1147.

Weisz, J. R., Rothbaum, F. M., & Blackburn, T. C. (1984). Standing out and standing in: The psychology of control in America and Japan. *American Psychologist, 39,* 955-969.

Appendix A

Mother Authoritativeness Scale

Please mark how well each statement describes your family (you and your children). Use the following scale: Describes my family (1) not at all; (2) a little; (3) fairly well; (4) well; (5) very well.

1. I usually give out chores for my child to do.

2. I have rules about when my child has to go to bed.

3. I have rules about not eating between meals.

4. I have rules about when my child can watch television and/or what programs can be watched.

5. When my child disobeys I might say "It hurts my feelings when you disobey".

6. When my child disobeys, say be writing on the walls, I might say, "We have a rule about not writing on the walls".

7. My child has learned to help out when work needs to be done around the house.

Marital Status and Well-Being: A Comparison of Widowed, Divorced, and Married Mothers in Israel

Ruth Katz

SUMMARY. This paper addresses itself to three main questions: (a) To what extent does single-parenthood enable a quality of life characterized by a sense of personal well-being? (b) What are the main components of well-being for single mothers? (c) Which background factors facilitate well-being in single mothers? In order to answer these questions a Depression Adjective Check-List (Lubin, 1965) was administered to a representative sample of 142 widows and 120 divorcées who had been single for a minimum of four years and who each had at least one minor child. The main findings: (a) measures of well-being were lower for single mothers than for married mothers; (b) there were negative, but also some positive components of well-being: a growing sense of loneliness, of material hardship, of anxiety about parental responsibilities, on the one hand, and a sense of occupational growth, on the other hand; (c) the background factors which affect well-being were properties such as schooling, earnings, and health as well as participation in familial decisions while still married. These results were interpreted in the context of the familistic orientations prevailing in Israeli society.

A person can become a single parent for a variety of reasons: separation, divorce, widowhood, adoption, and pre-marital motherhood are the most common. Following Norton and Glick (1986), we will define a type of family consisting of a lone parent maintaining a household with one or more minor children as a one parent family.

In the last generation, the single-parent family has become part of the

Ruth Katz, PhD, is on the faculty of the Department of Sociology and Anthropology and School of Social Work, University of Haifa, Mt. Carmel, Haifa 31999, Israel.

social landscape in most industrialized countries. This tendency has not skipped Israel, even though, here, it has evolved more slowly and at a relatively lower level compared to other countries. In 1981, about 5% of all the Jewish households in Israel with children under age 18 were single-parent households (Keren-Ya'ar & Souery, 1983) in comparison with 26% in the United States (U.S. Bureau of Census, 1985). In Israel, as in the United States, women head 89% of these families.

The internal constitution of these families in Israel is somewhat different from those in the United States. While, in the United States, a large proportion of the mothers were never married (20%), in Israel, this group is much smaller (we estimate them, according to various sources, as about 6%). On the other hand, widows in Israel constitute 29% of the single-parent mothers as compared to 9% in the United States. This is due mainly to the existence in Israel of relatively young war widows. The divorced mothers in both countries constitute the largest category—46% in both the United States and in Israel (Norton & Glick, 1986:11; Keren Ya'ar & Souery, 1983:31).

It is the intention of this article to study the relationship between marital status and well-being of the mother. This subject has been dealt with in a number of research studies, but their results are not unequivocal (e.g., Amato & Partridge, 1987; Menaghan & Lieberman, 1986; Pearlin & Johnson, 1977).

Possible reasons for the differences in the results of the studies are:

a. Faulty control of background factors, including the length of time which has elapsed since the dissolution of the family.
b. Differences in methods of measuring the dependent variable (well-being).
c. Insufficient detail concerning the dependent variable. The effect of the crisis may be different for different spheres of life. For example, it is reasonable to assume that the absence of a husband would affect the economic functioning of the mother more adversely than it would affect her relationship to her children. Such distinctions between changes in different spheres of life may even serve to locate beneficial effects of the dissolution of the family as well as the recognized costs. Some studies have claimed that successfully coping with the new role of being single again may result in personal growth and development (Chiriboga, 1979; Nelson, 1982; Salts, 1979; Weingarten, 1985).

In the present study the two largest categories of single-parent families in Israel—divorcées and widows—were compared both to married mothers and to each other. The comparison was made in regard to the personal well-being of the mother and to her perception of the changes which had occurred in different spheres of her family life. Important background factors such as age, education, ethnic origin, and time lapse since the dissolution of the marriage were also controlled.

From a sociological point of view, it is important to distinguish between direct effects of the family crisis on individual well-being and influences mediated by societal norms. In other words, the change in marital status causes a lowering of social status which in turn influences personal well-being. It is clear that the more familistically oriented the surrounding society, the greater the indirect influences of marital dissolution.

These reciprocal relations between the individual, the family in crisis, and the community necessitate a specific examination of the changes which have occurred in different spheres of life of the mothers.

This study will consequently address itself to the following questions: To what extent and under which conditions does single motherhood enable a quality of life characterized by a sense of well-being? What are the main components of the single mother's well-being? Which background factors facilitate the single mother's well-being?

METHOD

Population and Sample

The sample was planned to represent the population of Jewish one-parent families headed by either widows or divorcées (the two large categories among families headed by women), living in urban communities. From a list of urban communities in the central area of the country, fifteen whose socio-economic characteristics represent the urban population in Israel were selected (Egozi, 1978).[1] A complete list of all divorced and widowed mothers with minor children in these communities was obtained from the Ministry of the Interior. A systematic sample was drawn from this list.

Two hundred and sixty-two mothers constituted the research population. Of these, 142 were widows and 120 divorcées. Each subject had at least one child under 18 years of age and no permanent partner was living in her home. In order to examine personal well-being as a function of marital status rather than of marital dissolution, we excluded those very recently (i.e., less than four years) divorced or widowed. The average length of time our respondents had been heads of their households was about eight years. The average age of the widows in the sample was 44 and of the divorcées 38. The average number of children up to 18 years of age was two for both groups. The widows had on the average about eight years of education, while the divorcées had about ten. Among the divorcées 48% are employed full-time as are 26% of the widows. These percentages are identical to labor force survey data for the respective populations. A sample of 2476 married mothers, obtained from a previous survey (Peres & Katz, 1984), was used as a framework for comparison. This sample was matched with the present sample for age and number of children.

Measures

Questionnaire

A questionnaire was constructed in two parallel versions, for widows and for divorcées. The questionnaire is primarily composed of closed questions with a limited number of open ones.

Depression Adjectives Check List

A principal instrument for examining personal well-being was the Depression Adjectives Check List (DACL) developed originally by Lubin (1965). The test is based on self-description by means of 34 adjectives some of which express a feeling of well-being and confidence while others convey feelings of depression and self-negation. The respondent is awarded one point for each adjective of depression she circles and one point for each non-depressive adjective she did *not* mark. Thus, a higher score is indicative of lower well-being (more depressive adjectives). The test correlated with the clinical diagnosis of depression (Levitt & Lubin, 1975:7). The DACL was used in research dealing with the emotional state of widows (Smith, 1975), of women after childbirth (Heitler, 1975), of women after divorce (Vogel-Moline, 1979; Propst et al., 1986) and of unemployed individuals (Shamir, 1986).

A Hebrew version of the test was validated in the Israeli context (split-half reliability = .85; Cronbach's Alpha = .85 p ≤ .01). It was administered in the framework of ten national surveys after which norms for the Israeli Jewish population were constructed (Lomranz et al., 1981). Note that in the Lomranz survey a shortened version of the DACL was applied. This version contained 17 items (instead of 34). Consequently, when comparing single and two-parent mothers, we applied the same 17 items.

Depression is not the only indicator of personal well-being, but it is a most common and widely researched form of psychological distress. It is considered to be "a sensitive psychological barometer of life strains"

(Rose et al., 1983:810). Several studies report high correlations between depression and variables such as unhappiness, anxiety, and self-esteem.

We also tested the association between the DACL and other possible indicators of personal well-being and obtained the following results: DACL × job satisfactions, r = −.63; DACL × self-reported health, r = −.64; DACL × feeling tired and exhausted, r = .52; DACL × overall satisfaction, r = −.52, (p ≤ .01).

Following these findings, we use the terms depression and personal well-being interchangeably.

Independent Variables

Perceived Changes in Various Life Domains

The respondent was given a list of ten spheres of life (for example her economic situation, her relations with her children, social ties, etc.). Regarding each sphere she was asked whether any change had taken place since the divorce or husband's death; and in what direction—positive or negative.

- *Earnings* — average monthly salary calculated according to the previous three months, in dollars.
- *Health* — as evaluated by the respondent on a five-level scale.
- *Participation in Financial Decisions* — the question was phrased: "Who usually made the final decision about financial matters during the marriage?" Three answers were possible: 1 = only the husband; 2 = husband and wife jointly; 3 = only the wife.
- *Household Equipment* — the respondent was presented with a list of seven items (for example: washing machine, vacuum cleaner, color television) and was asked whether the family possessed each of the items. The number of items possessed by the family was then divided by seven.
- *Size of Dwelling* — the number of rooms in the home.
- *Schooling* — the respondents were grouped in five categories according to the number of years of schooling.
- *Ethnic Origin* — the respondents were divided into two categories: 1 = the respondent and/or her father were born in Europe-America; 0 = the respondent and/or her father were born in Asia-Africa. These are the two large ethno-cultural groups in the Jewish population of Israel. The socio-cultural gaps between them that were great in the 1950s are gradually narrowing but still exist (Smooha, 1978).
- *Time since widowhood or divorce* — number of years.

RESULTS

We first compare the personal well-being of widowed, divorced, and married mothers. For this purpose a one-way analysis of variance was carried out between these categories, first in a crude form and then controlling for background variables (education, age, ethnic origin) (see Table 1).

Both the gross and the controlled data indicate statistically significant differences between single-parent mothers and their two-parent counterparts, the latter scoring lower on the depression scale. The same results were obtained when divorcées and widows were compared, each group separately, with married mothers. Controlling for the background variables decreased the gap between the well-being of one and two-parent mothers. Nevertheless, the differences remain significant. On the other hand, we did *not* find net differences between the two categories of single-mothers (widows and divorcées: F = 1.04 N.S.). It would appear, therefore, that personal well-being is influenced chiefly by the presence or absence of a spouse and not by the way in which this situation came about (widowhood or divorce). The gross difference between the well-being of widows and that of divorcées may be attributed to the lower background characteristics of the widows.

The *variation* in depression is significantly greater among single mothers than among married mothers (variance of DACL: widows 16.3; divorcées 13.0; married mothers 5.33; F scores between widows and married mothers 3.06 and between divorcées and married mothers 2.44. p ≤ .01).

At this point several questions arise: Which life domains of the woman-mother are particularly impaired as a result of the dissolution of the marriage? And, (in spite of the negative balance) are there also areas in which an improvement is experienced? To what extent do these areas of life serve as components of personal well-being? In order to answer these questions the respondents were asked to evaluate whether a change had taken place in various areas of their lives since the dissolution of their marriage, and if so, whether it had been for the better or for the worse.

Table 2 presents the distribution of the changes in various areas of life as reported by the respondents. These changes were not unidirectional. The "cost" of single-parenthood is most salient in increased anxiety regarding raising and educating the children, in diminished economic resources and in increased feelings of loneliness and tension. On the other hand, the new situation includes benefits such as deepening relations with the children, increasing self-confidence and occupational success. On balance, the situation of the widows worsened, whereas in the case of the divorcées, positive and negative changes offset each other (see bottom row in Table 2).[2]

Table 1

One-way Analysis of Variance

Dependent Variable - mother's depression score[1]

Independent Variable - mother's marital status

Control Variables - mother's age, schooling and ethnic origin

[1] Married Mothers	[2] Single Mothers (Total)	[3] Widows	[4] Divorcees	F statistics	
				Crude	Controlled
n = 2476	n = 262	n = 142	n = 120	[2]-[1] = 222.24**	131.50**
X = 4.07	X = 6.03	X = 6.80	X = 5.28	[1]-[3] = 238.34**	152.50**
S.D. = 2.31	S.D. = 4.07	S.D. = 4.04	S.D. = 3.61	[1]-[4] = 45.33**	30.30**
				[3]-[4] = 12.78**	1.04

** p ≤ .01

1 The BDICL scores in this table are based on 17 adjectives.

Table 2

Perceived changes in various life domains
since marriage dissolution

Life Domain:	Widows (n=142)				Divorcees (n=120)				Tau(1)
	Direction of change:				Direction of change:				
	Positive	No-change	Negative	Totals	Positive	No-change	Negative	Totals	
Anxiety about children	10%	10	80	100%	9%	32	59	100%	-.19**
Material Hardships	16%	26	58	100%	24%	26	50	100%	-.10
Loneliness	13%	11	76	100%	26%	33	41	100%	-.33**
Burden of Responsibility	11%	18	71	100%	15%	44	41	100%	-.28**
Emotional Strain	17%	14	69	100%	23%	42	35	100%	-.29**
Quality of Social Relations	15%	60	25	100%	17%	39	44	100%	+.29**
Cheerfulness	9%	49	42	100%	40%	44	15	100%	-.42**
Occupational Growth	34%	52	14	100%	47%	38	15	100%	-.11
Quality of Relations with Children	39%	57	4	100%	54%	40	6	100%	-.13*
Self-confidence	53%	37	10	100%	64%	25	11	100%	-.09
Mean	22%	33	45	100%	32%	36	32	100%	

* p ≤ .05

** p ≤ .01

(1) Kendal's Tau is applied here to indicate an association between marital status (Widowed, Divorced) and direction of change. Tau < 0 denotes that widows' perceived situation worsened to a greater extent than did that of the divorcees.

A comparison of widows with divorcées shows that the direction of the change is usually identical. A prominent exception is the sphere of "cheerfulness" in which there is improvement for the divorcées, as against worsening for the widows. In all the areas in which there is a worsening, it is greater for the widows, with the exception of the sphere of social relations. In this area the widows' situation is somewhat preferable due to their greater ability to persevere in their previous social and family relations. A difficulty encountered by all the one-parent mothers is a deterioration in their economic situation. This finding replicates a long line of studies which reported a decline in living standard as a result of the dissolution of marriage (for example, Brandwein et al., 1974; Hyman, 1983).

It may be proposed that each sphere of change constitutes a component of the overall sense of well-being. To test this proposition, multiple regressions (for widows and divorcées) of the DACL on perceived changes in various domains are presented. Note that items denoting feelings of well-being or depression, similar to the DACL itself, were not included in these regressions (items such as emotional strain, cheerfulness, self-confidence).

Table 3 points to three items as components of the personal well-being of the widows: feelings of loneliness, occupational growth, and material hardships. The remaining areas did not show statistically significant associations and therefore were omitted from the regression. In the same format a multiple regression for the divorcées was computed. Here, four

Table 3

Multiple regression of widows' depression on perceived

changes in various life domains.

n = 142

Life Domains	Mean	S.D.	Pearson's r	Beta
Loneliness	2.64	.70	.40**	.34**
Occupational Growth	1.80	.66	-.35**	-.32**
Material Hardships	2.43	.75	.28**	.21*

* p ≤ .05 R^2 = .31**

** p ≤ .01   Constant = -5.6

items were found to constitute personal well-being: quality of social relations, anxieties regarding child-rearing, occupational growth, and loneliness (see Table 4).

In the case of both widows and divorcées, the feeling of personal well-being is a combination of components from functional and emotional spheres. The first component in both equations relates to social interaction. This, however, is perceived differently by each of the groups. The widows interpret insufficiency here as a sense of loneliness. What they mostly miss are intimate relations (Golan, 1981; Kivett, 1978; Lopata, 1969; 1973). Responses to other questions showed that 61% of the divorcées but only 33% of the widows have had romantic liaisons since becoming single-parent mothers. The divorcées suffer more from a lack of social relations as broadly defined. It is difficult for them to maintain good relations with mutual friends of theirs and their former husband or with the family of the husband. This difficulty was referred to as "the community divorce" by Bohannan (1971) and was also reported by others (Berman & Turk, 1981; Raschke, 1977; Weiss, 1979).

In the area of occupational growth, a *positive* change was found in both groups, contributing, indeed, to their well-being (lowering depression). Economic need along with concurrently increased responsibility bring about advancement and often even promotion at work. Material difficulties are a greater burden to the widows, who found themselves in the state of single parenthood with little or no prior warning. In the case of the divorcées, there is a greater fear of disturbance in their parental role. This

Table 4

Multiple regression of divorcees' depression on perceived changes in various life domains.

n = 120

Life Domains	Mean	S.D.	Pearson's r	Beta
Quality of Social Relations	1.73	.74	-.45**	-.23**
Anxiety about the Children	2.49	.67	.41**	.27**
Occupational Growth	1.67	.72	-.37**	-.23**
Loneliness	2.15	.81	.38**	.19*

*   p ≤ .05 R^2 = .37**

** p ≤ .01   Constant = -6.7

can be interpreted as resulting from the crisis in marital relations as well as from the problem of dual loyalty faced by the child (Steinzor, 1970).

After having identified the chief components of personal well-being, we attempted an examination of the background factors that would influence it. For this purpose regression equations for widows and divorcées have been constructed in which the background variables served as independent variables and the DACL as the dependent variable.

Background variables having a net effect on the well-being of the widows are earnings, health, and participation during the marriage in financial decisions (see Table 5). Additional variables were found to have a considerable *crude* correlation: The possession of household equipment ($r = -.40; p \le .01$) and schooling ($r = -.39; p \le .01$). Their influence, however, is already included in the first three factors.

Let us now turn to the factors which have an impact on the well-being of the divorcées.

Table 5

Multiple regression of widows' depression on background variables.

n = 142

Background Variables	Mean	S.D.	Pearson's r	Beta
Earnings	120.6	14.74	-.42**	-.21*
Health	1.90	1.14	-.34**	-.22**
Participation in Financial Decisions	1.55	.81	-.24*	-.23**
Household Equipment	.50	.20	-.40**	-.13
Size of Dwelling (rooms)	3.15	.83	-.23*	-.13
Schooling	8.00	3.60	-.39**	-.10
Ethnicity (+)	.75	.43	.31**	.05
Time Since Widowhood	9.00	3.70	.05	.03

* p ≤ .05 R^2 = .35**

** p ≤ .01   Constant = 22.04

(+) 0 = Europe-America
    1 = Asia-Africa

The two factors having a significant net effect in this case are: education and earnings. The household equipment has a considerable gross effect ($r = -.48$; $p \leqslant .01$), which is included in the previous factors. To sum up: background variables explain a considerable proportion (35%-38%) of the variance in personal well-being (see Table 6).

A much debated association which was *not* found is a net effect of the amount of time since the dissolution of the marriage on personal well-being. This fact contradicts several reports which mention a process of recovery and adaptation experienced by single-parent mothers (Golan, 1978; 1981; Raschke, 1977; Weiss, 1975; 1979). The gap between the two findings may be explained by the assumption that after several years the recovery process is completed. Thus, for divorcées or widows the emotional situation stabilizes but does not become equal to that of intact families.

DISCUSSION

The results of this research reconfirm the influence of marital status on the well-being of the individual, in this instance, the mother. Even after a prolonged period of recovery and adaptation the *overall* well-being of divorcées and widows remains lower than that of married mothers. Nonetheless, a closer examination reveals that along with the costs, there are also benefits in the single-parent situation. Dissolution of the marriage (even when caused by the death of the marriage partner) is at one and the same time a cause of stress and of emancipation. When single-parent mothers compare their present situation to the previous period of their marriage, they feel increased loneliness, overload, and a tangible lowering of their material living standard. On the other hand, an *improvement* is felt in the spheres of professional development, self-confidence, and parenthood. (Similar findings have been reported by Nelson, 1982.)

In the Israeli case the emotional dimensions associated with single parenthood are reinforced. Only 3% of the population of Israel were never married at the age of 50 (Population and Housing Census, 1983). Maintaining stability of the family is a socially recognized goal (Friedlander and Goldsheider, 1979). Under these circumstances, the single-parent life-style is often considered a deviation, especially for women. These familistic orientations create a social burden particularly for those divorcées who wish to establish new intimate relations (Katz & Pesach, 1985). Even the young widows who unwillingly became single parents, often find themselves ousted from their previous social niche. The loss of the

Table 6

Multiple regression of divorcees' depression
on background variables.

n = 120

Background Variables	Mean	S.D.	Pearson's r	Beta
Schooling	10.00	3.30	-.52**	-.25*
Earnings	200.3	15.25	-.43**	-.23*
Size of Dwelling (rooms)	2.94	.80	-.36**	-.16
Household Equipment	.42	.24	-.48**	-.17
Time Since Divorce	7.50	3.60	.14	.07
Health	2.5	1.30	-.24*	-.02
Participation in Financial Decisions	2.00	.90	-.01	-.01

* p $\leq$ .05 R^2 = .38**

** p $\leq$ .01   Constant = 22.55

husband almost automatically cuts some of her links in the social network (Shamgar-Handelman, 1986).

In traditional sectors of Israeli society, the widow faces an additional difficulty: she is expected to adjust to a well-defined role which keeps her in the protective but limiting framework of her late husband's family and consequently impedes her ability to remarry (Amir & Sharon, 1979).

The cause of single-motherhood (divorce or widowhood) does not itself influence personal well-being. This conclusion differs from the findings reported by Amato and Partridge, (1987:318). They indicated a significant gap between the personal well-being of widows and divorcées. This inconsistency might reflect the familistic orientations of Israeli society. The preference for conventional marriage seems to have an equally negative impact on the social standing, and thus, on the emotional well-being, of all those women who happen to live differently.

Well-being is influenced by the various background factors: In Israel divorce occurs more often in the higher socio-economic strata (Peres & Katz, 1981). Among the divorcées there is a larger proportion of those having resources and abilities which aid them in coping, practically as well as emotionally, with single-parenthood. Our findings point to the advantages of active as opposed to passive coping. Thus, for example, we found that the salary of the mother contributes more to her personal well-being than does her *income* (which includes various transfer payments: alimony, child allowances, etc.). Along with being a financial source, her salary constitutes a social recognition of her abilities. This same message is also embodied in the finding that a woman who exhibits independence and involvement during the period of her marriage (participation in the family's financial decisions) more easily copes with single-motherhood than does a woman who had concentrated on her traditional roles.

Several previous studies (Brown & Manella, 1978; Granvold et al., 1979; Keith & Schafer, 1982) maintained that adherence to traditional sex roles, which markedly differentiate activities of the spouses during marriage, is likely to cause difficulties in adapting to the situation of single parenthood. These difficulties are probably reflected in the lower well-being (or higher depression) of those single mothers who during their marriage adopted a rigid feminine role.

In the process of socialization for social roles, special emphasis should be placed on values and skills which enable functional independence and social flexibility while developing earning capabilities in particular. Such abilities will enable the individual (man or woman) more flexibility in coping with life situations in which s/he would need to fulfill social roles that traditionally had been assigned precisely to the opposite sex.

NOTES

1. The aggregate socio-economic score was calculated for each urban community according to the following five characteristics: income, education, ethnic origin, housing density, and family size. The communities included in the survey were classified into one of six levels according to their mean score. For each level of community the number of individual subjects in the sample was determined according to the proportion of this category in the Israeli urban Jewish population.

2. These conclusions are based on the assumption that each change has the same psychological weight. Therefore, they should be treated cautiously.

REFERENCES

Amato, P.R., and Partridge, S. (1987). Widows and divorcees with dependent children: Material, personal, family, and social well-being. *Family Relations*, 36(3), 316-320.

Amir, Y., and Sharon, I. (1979). Factors in the adjustment of war widows. *Megamot*, 25, 120-130 (Hebrew).

Berman, W., and Turk, D. (1981). Adaptation to divorce: Problems and coping strategies. *Journal of Marriage and the Family*, 43(1), 179-189.

Bohannan, P. (1971). The six stations of divorce. In P. Bohannan (ed.), *Divorce and After*, New York: Anchor Books, 33-63.

Brandwein, R., Brown, C. and Fox, E. (1974). Women and children last: The social situation of divorced mothers and their family. *Journal of Marriage and the Family*, 36(3), 498-514.

Brown, P., and Manella, R. (1978). Changing family roles: Women and divorce. *Journal of Divorce*, 1, 315-328.

Central Bureau of Statistics. (1983). Census of Population and Households; Jerusalem.

Chiriboga, D. (1979). Marital separation and stress: A life-course perspective. *Alternative Lifestyles*, 2, 461-470.

Egozi, M. (1978). The socio-economic composition of settlements in Israel according to *Census of Population and Households*, 1972, Ministry of Education and Culture, Jerusalem.

Friedlander, D., and Goldsheider, C. (1979). *Population of Israel*. New York, Columbia University Press.

Golan, N. (1978). *Treatment in crisis situations*; New York, Free Press.

Golan, N. (1981). *Passing through transitions*. New York: Free Press.

Granvold, D., Pedler, L. and Scheillie, S. (1979). A study of sex role expectancy and female post divorce adjustment. *Journal of Divorce*, 2(1), 383-393.

Heitler, S. (1975). Postpartum depression: A multidimensional study, Unpublished doctoral dissertation; New York University.

Hyman, H. (1983). *Of time and widowhood*. Durham, N.C.: Duke University Press.

Katz, R., and Pesach, N. (1985). Adjustment to divorce in Israel: A comparison between divorced men and women. *Journal of Marriage and the Family* 47(3), 765-773.

Keith, P., and Schafer, R. (1982). Correlates of depression among single parent, employed women. *Journal of Divorce*, 5(3), 49-59.

Keren-Ya'ar, H., and Souery, M. (1983). *Families with children in Israel 1970-1981*. The National Insurance Institute, Jerusalem, (Hebrew).

Kivett, V. (1978). Loneliness and the rural widow. *The Family Coordinator*, 27, 389-394.

Levitt, E., and Lubin, B. (1975). *Depression: concepts, controversies and some new facts*. New York: Springer Publishing Company.

Lomranz, J., Lubin, B., Eyal, N. and Medini, G. (1981). Hebrew version of the depression adjective check list: Reliability and validity. *Journal of Personality Assessment*, 45, 380-384.

Lopata, H.Z. (1969). Loneliness: forms and components. *Social Problems*, 17, 248-262.

Lopata, H.Z. (1973). *Widowhood in an American city*. Cambridge, MA: Schenkman Publishing Company.

Lubin, B. (1965). Adjective check lists for the measurement of depression. *Archives of General Psychology*, 12, 57-62.

Menaghan, E., and Lieberman, M. (1986). Changes in depression following divorce: a panel study. *Journal of Marriage and the Family*, 48(2), 319-328.

Nelson, G. (1982). Coping with the loss of father: Family reaction to death or divorce. *Journal of Family Issues*, 3(1), 41-60.

Norton, A. J., and Glick, P.C. (1986). One parent families: a social and economic profile. *Family Relations*, 35(1), 9-17.

Pearlin, L., and Johnson, J. (1977). Marital status, life-strains, and depression. *American Sociological Review*, 17, 459-463.

Peres, Y., and Katz, R. (1981). Stability and centrality: The nuclear family in modern Israel. *Social Forces*, 59(3), 687-704.

Peres, Y., and Katz, R. (1984). The Employed Mother and her Family—A research report submitted to the Ministry of Labor and Welfare; Jerusalem, (Hebrew).

Propst, L., Pardington, A., Ostrom, R. and Watkins, P. (1986). Predictors of coping in divorced single-mothers. *Journal of Divorce*, 9(3), 33-53.

Raschke, H. (1977). The role of social participation in post separation and post divorce adjustment. *Journal of Divorce*, 1(2), 129-141.

Rose, C.E., Mirowsky, J. and Huber, J. (1983). Dividing work, sharing work, and in-between: Marriage patterns and depression. *American Sociological Review*, 48, 809-823.

Salts, C. J. (1979). Divorce process: Integration of theory. *Journal of Divorce*, 2, 233-240.

Shamgar-Handelman, L. (1986). *Israeli war widows—beyond the glory of heroism*. Mass.: Bergin and Garvey Publishers.

Shamir, B. (1986). Unemployment and household division of labor. *Journal of Marriage and the Family*, 48(1), 195-207.

Smith, W. (1975). The desolation of Dido: Patterns of depression and death anxiety in the adjustment and adaptation behaviors of a sample of variably-aged widows. Unpublished doctoral dissertation, Boston University.

Smooha, S. (1978). *Israel: Pluralism and conflict*. London: Routledge and Kegan Paul.

Steinzor, B. (1970). *When parents divorce*. New York: Simon and Schuster.

U.S. Bureau of the Census. (1985). *Current Population Reports*. Series p-20, No. 398, Household and Family Characteristics; Washington, DC, US Government Printing Office.

Vogel-Moline, M. (1979). The effects of a structured group treatment on self-esteem and depression of divorced/separated persons. Unpublished doctoral dissertation, Brigham Young University.

Weingarten, H. (1985). Marital status and well-being: a national study comparing first-married, currently divorced, and remarried adults. *Journal of Marriage and the Family*, 47(3), 653-663.

Weiss, R. (1975). *Marital separation*. New York: Basic Books.

Weiss, R. (1979). *Going it alone*. New York: Basic Books.

Single Asian American Women as a Result of Divorce: Depressive Affect and Changes in Social Support

Young I. Song

SUMMARY. This article reveals findings of an exploratory study of the psychological and social experiences following divorce among Asian American women. In depth interviews were conducted with 50 women who were divorced within the last five years residing in the San Francisco Bay Area. The article focuses on neglecting dimensions of the adjustment problems among divorced Asian American women by investigating the perceptions, thoughts, and feelings over a broad range of questions. The study findings suggest that the newly divorced are significantly more depressed. This increased depression is affected by greater economic problems, lower perceived standard of living and lesser availability of close confiding relationships. Despite its increases, divorce remains an event that brings economic and emotional hardship to these women: The greater depressive effect reflects their worsened life conditions. These divorced Asian American women face complex problems of emotional, personal and social adjustment requiring further attention by researchers.

INTRODUCTION

Divorced Asian American women have traditionally been considered as outcasts by their ethnic community. They have suffered rejection, neglect, and blame for having failed the most important women's role as wife and homemaker according to cultural norm. This unjust persecution has

Young I. Song, PhD, is Assistant Professor, Department of Sociology & Social Services, California State University, Hayward, Hayward, CA 94542.

219

slowly subsided due to the occurrence of divorce as a universal phenomenon.

The dissolution of a marital relationship is frequently the result of numerous reasons and likely to create a variety of different outcomes (Baxter, 1984; Newcomb & Bentler, 1981; Thompson & Sparrier, 1983). Despite a still increasing divorce rate little is known about the patterns of divorced Asian women's experience in terms of social and psychological adjustment and its impact on those women.

The lives of Asian American women are very unique because they live as contemporary women in America while holding their traditional views. Those who have experienced marital transition, are caught in the crossfire of cultural conflict between Western views and the conservatism inherited from the predominantly Confucian tradition. Under these circumstances, the pain and suffering of the rapidly growing divorced women surely require much attention than ever before. The neglect of the hardships of divorced Asian women both in research and practice is a by-product of more concentrated efforts to explain and prevent divorce. The present study is an exploratory effort to examine the psychological and social dimensions of divorced Asian women. This paper begins with the description of cultural tradition of Asian women's lives. This is followed by the exploration of the needs and concerns of the problems of study participants and how they cope. This study attempts to highlight the practical and cultural aspects of marital transition, not its pathological ones. The assumption that divorce can be a problematic occurrence does not mean that the act itself is inherently detrimental or destructive to individuals.

ASIAN WOMEN'S LIVES
FROM A TRADITIONAL PERSPECTIVE

Asian immigrant women are confronted with Western culture and starting new lives in a Western country, and to a great degree, they have retained traditions that cannot be disregarded. Focusing on womanhood from traditional to current aspects will help to provide insightful understanding for divorced Asian women.

Asia is a country of morals, ethics, and conventions. Confucianism played a leading role, greatly influencing the degradation of women's status in Asian society. The function of the woman within the teaching of Asian traditional thoughts was simple and clear. The so-called "obey your father before your marriage, then your husband after the marriage, and after your husband dies, obey your son" (David and Vera Mace, 1959).

Women of Asia have never been regarded as autonomous human beings but only as appendages to the male members of the family. The only identity a woman had was as someone's daughter, wife, or mother, and she could live her life only through her father, husband, or son (Lee, 1977).

During the early socialization process, they should have a belief in the following: (1) Women are inferior to men; (2) Women must expect and acquiesce to the preferential treatment accorded males; (3) Women are subject to spatial constraints in movements; (4) Women must maintain proper social distance from men in their household and practice social avoidance with unrelated men; (5) Women must conceal emotions which are incompatible with their role requirements; (6) Women must cultivate covert strategies for goal realization, i.e., learn to "work the system"; (7) Women are married into strange households where their reception is uncertain; (8) Women who are valued by men and the society are those who uphold cultural values by their conformity and commitment to their female roles, and therein lies the traditionally most reliable social security for women. Almost by definition of their role, traditional Asian women were perpetually caught in restricted and unavoidable situations at the time of marriage. In traditional Asian society, women had nothing to say about their marriage. Marriage created a totally different status in a woman's life compared to a man's life as a husband.

In the West, one falls in love, then marries. In Asia, one marries, then falls in love. Asian young people must have patience to wait for the marriage arrangement or face the hatred of their parents, relatives, and neighbors. Thus, marriage in Asia does not involve the personal choice of the couple, but instead it involves the consideration of ancestors, descendents, property, and educational compatibility.

The marriage arrangement was generally achieved by first making marriage a matter of negotiation between two households with little or no personal participation by the prospective mates. Women were made utterly dependent on socially recognized relationships to men for their own duties and identities. Their existence was defined by reference to men and justified by their usefulness to them. Women were, for all their indispensability to the society, ancillary people and were readily replaceable as individuals.

Even when a woman marries, her continued right to remain in the husband's household was contingent upon others' evaluation of her performance. Thus women were not only socially tangential to men, but they also had to continually validate their duties in order to retain them. For example, women could not under any circumstance initiate divorce, but a woman could be divorced on any one of the seven legitimate standards and rules for marriage. If the woman broke any one of the rules, she was unconditionally divorced. The rules were: (1) if she does not serve her parents-in-law well; (2) if she cannot produce children, particularly male; (3) if she is lecherous; (4) if she is too jealous; (5) if she has an incurable disease; (6) if she talks too much; or (7) if she steals (Lee, 1967).

In traditional Asian society a woman's normative role was difficult to satisfy because it has been based on unrealistic expectations and over-whelming tasks where there can be little argument. Asian women married and continued to marry commandments rather than men. Even in Asia today, the husband and his family have the status of rights and privileges while the wife has the status of duties and obligations.

Above all, if she failed in marriage it usually meant that she was perma-nently deprived of the only legitimate role through which she could partic-ipate in the society. From this point of view, Asian women did not have any alternative but to endure and suffer.

At the time of a divorce, the property which was obtained during the marriage belongs to the husband and the worth of the wife's domestic labors is not considered at all. In case of divorce, the children are sent to the father, regardless of supporting capability. Asian women used to have no right over child custody. Therefore, even though a divorced mother raised her child, all the legal rights should be governed by her husband (i.e., school registry). Although continuous efforts have been made in promoting women's status, their position is still a visibly subordinate and oppressed one.

It is culturally inconceivable for women to remain unmarried. Women whose occupational roles forbade them to marry or made it difficult to marry were genuinely pitied and regarded as social non-persons. And once married, women no longer had any legitimate claim on their natal households. The best chances for socially acceptable survival for individ-ual women lay in completely identifying with the interests of their hus-bands and sons. The surest way for women's self-preservation lay in self-denial. For the majority of women, being forced to deny opportunities in life and to avoid unnecessary challenges was probably frustrating under many circumstances. These frustrations are confronted by many barriers such as educational, legal, and career opportunities.

In recent years, women were not generally denied the benefits of formal education, but were discouraged from developing any natural ability or talent which might be used for a career outside the home.

Even today, this situation remains largely unchanged in Asian society. Men have legally and socially bestowed authorities with all rights in fam-ily affairs. Women have always had an inferior status to that of men, serving primarily as child-bearers and child-carers in the system (Kim, 1976).

In such a cultural context, divorced women's lives are continually confronted with harsh reality. Given these considerations, the primary objective of this study is to investigate the psychological and social experiences following divorce among Asian American women.

THE METHODS OF THE STUDY

The present study attempts to broaden and deepen our understanding of divorced women's experiences and recovery by means of depth interviews of the women in which they talk at length about their personal experiences and feelings. Although the interviews implied some open-ended questions, I employed a semistructured format by outlining my goals and specifying the particular areas I hoped to cover.

Fifty divorced women were interviewed for approximately one and a half hours by the author. All those interviewed lived in the San Francisco Bay Area. All had been divorced within the last five years. The social composition of the sample was as follows: 20 Koreans; 16 Chinese; 8 Vietnamese; 3 Japanese; 28 were college-educated and 22 were high school-educated respondents; 12 were professionals, 28 nonprofessionals, 6 were students, and 4 were unemployed; and age range was between 23 to 56. The present study investigates the major features of the divorced women's predicament. This is done by focusing on the perceptions, thoughts, and feelings of the women.

THE PSYCHOLOGICAL SITUATION OF THE DIVORCÉE DEALING WITH DEPRESSION

In this section, the complex psychological situation divorce creates for the women will be discussed. Through a torrent of painful emotions, divorcées struggle to cope with depression. Among the distresses and dislocations that accompany divorce is the tendency for a woman to blame herself for the failure of her marriage. For most Asian women, marriage continues to be, as it was for their grandmothers, a social statement that affirms and assures them of a recognized place in women's life. Those women have not been liberated much from the traditional patriarchal burden of homemaker and housewife. As females, from a very young age they are taught to define themselves in terms of being married or attached to a man.

In all societies, particularly Asian culture which can be considered as an outstanding example of the male dominated society for many centuries, women have been treated as second class citizens. The traditional notion that women are inferior, subordinate — indeed "the Second Sex" is still deeply rooted in Asian culture. In fact, the independent, strong woman is labeled as the "castrating bitch," society's outcast culturally. Women who choose not to be dependent on men have been viewed with fear, hostility, and/or pity. Many Asian women learned to make themselves an acceptable woman for men by sacrificing and degrading their minds.

Respondents expressed that they enabled their ex-husbands to put time and energy into the pursuit of occupational success by taking on heavy responsibility for care of the home and children. They seemed to agree that they made many sacrifices for men since they considered the husband's occupation and social status to be a priority in the community's evaluation of their family.

The emotional trauma that accompanies such a break-up left those women feeling that they were failures as women. They tended to think that it was their fault. This is found to be especially true if they have seen taking care of home, husband, and children as their primary occupation. Divorce can be considerably more painful for the woman who has not learned adequate rational methods of dealing with reality. If too many situations arise that they cannot handle, they began to consider themselves as failures and fall into a pattern of behaving like a failure.

In describing the immediate response of the divorce, most of them (92%) recalled that it has been a painful experience. Shock, disbelief, fear, anger, were commonly mentioned as they recounted the early phases of their experience. The end of any relationship is a loss that leaves an empty space in one's life. The Social Readjustment Rating Scale (Holmes and Rahe, 1967) lists death of a spouse as the most stressful transition, with divorce and marital separation being second and third. Kubler-Ross (1975) also described that the stages of dying apply equally to divorce as significant changes occur in a person's life. Most divorce theorists maintain that recovery from divorce is both painful and slow. Robert Weiss (1975), for example, estimates that two to five years will elapse after separation before the individuals are "fully themselves again" with the average recovery time closer to the four year mark. Moreover, he postulated that there are two definitive phases in the course of recovery: transition and recovering. During the transition period in early phase the individual has to contend with the "crisis of identity" and begin the process of reordering the life as a single person. The recovery phase is a far longer period.

Although there are few women for whom divorce is not a crisis, Asian women have been conditioned to believe that marriage is their highest goal as female, that status of wife and mother is their most important role. Because the effects of marriage are usually broader and deeper for women than for men, it follows that the psychological effects of divorce are also deeper. For those women (60%) who feel that life is hardly worthwhile without a partner, it may take a longer time to recover from the depression and to give up the belief that they are incomplete as single persons.

Self-blame is usually accompanied by feelings of guilt (Dorpat, 1973; Charmaz, 1980) or the emotional or psychological pain connected with a belief that one has done something unacceptable. However, feelings of guilt were reported in only 22 of the interviews. On the other hand, regret was reported by most of the women (92%). Apparently, not everyone who placed blame on themselves necessarily felt guilt, or were perhaps unable or unwilling to express it. In several cases, women expressed that they feel guilty and angry when the stigma of divorce weighed heavily upon them. This suggests that guilt can be an emotional response to feelings of powerlessness as well as an outcome of self-blame.

There were some feelings which were commonly found in all women regardless of their background. Women reported their fears about being lonely. Most women reported that they are resentful that their ex-husbands seem to have many more options for getting decent jobs, meeting new women, and in general putting their lives together. Older women felt especially vulnerable. Many of them have devoted their lives to "doing the right thing" by taking care of their families and homes, and now find themselves with very few options.

The variety of psychological situations divorced women live through were discussed. Pain seems to be one of the primary feelings during the time of doubt, guilt, isolation, fear, insecurity, overwhelmed frustration, and resentful feelings. The degree of pain is influenced by how dependent women have been on their husbands. There are a number of different psychological stages among women who are working through feelings of depression. During the early days after the divorce (weeks, months to years), many women felt abandoned, inadequate, panicky, isolated, and lonely. They experienced fear, guilt, feeling of failure, and anger as they went through the grief and mourning process which follows the death of a relationship.

THE SOCIAL SITUATION OF THE DIVORCED WOMEN: CHANGES IN SOCIAL SUPPORT

This section focuses on divorcées' experience in social or economic situations and the impact these changes have on women. What emerges is a complex and painful portrait of the women's social reality, which is characterized by confusion, frustration, and occasionally resentment.

The dominant theme among subjects was lack of support. Repeatedly, respondents confessed that others failed to understand or respond to their needs in meaningful and helpful ways. At the same time, the women indicated they themselves frequently denied their own needs by withdrawing from others and thus avoiding the topic of their social or economic situation.

While married, these women felt they belonged to a social unit. They have become accustomed to thinking of themselves as part of a unit and now they must return to thinking of the self as I. After divorce women became alone, without status, comfort, or security that social unit provided. Such experiences among divorced women may be accompanied by dislocation in social activities and friendships. Accustomed to being part of a couple, a divorced woman becomes an "extra" guest or third wheel, a source of discomfort to her acquaintances. A few women reported that they discovered a negative attitude toward them because they present a threat to wives who may believe divorced women are after their husbands, and to husbands who may fear she will encourage their wives to get divorces too.

Beyond such problems, the most clearly established aftermath of divorce is the economic hardship suffered by women. The disadvantaged status of female-headed households and the economic consequences of divorce for women have been well documented in the social science literature (Bane, 1976a, 1976b; Bradbury et al., 1979; Brandwein et al., 1974; Espenshade, 1979; Driesberg, 1970). Lenore Weitzman (1985) after a 10 year study of divorce in California concluded that divorced women suffer an average immediate 73 percent drop in standard of living while that of their husbands increase in the first year after divorce by an average of 42 percent. In the United States today, less than 15 percent of divorced women receive alimony. The average child support award is $200 a month for two children. Forty-four percent of divorced mothers are awarded child support (Lott, 1987). One word used by many mothers in transition to describe their feelings is "trapped." Mothers of younger children expressed feeling trapped because of their children's greater dependence on them. On the other hand, divorced women without young children and without jobs found themselves suffering the consequences of being "displaced homemakers . . . women who have been forcibly exiled from a role, an occupation, dependency status, and a livelihood" (Sommers & Shields, 1978). Such women lose their sole source of income, are ineligible for unemployment insurance, do not qualify for Aid to Families with

Dependent Children, and find it extremely difficult to get jobs because of their age and lack of recent paid employment experience. Especially older women who have accepted the traditional role of housewife and their entire life has revolved around their husbands the changes are particularly hard. A few women confessed that they have seen themselves as "Mrs. Jones" for thirty years, and the welfare of their husbands and children were their only career. They felt that they had no role in life anymore.

Women who are overworked heads of households reported that they received less help and sympathy from friends and neighbors than divorced men. People are likely to offer help to a newly single man with dinner invitations more readily than to a divorced woman who can cook but may be just as lonely as her male counterpart. Studies of divorced women have found that the majority are interested in remarriage, but the chances of such for women are considerably low compared to men (Phillis & Stein, 1983).

Some women, especially those with professional credentials with high educational background, were able to manage without significant financial hardship, especially those who have worked prior to divorce. Other women however, who have been described as "middle class" by their husband's job and status, found themselves with little or no financial resources and few marketable skills with which to support themselves and their children.

For women who have several children, or who are older, or who are experiencing cultural and language barriers, they found there is not any realistic option for their future. Much of the research on divorce focuses on the economic impact of the divorce, but the financial status of the respondents did not seem to be the critical factor affecting their ability to adjust to marital transition. Rather, differences in their relationship with ex-spouses, family, neighbor, and friends, the circumstances surrounding the divorce, whether they were employed and/or had interests outside the house, their own resiliency, and even the passage of time appeared to be the key determinants of a successful adaptation to single life.

STRESS RELATED SYMPTOMS
EXPERIENCED BY DIVORCED WOMEN

Women alone face grave dangers emotionally and physically. Divorce, a major crisis in any individual's life, can sure bring emotional and physical changes. The "loneliness and isolation" that characterize their lives can lead to emotional deterioration and then physical deterioration. Indeed, widowed, divorced, and single people have far more heart disease, strokes, lung cancer, and cirrhosis of the liver than married people do

(Smith, 1979). Improperly handled stress causes wear and tear to the organs of the body, interferes with life goals, reduces energy, can cause neurotic symptoms and withdrawal and the development of psychosomatic ailments.

Stress related symptoms were measured by responses to a twenty-two screening score which was originally developed in New York City. All of the divorced women in the sample reported experiencing at least some stress related symptoms (i.e., difficulty sleeping, occasional headaches, loss of appetite, ulcer, etc.). Even though some women could have experienced some symptoms prior to the divorce, there were a highly significant number (42 out of 50) who experienced some stress related symptoms. The respondents of newly divorced (less than two years) reported severe levels of stress related symptoms. At the same time, the women who have been divorced more than four years ago reported less stress related symptoms.

COPING WITH MARITAL TRANSITION

In this section, we shall be concerned about what our respondents do to cope with divorce in terms of their knowledge of problem solving methods, service needs, utilization patterns, sources of help, and barriers to the use of formal services.

Problem Solving Methods: Problem solving methods were assessed by asking the women to indicate the most preferred methods of solving problems from the five suggested methods. The most preferred ways of problem solving for the divorced women respectively were: (1) Time will solve the problem 34%; (2) Keep the problem in the family 26%; (3) Praying 20%; (4) Consulting friends and relatives 12%; (5) Seek professional help 8%. Interestingly, thirty-four percent of the women indicated that time will solve the problem. This appears to be a cultural pattern of problem solving methods for Asians.

Crisis Management: In order to identify the patterns in crisis management a question was asked: When you are in a crisis where would you go for help? It is interesting to note that over half of the divorced women reported they would turn to parents or ministers. They were less likely to turn to their friends, relatives and neighbors for help. Surprisingly, only two women indicated they would turn to social service agencies for managing their crises. The majority of women did not express wanting help from their friends, relatives or neighbors. As indicated by Koh (1983), Asian immigrants seem to have less intimate relations with their relatives, friends, or neighbors to whom they can freely ask for help in the crisis situation. The results seems to reveal that there is evidence of tremendous underutilization of social service agencies by divorced Asian women.

CONCLUSION

Results from the present study indicate that divorced Asian women experience many types of problems and in fact have problems unique to the Asian community. The results also indicate a social response to the needs of divorced Asian women is generally inadequate. Therefore, society needs to incorporate the concerns for the uniqueness of the Asian divorced women and their families in order to resolve the problems and suggest different options.

On the positive side, the experience of divorce provides a woman with the opportunity to reevaluate her lifestyle and goals. The upheaval and the impossibility of continuing in their previous roles may leave people open to examine their identities, personalities, and values. Helping professionals can help the women to increase understanding of strengths and weaknesses so that the client can develop a satisfying new identity and find life rewarding with or without a partner. Professionals will be able to help the newly divorced woman to focus on future possibilities and to accept the challenge of the new life roles.

Most of these women have been accustomed to controlling their negative feelings and have not been used to expressing their emotions. Professionals must be sensitive to the issues of shame and guilt which these divorced Asian women are experiencing. The professional who is bilingual and bicultural or who has special knowledge of cross-cultural approaches, would also help for a better assessment and planning for its required intervention.

REFERENCES

Bane, Mary Jo. *Here to Stay: American Families in the Twentieth Century*. New York: Basic, 1976a.

_____. "Marital Disruption and the Lives of Children." *Journal of Social Issues*. 32:1, pp. 103-107, 1976b.

Bradbury, Katherine; Danziger, Sheldon; Smolensky, Eugene; and Smolensky, Paul. "Public Assistance—Female Hardship and Economic Well-being." *Journal of Marriage and Family*. 36:3, pp. 498-532, 1974.

Charmaz, K. *The Social Reality of Death*. Reading, MA: Addison-Wesley, 1980.

Dorpat, T. L. "Suicide, Loss and Mourning." *Life-Threatening Behavior*. 3., pp. 213-224, Fall 1973.

Espenshade, Thomas J. "The Economic Consequences of Divorce." *Journal of Marriage and the Family*. 41:3, pp. 615-625, 1979.

Holmes, Thomas and Rahe, R. H. "The Social Readjustment Rating Scale." *Journal of Psychosomatic Research*. 11, pp. 213-218, 1967.

Koh, K. and Koh, H. *Koreans and Korean-Americans in the United States: A Summary of Three Conference Proceedings*. New Haven: East Rock, 1974.

Kriesberg, Louis. *Mothers in Poverty: A Study of Fatherless Families*. Chicago, IL: Aldine, 1970.

Kubler-Ross, Elisabeth. *Death: The Final Stage of Growth*. Englewood Cliffs, NJ: Prentice-Hall, 1975.

Lott, Bernice, *Women's Lives*. Monterey, CA: Brook/Cole Publishing, 1987.

Phillis, Diane E. and Stein, Peter J. "Sink or Swing? The lifestyles of single adults." In E. R. Allgeier and N. B. McCormick (Eds.) *Changing Boundaries: Gender Roles and Sexual Behavior*. Palo Alto, CA: Mayfield, pp. 202-205, 1983.

Smith, Ralph E. (Ed.) *The Subtle Revolution: Women at Work*. Washington, D.C.: Urban Institute, 1979.

Simmers, T. and Shields, L. "Displaced homemakers." *Civil Rights Digest*. Winter, pp. 33-39, 1978.

Weiss, Robert. *Marital Separation*. New York: Basic, 1975.

Weitzman, Lenore J. *The Divorce Revolution*. New York: Free Press, 1985.